As is well known the Human Rights Act 1998 (HRA) is a constitutional innovation, but can its scheme deliver? This timely and provocative book probes the extent to which the HRA is guaranteeing rights and whether it is transforming the legal landscape.

This companion text to *Understanding Human Rights Principles* (Hart Publications 2001) is the culmination of a six-month project where key elements of the HRA were analysed and subjected to detailed scrutiny by expert practitioners and academics. The result is seven chapters of the highest quality which examine the following subjects including the reach of the Act and its jurisdictional scope and how to strike the balance under the HRA between interpretation and incompatibility. Two chapters look at remedies for breach of human rights. The first under the HRA and the second using Community law principles. The text then goes on to consider assessment of fact, due deference, and the wider impact of the Human Rights Act in administrative law. It then asks what is public power? And looks at the courts' approach to the public authority definition under the Act. Finally access to court under the Human Rights Act is examined including standing, legal assistance and third party intervenors.

The book's contributors are the leading experts in the field including Dinah Rose, Nathalie Lieven, Janet Kentridge, Kate Markus, Richard Clayton QC, Peter Roth QC, and Tim Owen QC. It provides an unparalleled examination of the scheme of the Human Rights Act and its component parts and it is of direct relevance to the practitioner and academic.

DELIVERING RIGHTS

How the Human Rights Act is Working

Edited by

JEFFREY JOWELL QC
Professor of Public Law, University College London

AND

JONATHAN COOPER
Barrister, Doughty Street Chambers

·HART·
PUBLISHING

OXFORD – PORTLAND OREGON
2003

Hart Publishing
Oxford and Portland, Oregon

Published in North America (US and Canada) by
Hart Publishing c/o
International Specialized Book Services
5804 NE Hassalo Street
Portland, Oregon
97213-3644
USA

Hart Publishing is a specialist legal publisher based in Oxford,
England.
To order further copies of this book or to request a list of other
publications please write to:

Hart Publishing, Salter's Boatyard, Folly Bridge,
Abingdon Road, Oxford OX1 4LB
Telephone: +44 (0)1865 245533 or Fax: +44 (0)1865 794882
e-mail: mail@hartpub.co.uk
WEBSITE: http//www.hartpub.co.uk

British Library Cataloguing in Publication Data
Data Available
ISBN 1–84113–287–X (paperback)

Typeset by Hope Services (Abingdon) Ltd.
Printed and bound in Great Britain on acid-free paper by
Page Bros, Norwich, Norfolk

Foreword

These excellent papers are based on drafts that were presented by their authors at seminars that were held in 2002 at University College, London. They have been honed and expanded to reflect ideas that emerged during the debates that they generated, and have been updated to take account of more recent case-law. The papers are scholarly and extremely well reasoned. They will undoubtedly provide nourishing food for thought for those who are interested in human rights law; and, for a short time at least, they will furnish them with a rich mine of material. I say "for a short time at least", because several of the authors themselves make the point that the development of the law in this field is still relatively in its infancy. The Human Rights Act has been in force for almost 3 years. And yet there have already been many important decisions at the highest level on the meaning and application of the Act. The fact that we are witnessing a fast-moving scene is well demonstrated by the number of references to cases which have been decided since the seminars were held last year.

One noteworthy feature of these papers is that a number of the authors are somewhat critical of what they consider to be the excessively cautious approach that has been adopted by the courts so far to issues raised by the Act. Thus, for example, Kate Markus mounts a powerful attack on the decisions as to the meaning of "public authority" in *Poplar* and *Leonard Cheshire*. She argues that, by failing to develop a functional approach to the definition of "public authority", the courts have ignored the reality of increased reliance by local and central government bodies on private contractors to discharge their statutory duties.

In their discussion on sections 3 and 4 of the Act, Dinah Rose and Claire Weir suggest that the House of Lords "got it right" in *R v A (No 2)*. They deprecate the retreat into conservatism and a more traditional, cautious approach to interpretation that is evident in some of the more recent cases. They suggest that by adopting the interpretative techniques of "reading down" or "reading in", the courts could and should have arrived at interpretations in a number of cases which would have obviated the need for declarations of incompatibility.

On the other hand, Nathalie Lieven and Charlotte Kilroy welcome the way in which the courts have escaped from the shackles of the "victim" test in section 7. The approach of the courts has been to try not to exclude cases on the grounds that there may be said to be no victim, and to take a relaxed attitude to third party interventions. The rise of the third party intervention is one of the most important developments in public law. From my own experience, I can testify that the quality of such interventions by bodies such as JUSTICE, Liberty and Amnesty has been most impressive, and of real value to the court.

The international dimension is covered by Janet Kentridge in a thought-provoking paper about the extent to which the Act reaches beyond the borders of the United Kingdom. Peter Roth QC looks at the issue of remedies through the prism of Community Law.

Each of these papers is very well written and carefully researched. Every person interested in the Human Rights Act will benefit from reading them. As a judge, I can say that, although I do not necessarily agree with everything that is in these papers, I have found reading them most instructive and rewarding.

Lord Justice Dyson
London, 2003

Preface

This latest series of JUSTICE seminars on the out-workings of the Human Rights Act is the second with which Clifford Chance has been pleased to be associated.

Few can doubt that the rights guaranteed by the European Convention on Human Rights now suffuse virtually every area of legal practice, sometimes with surprising results. Who would have predicted, before the Act came into force, that the business of pawn-broking would give rise to human rights challenges (engaging the attention of the Law Lords no less) and the making of a declaration of incompatibility?

The claim that the legislation would result in a bean-feast for the legal profession has been shown to be misplaced. Equally it is clear that those who hoped, for whatever reasons, that the decision to make the European Convention's guarantees directly justiciable in the UK courts would settle the boundaries of domestic rights for the foreseeable future are likely to be disappointed.

As I write, the centre of attention appears in the coming period likely to move to Brussels rather than Strasbourg. In the next year much will be heard about EU enlargement, the framing of an EU constitution and the EU Charter of Rights. Human rights considerations underpin all of these.

All that is to come. For the moment it is a pleasure to have been able to facilitate, in a very small way, the holding of these seminars and the publication of the stimulating contributions that follow.

Michael Smyth
Partner and Head of Public Policy
Clifford Chance LLP

Contents

List of Contributors

Richard Clayton QC practises in the fields of public and employment law. His public law practice covers a wide range of advisory and litigation work in the administrative and public law fields. He undertakes disciplinary/regulatory work, discrimination law, local government, health care, prisoners' rights and criminal judicial review. He acts both for and against public bodies. He has a particular expertise in human rights law and is the co-author of *The Law of Human Rights* (Oxford University Press, 2000), as well as *Judicial Review Procedure* (Hart Publishing, 1997). He writes and lectures extensively on public law topics and is a Visiting Fellow at the Centre for Public Law, University of Cambridge.

Jonathan Cooper is in practice at the Bar at Doughty Street Chambers, but prior to returning to the Bar he was Assistant Director of JUSTICE. He has taken several cases to the European Court of Human Rights. He is editor of the *European Human Rights Law Review* (Sweet & Maxwell), co-editor of *Legislating for Human Rights, a Guide to the Parliamentary Debates on the Human Rights Act 1998* (Hart Publishing) and co-editor of *Understanding Human Rights Principles* (Hart Publishing). Jonathan has been instrumental in training public authorities and lawyers in the UK on the implementation of the Human Rights Act 1998 and was responsible for devising and carrying out human rights training for various government departments. He is often asked to train judges and lawyers in human rights principles in other jurisdictions. These have included Serbia, Croatia, Albania, Lithuania and the Gambia.

Jeffrey Jowell QC is Professor of Public Law at University College London and a member of Blackstone Chambers. He is a member of the Royal Commission on Environmental Pollution and the UK's member on and a Vice President of the Council of Europe's Commission for Democracy Through Law (the Venice Commission).

He was a member of the Bowman Committee on the Crown Office (now the Administrative Court Office). He is an Honorary Professor at the University of Cape Town and has received a number of Honorary degrees and awards including Hon. Queen's Council and Hon. Bencher of the Middle Temple. He is co-author with Lord Woolf of de Smith, Woolf and Jowell's *Judicial Review of Administrative Action* and many other books and articles on public law.

Janet Kentridge was called to the Bar in London in 1999 having previously been called in Johannesburg in 1994. She has practised in a range of areas, and specialises in administrative, human rights, constitutional and media law, acting for and against a range of public bodies and regulatory authorities. She is a co-author and editor of *Constitutional Law in South Africa*, which is frequently cited by courts at all levels in South Africa.

Charlotte Kilroy was called to the Bar in 1999 and as a junior practitioner has developed a practice in education, human rights, immigration and asylum, public law, public international law and EU law. She is building a reputation in international and human rights law and published joint opinions with Rabinder Singh QC for the Campaign for Nuclear Disarmament on the legality of the war with Iraq. Prior to joining Matrix in October 2002 she was a member of 4 Breams Buildings.

Nathalie Lieven specialises in public law (including education, mental health, community care, most aspects of local government and compulsory purchase), planning law and social security law. She has been involved in a number of cases involving human rights issues, and was appointed to the "A Panel" of Treasury Counsel in 2000, having previously been on the "B Panel". She appears regularly in the High Court, Court of Appeal, and before the Social Security Commissioners and the Mental Health Review Tribunal. She is listed as a leading specialist in Administrative and Public Law, Education, Local Government and Planning in both *Chambers & Partners Directory* and the *Legal 500*. She is a contributor to the *Town and Country Planning* volume of *Halsbury's Laws*.

Kate Markus specialises in public law and human rights. Her practice spans a wide range of public law fields: social welfare (housing, social security and welfare benefits, health and social services including community care), education, planning and environment, magistrates' decisions, prisoners' rights and mental health. She also acts in a wide range of other local government and community issues such as tenant consultation rights, funding and local service provision. Her practice also embraces other diverse public law and human rights issues, such as registration of political parties and data protection. Her housing law practice includes appeals as well as judicial review. She also has a general civil litigation practice, particularly in relation to the activities of public bodies such as claims for breach of statutory duty, breach of contract or negligence by public bodies.

Tim Owen QC specialises in public law (especially prison, police, criminal and inquest law), human rights law, criminal law (especially political offences, cases involving police malpractice, public order and appellate work as well as asset restraint, money laundering and confiscation law), international human rights law and civil litigation involving abuse of power by public bodies. He has litigated before the European Court of Human Rights and has lectured on the domestic application of the ECHR and the Human Rights Act for both the Judicial Studies Board and the Bar Council. He is co-author of *Prison Law* (2nd edn, Clarendon, 1999), co-editor of *Halsbury's Laws of England*, Vol. 36 (*Prisons and Prisoners*) and co-author of *Criminal Justice, Police Powers and Human Rights* (Blackstone, 2001).

Dinah Rose is a barrister practising at Blackstone Chambers specialising in public and administrative law, human rights and employment law.

P.M. Roth QC of Monckton Chambers, Gray's Inn, practises in the fields of public law, EC and competition law, and commercial law. He is Visiting Professor at King's College, University of London, and was previously a Visiting Associate Professor at the University of Pennsylvania Law School. He is chairman of the Competition Law Association and sits as a Recorder in the Crown Court.

Claire Weir is a barrister at Blackstone Chambers specialising in human rights, public law and employment and discrimination law.

Introduction

Jeffrey Jowell QC and Jonathan Cooper

History is packed with examples of fine constitutional documents which have been honoured mainly in their breach. The drafters of these documents have congratulated themselves on the contours of their institutional design, but bothered little about their subsequent implementation.

By contrast, the impact of the UK's Human Rights Act 1998 ("The Act") has been immediate. Its implementation has no doubt been assisted by the fact that a small army of lawyers was awaiting, with sharpened pencils, to challenge the compatibility of longstanding practices and new proposals with the new Convention rights. In addition the government had, uniquely, before the coming into effect of the Act in England and Wales, generously financed a training programme which ensured that the scheme of rights against the state was well understood by judges as well as by a wide variety of public decision-makers.

Following the book we edited two years ago,[1] this book reflects upon the delivery of rights in the period immediately following its initial implementation. The material now exists to begin to assess how uncertain aspects of the Act have been interpreted in practice. The chapters that follow deal with the issues which we considered most deserving of analysis at this point in the Act's history. As with the previous volume, all the papers were presented at a series of seminars held at University College London under the auspices of JUSTICE and UCL, this time chaired by Lord Justice Dyson. The seminars were attended by leading academics and practitioners and the papers were edited so as to absorb the intense discussion following their delivery.

Underlying all the papers, but perhaps not engaged directly by any of them, is the key question of the constitutional status of the

---

[1] *Understanding Human Rights Principles* (Oxford: Hart Publishing, 2001).

Human Rights Act. Is it a statute like any other, or is it a "super statute"?[2] The Act has not expressly been accorded any specific status over- and-above any other law which constrains the state and enables individuals to hold government to account. Yet a number of judicial pronouncements have confidently asserted that it does possess constitutional status.[3] The reasons, however, for these assertions have rarely been spelled out. After all, why should the Act be considered any more important, constitutionally, than a statute providing rights of way or establishing environmental standards? And if it does possess constitutional status, in a country without a written constitution, what follows from that?

Before touching upon this issue, we should note that the new rights-culture has been severely tested by the events of September 11 2001. No-one in 1998 could have foreseen that within the first two years of the Act's implementation Parliament would agree to a derogation from the European Convention on Human Rights (under Article 15 of the Convention), in order to permit detention without trial.[4] As this book goes to press, controversy is raging about the proper role of judges in interpreting the scope of the Act (and of judicial review more broadly). The Home Secretary, David Blunkett is, in particular, publicly rebuking judges for interfering in what he regards as the proper role of Parliament and the executive.[5]

The Home Secretary's statements themselves focus attention upon the Act's status. Although courts may not, under the Act, strike down statutes, Parliament itself has conferred upon them a new power to

---

[2] See W. Eskridge and J. Frerejohn, "Super Statutes" (2001) 50 *Duke Law Journal* 1215. See also Laws LJ in *Thoburn and others* v. *Sunderland City Council* [2001] EWHC Admin. 934, [2002] Eu LR 253, where Sir John Laws made a distinction between ordinary statutes and "constitutional statutes".

[3] See eg Lord Bingham in *Brown* v. *Stott* [2001] 2 WLR 817 at 835; Lord Woolf in *R* v. *Offen* [2001] 1 WLR 254 at 275; Laws LJ in *Roth and others* v. *Secretary of State for the Home Department* [2002] EWCA at paras 69–75 and in *Thoburn* (above, note 2).

[4] This may be done where there is a "war or other public emergency threatening the life of the nation" and where the measures are "strictly required by the exigencies of the situation". In *A, X Y and others* v. *Secretary of State for the Home Department* (CA, 25 October 2002), the Court of Appeal upheld the Home Secretary's submission that the criteria for satisfying a derogation under Article 15 was satisfied and therefore permitted legislation to detain immigrants suspected of terrorist activities without trial.

[5] For example in the *Evening Standard* 12 May 2003.

review legislation and to issue declarations of their incompatibility with Convention rights.[6] In what has been considered a subtle compromise, Parliament has the ultimate power as to whether to comply with such a declaration. However, the Act's subtlety transcends even that formal re-arrangement of powers. It introduces new constitutional expectations. It is clearly expected that Parliament, as well as public officials, should conform with Convention rights. This is because these rights are not a mere catalogue of unrelated freedoms. They assert the necessary requirements of a modern democracy; requirements, such as freedom of expression and equality, which are integral to a constitutional democracy and a necessary and not antithetical supplement to the power of a freely elected Parliament.

It is this new, constitutional or rights-based democracy with which our lawmakers will have to come to terms. Parliament itself conferred the role of constitutional umpire upon the courts. Yet some judicial pronouncements have suggested that the courts ought still to defer to Parliament for reasons of *constitutional principle*.[7] On the contrary, the courts would be abdicating their responsibility under the Act if they deferred to Parliament on the ground alone that Parliament has been elected, or that it represents the popular will. The very essence of a constitutional democracy lies in the fact that it protects the citizen's rights even against overwhelming popular will. It is the courts which, under this dispensation, possess full authority to determine the scope of those rights.

The absence of need for constitutional deference does not, however, mean that judges should not recognize on occasion a "discretionary area of judgment"[8] on the part of Parliament or the executive with which the courts should not interfere. This area is based, however, not on lack of judicial authority to decide the matter but on the lack of institutional capacity. Lord Hoffmann, in a recent case, implies that the contours of this discretionary area are brightly lined and that "when a court decides that a decision is within the proper competence of the legislature or the executive, it is not

---

[6] Sections 3 and 4 of the Act.

[7] See Lord Woolf in *R* v. *Lambert* [2001] 2 WLR 211 at 219.

[8] A term employed by A. Lester and D.Pannick, *Human Rights Law and Practice* (London: Butterworths,1999), p 74 para 3.21 and cited by Lord Hope in *R* v. *DPP, ex p Kebilene* [2000] 2 AC 326, 380–81 and by Lord Bingham in *Brown* v. *Stott* (above, note 3, at 834–5.

showing deference. It is deciding the law."[9] Lord Hoffmann's stance on this question seems in part to be based upon his avowed dislike of the term 'deference', which he describes as having "overtones of servility, or perhaps gracious concession". Instead, he identifies two legal principles, the first of which contains the principle that "the independence of courts is necessary for a proper decision of disputed legal rights or claims of violation of human rights". His second legal principle is that "majority approval is necessary for a proper decision on policy or allocation of resources".

The vocabulary of legal principle to indicate the scope of judicial competence in judging human rights may have its attractions. But it also has its dangers, insofar as it implies that the courts have no legal right to intervene in certain matters which engage majority choice. It is the judges now who define the scope of all Convention rights (although Parliament may defy their decisions). And it is for the courts to decide whether and under what circumstances to concede competence to other branches of government. If this be deference then so be it, but any concession on the part of the courts, gracious or otherwise, is based less upon the law than upon a developing sense of when to recognize the limits of the courts' own fact-finding capability or expertise, and an appreciation of those matters which are most appropriately decided by Parliament or the executive.

The editors are very grateful to Clifford Chance for their support of the seminars, to Sir John Dyson for so skillfully chairing them and to Richard Hart for his characteristically efficient and speedy publication of this volume.

Jeffrey Jowell
Jonathan Cooper

May 2003

---

[9] *R* v. *BBC, ex p Prolife Alliance* [2003] UKHL 23, at paras 74–77.

The Reach of the Human Rights Act 1998: Its Jurisdictional Scope

Janet Kentridge*[1]

INTRODUCTION

Does the Human Rights Act 1998 ("HRA") reach beyond the borders of the United Kingdom? If so, how far, to whom and in what circumstances? This chapter seeks to deal with these questions by considering:

1. the express provisions of the HRA dealing with its scope of application;
2. the relevance of the presumption against extraterritorial application of statutes;
3. the Strasbourg jurisprudence on the extraterritorial application of the European Convention on Human Rights and Freedoms ("the Convention");
4. the extent to which the scope of application of the Convention determines the scope of application of the HRA;
5. briefly, the approach taken by Canadian courts in determining the territorial reach of the Canadian Charter of Rights and Freedoms ("the Charter") and that adopted by the United States to the extraterritorial application of the US Constitution.

Before doing so, it is as well to set out a range of potential answers to these questions. Various candidate "theories of reach" may be identified:

---

* Matrix Chambers.
[1] I am grateful to Philippe Sands, Raza Husain and Max du Plessis for their assistance. Any error or omission is my own.

1. the "purely territorial" or "border" theory, according to which the HRA applies within the borders of the United Kingdom, but no further;
2. the "effective territorial control" theory identified by the European Court of Human Rights ("ECHR") in *Bankovic* v. *Belgium and Others* ("*Bankovic*").[2] This would accept the application of the HRA beyond the borders of the United Kingdom in circumstances in which, on foreign territory, British public authorities exercise some or all of the powers normally exercised by the government of that territory through the effective control of that territory and its inhabitants, as a consequence of military occupation or through the consent, invitation or acquiescence of the government of that territory;[3]
3. the "actual authority" approach, favoured by the ECHR in the decisions on extraterritorial application of the Convention which preceded *Bankovic*,[4] accepts that the HRA applies to the acts and omissions of British public authorities exercising actual authority or control over persons or property;
4. according to the "causation based" theory of reach, the acts of public authorities in the United Kingdom may be unlawful if Convention rights are violated as a direct consequence or effect of such acts – even if the violation is perpetrated by and in another State;[5]
5. according to the "mutuality" principle, those made subject to the laws of the United Kingdom, whether at home or abroad, are entitled to claim the protection of the HRA in the way in which the law or laws in question are applied to them. As stated by Lord Scarman in *R* v. *Home Secretary ex parte Khawaja*: "He who is subject to English law is entitled to its protection."[6] So too, those who are brought under the direct control, authority or power of a United Kingdom public authority are entitled to the protection of the HRA in relation to the exercise of that control, authority or power over them. Hence public authorities of the United

---

[2] Application no 52207/99, decision of 12 December 2001; (2001) 11 BHRC 435.
[3] *Bankovic* at para 71.
[4] Discussed below.
[5] See *Soering* v. *UK* 11 EHRR 439, and the cases which followed, discussed below.
[6] [1984] 1 AC 74 at 111.

Kingdom must act[7] compatibly with Convention rights, not only within the United Kingdom, but when they exercise power, control or authority beyond the borders of the United Kingdom.

The principle of mutuality has the virtue that it provides a principled basis upon which the existing authorities may be explained. It allows for a more nuanced, flexible and principled approach to individual cases than any one of the other theories permits. It does not entail that anyone adversely affected by an act imputable to a public authority of the United Kingdom, wherever in the world that act may have been committed or its consequences felt, may bring a claim under the HRA.[8] The exercise of power, control or authority over the alleged "victim"[9] must be direct or effective for the principle of mutuality to be engaged.

These theories are not mutually exclusive. The view of the ECHR, as articulated in *Bankovic*, is that the Convention is essentially territorial in its application. The causation based cases, relating as they do to the decisions of public authorities within the borders of the State in question, fall within the territorial approach. Instances of extraterritorial application, such as those predicated on effective authority or control of persons or property, or relating to the activities of diplomatic or consular agents, are said to be exceptional.[10]

This chapter argues that the Court in *Bankovic* adopted a particularly narrow reading of its own jurisprudence on the extraterritorial application of the Convention, and that the concept of mutuality would provide a more consistent and principled approach to the application of the HRA.

EXPRESS PROVISIONS

It is unlawful, according to section 6(1) of the HRA, "for a public authority to act in a way which is incompatible with a Convention

---

[7] An act includes a failure to act (but not a failure to introduce to Parliament or enact a statute) – s 6(6) of the HRA.

[8] cf *Bankovic and others* v. *Belgium and 16 other Contracting States* Application no 52207/99, decision of 12 December 2001; (2001) 11 BHRC at para 75.

[9] Section 7 of the HRA read together with Art 34 of the Convention.

[10] *Bankovic*, paras 67–73.

right".[11] Nowhere in section 6 of the HRA is its reach confined to the borders of the United Kingdom. Section 22 of the HRA deals with the application and extent of the HRA. Subsection (6) provides that the Act extends to Northern Ireland. Section 22(7) provides that the reach of section 21(5) of the HRA, which abolishes the death penalty for military offences, is coterminous with the extra-territorial application of the enactments to which it refers. These apply to members of the army, the air force and the navy – and not to those affected by the operations or activities of the forces or their members.

PRESUMPTION AGAINST EXTRATERRITORIAL APPLICATION

That section 22 deals thus expressly with the extraterritorial application of section 21(5) only could be taken to indicate that the Act as a whole does not apply beyond the territory of the United Kingdom.[12] This might be thought to reinforce what is often called "the presumption against extraterritorial legislation". As Lord Bridge pointed out in *Holmes* v. *Bangladesh Biman Corporation* [1989] AC 1112 (HLE) at 1126, this expression may be misleading. The presumption limits "the scope which should be given to general words in United Kingdom statutes in their application to the persons, property, rights and liabilities of the subjects of other sovereign states who do not come within the jurisdiction of the United Kingdom Parliament". Parliament is presumed not to intend to usurp an "illegitimate authority over the subjects of foreign states".[13] Hence the presumption may more accurately be described as a "presumption that Parliament is not to be taken, by the use of general words, to legislate in the affairs of foreign nationals who do nothing to bring themselves within its jurisdiction".[14]

---

[11] That is the rights listed in s 1(1) and set in sch 1. See also s 21(1), interpretation.

[12] cf Lester and Pannick *Human Rights Law and Practice* (London: Butterworths, 1999), 2.22.4.

[13] *Holmes* v. *Bangladesh Biman Corporation* [1989] AC 1112 (HLE) at 1127.

[14] Ibid at 112, and see generally at 1126–28; Lord Griffiths at 1135–38; Lord Jauncey at 1146–48. The presumption against extra-territorial application in relation to the HRA is mentioned by Stanley Burnton J in *R* v. *Secretary of State for Work and Pensions ex parte Carson* [2002] EWHC 978 at para 19; upheld on appeal at [2003] EWCA Civ 797.

The authorities on the reach of enactments of the United Kingdom indicate that such enactments are, in the absence of express words to the contrary, presumed to apply to British subjects whatever their location, but to foreigners only when they bring themselves within the territorial jurisdiction of the United Kingdom.[15] Properly understood, the so-called presumption against extra-territoriality has no bearing on the reach of a statute imposing obligations upon public authorities of the United Kingdom,[16] and conferring rights upon the "victims" of the "acts" of such public authorities. The HRA does not interfere with the affairs of foreign nationals, nor with the sovereignty of other states – but it may provide certain protections to persons outside the United Kingdom who are adversely affected by the acts of British public authorities.[17]

The concept of extraterritorial jurisdiction usually refers to a claim of jurisdiction over foreign persons or entities in respect of acts which, although performed outside the territory of the state asserting jurisdiction, have effects within the territory of that State.[18] This chapter is not concerned with extraterritoriality in the usual sense, but with its mirror image – the ability of individuals and entities beyond the borders of a State to found a claim before its courts arising from the extraterritorial acts or omissions of that State.

WHO ARE THE VICTIMS OF THE UNLAWFUL ACTS OF PUBLIC AUTHORITIES

Only a victim or potential victim of an unlawful act by a public authority may bring proceedings under the HRA (section 7(1)). And

[15] cf. *The Zollverein* Swab. 96 at 98; *Ex parte Bain* (1879) 12 Ch D 522 (CA) at 526, 528, 532–33, 544–45; *Clark* v. *Oceanic Contractors Inc* [1983] 2 AC 130 (HLE) at 151–52.

[16] The policy concerns underlying the presumption do, however, elucidate why a "public authority" for the purposes of the Act can be only a public authority of the United Kingdom.

[17] Compare Justice Blackmun's dissenting views on the applicability of the presumption in the interpretation of the US Refugee Act, 1980 – *Sale* v. *Haitian Ctrs. Council, Inc.* 509 US 155 (1993) at 205–07.

[18] See, eg *United States* v. *Aluminium Co of America* 148 F. 2d 416 (1945) at 443; *United States* v. *Nippon Paper Industries Co Limited* 109 F. 3d 1 (1997); *Re the Wood Pulp Cartel* [1988] CMLR 901 (ECJ); *Gencor Ltd* v. *EC Commission* (Case T–102/96 of 25 March 1999) [1999] ECR II–753 (CFI).

only if a person would be a victim for the purposes of Article 34 of
the Convention in proceedings before the ECHR is he or she a victim for the purposes of section 7 (section 7(7)). Can a person
adversely affected by state conduct in another territory be a victim for
the purposes of Article 34?

Article 34, previously Article 25, sets out the right of individual
application in the following terms:

> The Court may receive applications from any person, non-governmental
> organisation or group of individuals claiming to be the victim of a viola-
> tion by one of the High Contracting Parties of the rights set forth in the
> Convention or the protocols thereto. The High Contracting Parties
> undertake not to hinder in any way the effective exercise of this right.[19]

Article 34 of the Convention does not speak to the question of
whether a person may complain of a violation by a High Contracting
Party outside the territory of the party in question. Article 1 deals
with the application of the Convention, requiring the High
Contracting Parties to secure the Convention rights "to everyone
within their jurisdiction."[20]

Article 1 is not one of "the Convention rights" included in section
1(1) of the HRA.[21] This must be borne in mind in assessing the
Strasbourg jurisprudence on the application of the Convention,
which turns on the interpretation of Article 1. The weight of such
authorities could arguably be diminished by the non-inclusion of
Article 1. Arguably, however, in determining what constitutes a victim for the purposes of section 7 of the HRA, Article 34 of the
Convention should be read subject to Article 1. This would mean
that a person adversely affected by a "violation" which occurs beyond
the jurisdiction of the respondent state could not be considered to be
a victim for the purposes of Article 34; nor, in consequence, for the
purposes of section 7 of the HRA. Such was the analysis accepted by

---

[19] The ECHR jurisprudence on what constitutes a "victim" under Art 34 is outlined in Lester and Pannick, above n 12, at 2.7.2.

[20] The wording in the French text is "*relevant de leur jurisdiction*" which suggests
a more expansive, and not exclusively territorial, scope of application. – See *Carson*,
above n 14 at para 20.

[21] This was said to be because the HRA itself gives effect to Art 1 by its incorporation of the Convention Rights – Lord Chancellor, 583 HL Official Reports (5th
series) col 475 (18 November 1997).

the Court in *R* v. *Secretary of State for Foreign and Commonwealth Affairs ex parte Quark Fishing Ltd* [2003] EWHC 1743 (Admin) at paras 18–19.

In *Bankovic*,[22] considered in detail below, the Court underlined at paragraph 62 that the determination of whether an individual falls within the jurisdiction of a contracting state must not be equated with the question of whether that person could be considered to be a victim of a violation of rights guaranteed by the Convention. These were said to be separate and distinct provisions, each of which had to be met consecutively before an individual may invoke the provisions of the Convention against a contracting state. Before the ECHR, therefore, the question of victimhood does not even arise unless jurisdiction is established.

Notwithstanding the Court's assertion that Article 1 and Article 34 raise separate and distinct admissibility conditions, in effect persons or entities cannot be victims for the purposes of article 34 of the Convention unless a jurisdictional link for the purposes of section 1 has been established.

But even if Article 34 is not implicitly limited in this way, section 2(1) of the HRA provides that a court or tribunal determining a question which has arisen in connection with a Convention right must take Strasbourg jurisprudence into account in so far as it considers such to be relevant to the proceedings at hand. In proceedings in which an extraterritorial violation of a Convention right is claimed, the extraterritorial reach of the HRA is a question which arises in connection with a Convention right, in respect of which the decisions and opinions of the ECHR and the Commission are clearly relevant.[23] Indeed, as pointed out in *R* v. *Special Adjudicator ex parte Ullah* [2002] EWCA Civ 1856 at paragraph 17, English courts have proceeded on the basis that the obligation imposed by section 6 of the HRA is subject to the limitation defined in Article 1 of the Convention.

---

[22] (2001) 11 BHRC 435.

[23] This obligation to "take into account" ECHR jurisprudence does not mean that the scope of the Convention rights is necessarily determined by the decisions and opinions emanating from Strasbourg. (Compare *R* v. *Broadcasting Standards Commission ex p British Broadcasting Corporation* [2000] 2 WLR 1327 (CA)). Nor does it detract from the value of considering how courts in other jurisdictions have dealt with similar and related questions of principle.

Embedded in the question of what constitutes a victim for the purposes of the HRA is the further question of whether, if the HRA applies at all beyond the territory of the United Kingdom, it benefits only British citizens or nationals, or extends to any person affected by an act of a British public authority. There is no such distinction in the level of protection afforded to those within the territory of the United Kingdom, and there is no principled basis upon which such a distinction could be maintained outside that territory.[24]

BANKOVIC INTRODUCED

The most recent Strasbourg decision on the reach of the Convention is the admissibility decision of the Grand Chamber of the ECHR in *Bankovic* v. *Belgium and 16 Other Contracting States*.[25] The claim was brought in respect of the NATO bombings of Belgrade, in particular the bombing of one of the Radio Televizije Srbije ("RTS") buildings on 23 April 1999. One of the applicants was injured in the bombing, the others were immediate relatives of people who were killed. The Court declared the application to be inadmissible on the ground that there was no jurisdictional link between the victims of the bombing and the respondent states. In reaching the conclusion that the Convention did not apply to the extraterritorial act of the respondent states in bombing Belgrade, the Court, from a number of strands in previous decisions and determinations on the question of extraterritorial application of the Convention, drew upon that strand which regarded extraterritorial jurisdiction as "exceptional" and founded such jurisdiction firmly upon a high degree of effective control or actual authority by the respondent state over the territory in which the violation is alleged to have occurred.

---

[24] Beyond the territory of the United Kingdom, a distinction could conceivably be drawn between those who owe allegiance to the Crown and those who do not. cf *Nissan* v. *Attorney-General* [1970] AC 179 (HLE) esp at 207–08, 213 (Lord Reid), 221 (Lord Morris), 225 (Lord Pearce). Another basis upon which the protection of the HRA could be claimed, however, is the principle of mutuality identified in the dissenting opinion of Brennan J in *United States* v. *Verdugo-Urdiquez* 494 US 259 at 284–85.

[25] Application no. 52207/99, decision of 12 December 2001; (2001) 11 BHRC 435.

The Court in *Bankovic* accepted that the Convention may, in exceptional circumstances, have extraterritorial application, but it considerably narrowed the scope for bringing claims in respect of extraterritorial acts by the High Contracting Parties. A brief overview of the cases in which extraterritoriality was considered prior to *Bankovic* illustrates the significance of the recent decision.

BANKOVIC'S PREDECESSORS

The Commission has long accepted that there may be circumstances in which a State may be held responsible under the Convention for its actions outside its national territory. In *Hess* v. *United Kingdom*,[26] the Commission considered the responsibility of the UK for the administration of the Allied Military Prison in Berlin, where the applicant was detained. The Commission expressed the opinion that,

. . . there is in principle, from a legal point of view, no reason why acts of the British authorities in Berlin should not entail the liability of the United Kingdom under the Convention.[27]

The administrative structure of the prison, however, was such that all decisions were taken jointly by all four powers. In the view of the Commission, this joint authority could not be divided into four separate jurisdictions. Consequently, the administration of the prison was not "within the jurisdiction" of the United Kingdom for the purposes of Article 1.

In *Cyprus* v. *Turkey* the Commission considered the applicability of the Convention to the actions of the occupying Turkish army in Cyprus.[28] It noted that Article 1 was drafted in broad terms. In particular, the language of the French text, "*relevant de leur jurisdiction*" suggested that a State was bound to secure the Convention rights of all those who fell under its actual authority and responsibility, whether such authority is exercised within the borders of the State or abroad.[29]

---

[26] Commission Admissibility Decision, 28 May 1975, 2 DR 72.
[27] Ibid at 73.
[28] Commission Admissibility Decision, 26 May 1975, 2 DR 125.
[29] See also *Mrs W* v. *Ireland* Commission Admissibility Decision, 28 February 1983, 32 DR 211; *Mrs W* v. *United Kingdom* Commission Admissibility Decision, 28 February 1983, 32 DR 190.

The Commission noted that,

> nationals of a State, including registered ships and aircrafts, are partly within its jurisdiction wherever they may be, and . . . authorised agents of a State, including diplomatic or consular agents and armed forces, not only remain under its jurisdiction when abroad but bring any other persons or property "within the jurisdiction" of that State, to the extent that they exercise authority over such persons or property. Insofar as, by their acts or omissions, they affect such persons or property, the responsibility of the State is engaged.[30]

The Commission therefore considered that the actions at issue in the case did engage the responsibility of Turkey under the Convention, despite the fact that Turkey had not annexed the territory or established either military or civil government there.

In *X and Y* v. *Switzerland*,[31] the Commission considered the admissibility of an application against Switzerland, in relation to the refusal of a residence permit to the first applicant to remain in Liechtenstein. The decision to refuse the permit was taken by the Swiss authorities, under the terms of a treaty between Switzerland and Liechtenstein, which made the Swiss authorities competent in relation to matters concerning the aliens police in Liechtenstein. The Commission referred to its decisions in *Hess* and *Cyprus* v. *Turkey* as establishing that,

> the Contracting Parties' responsibility under the Convention is also engaged insofar as they exercise jurisdiction outside their territory and thereby bring persons or property within their actual authority or control.[32]

The Commission noted that under the terms of the treaty, the Swiss authorities did not act "in distinction from their national competences."[33] They acted exclusively in conformity with Swiss law, though with effect on the territory of Liechtenstein. As a result, it was held, the authorities in question had exercised a Swiss jurisdiction, and acts by the Swiss authorities with effect in Liechtenstein would

---

[30] *Cyprus* v. *Turkey* Commission Admissibility Decision, 26 May 1975, 2 DR 125, p 136, para 8.
[31] Commission Admissibility Decision, 14 July 1977, 9 DR 57.
[32] Ibid at 71.
[33] Ibid at 73.

bring all those to whom they applied under Swiss jurisdiction within the meaning of Article 1 of the Convention. In *Mrs W* v. *Ireland*,[34] the Commission reiterated a generous construction of the territorial jurisdiction established in Article 1. However, in that case it was held that complaints against Ireland were inadmissible in respect of a murder which had taken place in Northern Ireland, and which had been committed by a Northern Ireland resident. The Commission found that the applicants had failed to show that the acts or omissions of the Irish authorities had contributed in any way to the murders; therefore the alleged violations were outside the jurisdiction of the State. The Commission said:

> it emerges from the language, in particular of the French text, and the object of [article 1] and from the purpose of the Convention as a whole, that the High Contracting Parties are bound to secure the said rights and freedoms to all persons under their actual authority and responsibility, not only when the authority is exercised within their own territory but also when it is exercised abroad.

In a related case against the United Kingdom, *Mrs W* v. *United Kingdom*,[35] it was found that a second murder which took place in the Republic of Ireland did not engage the jurisdiction of the United Kingdom, since no acts or omissions of the UK government could have contributed to the murder.

In *Reinette* v. *France*,[36] the Commission considered a complaint regarding the actions of the French authorities on the territory of St Vincent in the course of the extradition of the applicant from St Vincent to France. It was found that the initial deprivation of liberty, which took place on the territory of St Vincent without the involvement of the French authorities, did not fall within the jurisdiction of France and did not engage French responsibility under the Convention. However, from the moment when the French authorities took the applicant into custody, and when he was detained on a French military aircraft, the Commission considered him to have been within French jurisdiction.

---

[34] Commission Admissibility Decision, 28 February 1983, 32 DR 211.
[35] Commission Admissibility Decision, 28 February 1983, 32 DR 190.
[36] Commission Admissibility Decision, 2 October 1989.

In *Drozd and Janousek v. France and Spain*,[37] both the Commission and the Court confirmed the extra-territorial application of the Convention. That case concerned allegations of unfair trial in the Andorran courts. The Court examined the ambiguous status of Andorra in international law. The question arose whether the acts complained of by the applicants could be attributed to France or Spain or both, even though they occurred outside the territory of those states.

With reference to its previous decisions on the interpretation of Article 1, the Commission pointed out that:

> the term "jurisdiction" is not limited to the national territory of the High Contracting Parties concerned. It is clear from the wording, particularly of the French text, and the object of this Article, and from the purpose of the Convention as a whole, that "the High Contracting Parties are bound to secure the said rights and freedoms to all persons under their actual authority and responsibility, whether that authority is exercised within their own territory or abroad" and even that "the responsibility of a High Contracting Party can be engaged by acts of its authorities producing effects outside its own territory".[38]

To similar effect, the Court noted that:

> The term jurisdiction is not limited to the national territory of the High Contracting Parties; their responsibility can be involved because of acts of their authorities producing effects outside their own territory.[39]

This principle was expressly reaffirmed by the Court in *Loizidou v. Turkey*,[40] which concerned the responsibility of Turkey for alleged breaches of the Convention in Northern Cyprus. The Court said that although Article 1 sets limits on the reach of the Convention, the concept of "jurisdiction" under this provision is not restricted to the national territory of the High Contracting Parties. This principle was illustrated by case law holding that the extradition or expulsion of a person by a Contracting State may give rise to an issue under Article 3 and hence engage the responsibility of that State under the

---

[37] [1992] 14 EHRR 745.
[38] Ibid para 79, p 764.
[39] Ibid para 91, p 788.
[40] 20 EHRR 99 at para 62.

Convention[41] as well as that holding that the responsibility of Contracting Parties can be involved because of acts of their authorities, whether performed within or outside national boundaries, which produce effects outside their own territory.[42]
The Court went on to hold :

> Bearing in mind the object and purpose of the Convention, the responsibility of a Contracting Party may also arise when as a consequence of military action – whether lawful or unlawful – it exercises effective control of an area outside its national territory. The obligation to secure, in such an area, the rights and freedoms set out in the Convention derives from the fact of such control whether it be exercised directly, through its armed forces, or through a subordinate local administration.[43]

On the merits, the Court did not consider it to be necessary to determine whether Turkey actually exercised detailed control over the policies and actions of the authorities of the "Turkish Republic of Northern Cyprus" ("TRNC"). The large number of Turkish troops engaged in active duties in northern Cyprus meant that the Turkish army obviously exercised effective overall control over that part of the island. In the circumstances, Turkey was found to be responsible for the policies and actions of the TRNC with the result that those affected by such policies or actions therefore came within the jurisdiction of Turkey for the purposes of Article 1 of the Convention. Turkey's obligation to secure the rights and freedoms set out in the Convention was found therefore to extend to northern Cyprus.

In a subsequent decision, *Cyprus* v. *Turkey*,[44] the Court added that since Turkey exercised "effective control" over northern Cyprus, its responsibility went beyond the acts of its own agents therein and extended to the acts of the local administration which survived by virtue of Turkish support. Hence Turkey's jurisdiction under Article 1 was held to extend to securing the entire range of substantive Convention rights in northern Cyprus.

---

[41] For example, *Soering* v. *United Kingdom* (1989) 11 EHRR 439 at para 91; *Cruz Varas* v. *Sweden* (1992) 14 EHRR 1, paras 69–70; *Vilvajarah* v. *UK* (1992) 14 EHRR 248 para 103. These cases are considered briefly below.

[42] *Drozd and Janousek* v. *France and Spain* [1992] 14 EHRR 745 at para 91.

[43] Ibid at para 62.

[44] [GC], no 25781/94, ECHR 2001; and see the ECHR decision of 9 July 2003 in *Djavit AN* v. *Turkey* (Application no. 20652/92) at paras 21–23.

CAUSATION AND RESPONSIBILITY – EXTRADITION OR EXPULSION TO FACE ILL-TREATMENT ABROAD

Soering v. *UK*[45] establishes the principle that states are responsible under the Convention for the extradition or expulsion of individuals to states where they will face breaches of absolute rights such as those in Article 3. In *Soering*, the Court held that the decision by a State to extradite an accused may give rise to liability under Article 3, where there are substantial grounds for believing that, if extradited, the person faces a real risk of being subjected to inhuman or degrading treatment or punishment in the requesting country.

The Court noted that Article 1 set a territorial limit on the application of Convention rights:

> Article 1 sets a limit, notably territorial, on the reach of the Convention. In particular, the engagement undertaken by the Contracting State is confined to "securing" . . . the listed rights and freedoms to persons within its own "jurisdiction". Further, the Convention does not govern the actions of States not Parties to it, nor does it purport to be a means of requiring the Contracting States to impose Convention standards on other States.[46]

Although it was common ground that the United Kingdom had no power over the practices and arrangements of the US authorities in holding prisoners on death row, this did not absolve the UK from its responsibility under Article 3 to ensure that the foreseeable consequences of its extradition did not amount to inhuman and degrading treatment or torture.

In *Soering*, a number of basic characteristics of the Convention were used to support the Court's interpretation of the obligations imposed by Article 3:

1. the "special character" of the Convention as a treaty for the collective enforcement of human rights and fundamental freedoms;
2. the need to ensure that the Convention's provisions be interpreted and applied so as to make its safeguards "practical and effective";
3. the need to interpret Convention rights in a way that is consistent

---

[45] 11 EHRR 439.
[46] Para 86.

with "the general spirit of the Convention, an instrument designed to maintain and promote the ideals and values of a democratic society";[47]

4. the need to interpret the Convention's provisions in accordance with its underlying values referred to in the preamble, the "common heritage of political traditions, ideals, freedom and the rule of law." In relation to absolute rights such as freedom from torture, the Court considered that these values would require a state to refrain from extradition to a State where there was a foreseeable risk of torture or inhuman and degrading treatment.[48]

The principles set out in *Soering* were reaffirmed in *Cruz Varas* v. *Sweden*,[49] where the Court, referring to *Soering*, found that the same principle applied to a decision to expel a non-national from the territory. This was again affirmed in *Vilvarajah* v. *UK*.[50] The Court has also made it clear that the risk of inhuman and degrading treatment does not have to involve deliberate breaches of human rights on the part of the State to which the applicant is being expelled, but may instead involve risks from non-governmental sources,[51] or from the absence of adequate medical treatment.[52]

Soering and its progeny[53] establish that the Convention is violated by the *decision* to extradite or expel – a decision which is made within the territory of the Contracting State.[54] Hence these cases are not, in fact, instances of the extraterritorial application of the Convention.[55] They simply acknowledge that an act may be unlawful if it has as its direct consequence harm which itself violates a core

---

[47] Para 87.

[48] Para 88.

[49] [1991] 14 EHRR 1, paras 69–70.

[50] [1991] 14 EHRR 248, para 103.

[51] *Ahmed* v. *Austria* (1997) 24 EHRR 728, paras 39–47.

[52] *D* v. *UK* [1997] 24 EHRR 423.

[53] *Ahmed* v. *Austria* (1997) 24 EHRR 728, paras 38–39; *HLR* v. *France* (1997) 26 EHRR 29; *Hatami* v. *Sweden* 27 EHRR CD 8; *Jabari* v. *Turkey* (2000) BHRC 1; *Hilal* v. *UK* (2001) 33 EHRR 2, para 59; *Bensaid* v. *UK* (2001) 33 EHRR 10, para 32.

[54] Mere physical presence within the contracting state is sufficient to bring an individual within jurisdiction for the purposes of Art 1 – see eg *D* v. *UK* (1997) 24 EHRR 423, para 48.

[55] cf *R* v. *Special Adjudicator ex parte Ullah* [2002] EWCA Civ 1856 at para 29.

value underlying the Convention.[56] Where the harm eventuates is irrelevant. The Convention is not in these cases being applied to acts governed by the laws of States of non-contracting parties. Nor are Contracting States being held vicariously liable for the acts or omissions of non-contracting states. A causal nexus establishes liability – the Contracting State is held liable for the foreseeable consequences of extradition or expulsion.[57] *Al-Adsani v. United Kingdom*[58] establishes, however, that where torture is alleged to have occurred abroad, and was not caused by the acts of United Kingdom public authorities, the Convention is not breached by the failure to allow a claimant to bring a claim in England against the foreign state which is alleged to be responsible.[59]

Strasbourg jurisprudence distinguishes between the full panoply of Convention safeguards and its fundamental values.[60] The prohibition of torture and of inhuman or degrading treatment or punishment is one such value. The prohibiton of torture and of inhuman or degrading treatment or punishment is one such value. In *R v. Special Adjudicator ex parte Ullah* the Court of Appeal held that a decision to remove an alien to a country that did not respect the right to freedom of religion would not infringe the HRA where the nature of the foreseeable interference with that right in the receiving state fell short of ill-treatment within Article 3.[61] The wider implication of this conclusion, the Court pointed out at paragraph 64, was that regardless of the right invoked, an apprehension of ill-treatment falling short of Article 3 would be insufficient to bring a claimant within the limited "extension" to the territorial principle wrought by the *Soering* line of authority (and see paragraph 47).

In *R v. Secretary of State for the Home Department ex parte Razgar and other cases* the Court of Appeal stated that although the *Ullah* approach could be applied without difficulty in many cases, claims under Article 8 could be more difficult to analyse.[62] The Court concluded at paragraphs 22–24 that a threat of ill-treatment with a sufficiently adverse

[56] *Soering* (1989) 11 EHRR 439 at paras 86, 88.
[57] *R v. Special Adjudicator ex parte Ullah* [2002] EWCA Civ 1856 at para 29.
[58] (2002) 34 EHRR 11.
[59] The applicant had joint British and Kuwaiti citizenship.
[60] *Soering*, above n 56 para 86.
[61] [2002] EWCA Civ 1856, [2003] 1 WLR 770 at para 63 and see 39, 61–63.
[62] [2003] EWCA Civ 840 at para 17.

effect on physical and mental integrity, even if it fell short of Article 3, could in principle engage the responsibility of the expelling state under Article 8, provided that the claim met a threefold test as to the nature of the harm apprehended, the severity of such harm and the likelihood of the harm eventuating. The Court pointed out that even if a removal case engages Article 8(1), a claim could nevertheless be defeated by Article 8(2) considerations (paragraphs 25–27).

The causal analysis in relation to the risk of torture has recently been adopted by the Canadian Supreme Court in construing section 7 of the Charter[63] in the context of an expulsion case, *Suresh v. Canada (Minister of Citizenship and Immigration)* (2002) SCC 1. The Court held that the deportation of a refugee facing a risk of torture abroad was contrary to the principles of "fundamental justice" within the terms of the Charter if there was a sufficient causal connection between the treatment abroad and the acts of the Canadian government. A similar causal analysis was applied by the Irish Supreme Court in *Finucan v. McMahon* (1990) 1 INLR 165 (SC). The Court held that it would be failing in its duty to protect an extraditee's rights were it to permit him to return to Northern Ireland's Maze Prison where, it was alleged, there was a probability that he would be subject to assaults and inhuman treatment.[64]

The Canadian Supreme Court has also applied the causal analysis in adjudicating the lawfulness or otherwise of the extradition of fugitives to a country where they would face the death penalty. In *United States v. Burns*[65] the Court held that before extraditing a person to be tried for a capital offence in a country in which the death penalty is competent, there is now an obligation on the Canadian government, in the absence of exceptional circumstances, to obtain from the country requesting extradition an assurance that the death penalty would not be applied.[66] Like the decision in *Suresh*, *Burns* turned on section

[63] Section 7: "Everyone has the right to life, liberty and security of the person and the right not to be deprived thereof except in accordance with the provisions of fundamental justice."

[64] At p 206.

[65] [2001] 1 SCR 283; (2001) 81 CRR (2d).

[66] The Court did not anticipate what might constitute exceptional circumstances (para 65). The Court in *Burns* reconsidered the majority decisions in *Kindler v. Canada (Minister of Justice)* [1991] 2 SCR 779, (1991) 6 CRR (2d) 193 and *Reference re Ng Extradition (Canada)* [1991] 2 SCR 858, (1991) 6 CRR (2d) 252 holding that such assurances were not a prerequisite to a lawful extradition.

7 of the Charter. The Court pointed to the causal nexus between the minister's decision and the eventual result:

> While the Canadian government would not itself inflict capital punishment, its decision to extradite without assurances would be a necessary link in the chain of causation to that *potential* result.[67]

The language of causation is employed by the South African Constitutional Court in dealing with the legality of a suspect's extradition by the South African Government to stand trial in the United States for involvement in the bombing of the US embassies in Africa. The Court found in *Mohamed and Another* v. *President of the Republic of South Africa and Others* 2001 (3) SA 893 (CC),[68] that the government had not complied with its constitutional obligation to seek an assurance from the United States that the death sentence would not be imposed on Mohamed:

> The fact that Mohamed is now facing the possibility of a death sentence is the direct result of the failure by the South African authorities to secure such an undertaking. The causal connection is clear between the handing over of Mohamed to the FBI for removal to the United States for trial without securing an assurance against the imposition of the death sentence and the threat of such a sentence now being imposed on Mohamed.[69]

It is in the jurisprudential setting described above that the *Bankovic* decision should be read.

BANKOVIC REVISITED

The applicants in the *Bankovic* case relied on the line of Strasbourg authority from *Hess* to *Loizidou*, including *Soering*, in support of their claims that their rights under the Convention were violated when their close relatives were killed or they were themselves injured by the NATO bombings in Belgrade.[70]

---

[67] *Burns*, para 54.

[68] Available at www.concourt.gov.za.

[69] Paras 54–55.

[70] In addition, they relied on the admissibility decisions in the cases of *Issa and Others* v. *Turkey* (dec), no 31821/96, 30 May 2000, unreported and *Öcalan* v. *Turkey* (dec), no 46221/99, 14 December 2000, unreported (both of which concerned the

In assessing whether the applicants and their relatives were, by the bombing of Belgrade, brought "within the jurisdiction" of the respondent states, the Court began by reviewing the rules applicable to the interpretation of the Convention.[71] As to the ordinary meaning of "jurisdiction" in Article 1, the Court considered that it reflected the essentially (although not exclusively) territorial notion of jurisdiction which prevailed in public international law.[72] Moreover, the practice of Contracting States was at odds with the applicants' argument that, in the absence of a derogation under Article 15, the Convention would apply to extraterritorial wars and states of emergency.[73]

In confirmation of this primarily territorial conception of jurisdiction the Court turned, as neither it nor the Commission had felt the need to do in previous cases on the point, to the *travaux préparatoires*. These indicated that in the drafting of Article 1, the present formulation ("within their jurisdiction") had replaced the words "all persons residing within their territories" in order to expand the application of the Convention to persons actually present within the territory of the Contracting States, although not necessarily legally resident there.[74]

The Court went on to review its case law on the question of extraterritorial jurisdiction, which exercise was introduced as follows:

> In keeping with the essentially territorial notion of jurisdiction, the Court has accepted only in exceptional cases that acts of the Contracting States performed, or producing effects, outside their territories can constitute an exercise of jurisdiction by them within the meaning of Article 1 of the Convention.[75]

Of the *Soering* line of authorities, the Court pointed out that these were not instances of the extraterritorial jurisdiction of the respondent states. Rather,

arrest and detentions of the applicants outside the territory of the respondent state) and *Xhavara and Others* v. *Italy and Albania* (dec), no 39473/98, 11 January 2001, unreported, which concerned the alleged deliberate striking of an Albanian ship by an Italian naval vessel 35 nautical miles off the coast of Italy, and *Ilascu* v. *Moldova and the Russian Federation* (dec.) no 48787/99, 4 July 2001, unreported.

[71] Paras 55–58.
[72] Paras 59–63.
[73] Paras 49, 62.
[74] Para 63.
[75] Para 67.

liability is incurred in such cases by an action of the respondent State concerning a person while he or she is on its territory, clearly within its jurisdiction, . . . such cases do not concern the actual exercise of a State's competence or jurisdiction abroad.[76]

Of its dictum at para 91of the *Drozd and Janousek* case, affirmed at paragraph 62 of the *Loizidou* case, stating that the responsibility of Contracting States could in principle be engaged if such acts produced effects outside their own territory, the Court simply pointed out that in *Drozd* the acts in question could not in fact be attributed to the respondent states.[77]

The *Loizidou* admissibility decision, said the Court, had held that the responsibility of a Contracting State was capable of being engaged when as a consequence of military action (lawful or unlawful) it "exercised effective control of an area outside its national territory." Such control, whether exercised directly, through the respondent state's armed forces, or through a subordinate local administration, gave rise to an obligation to secure the Convention rights and freedoms in such an area.[78]

The Court concluded its review of the Article 1 admissibility decisions thus:

> In sum, the case-law of the Court demonstrates that its recognition of the exercise of extra-territorial jurisdiction by a Contracting State is exceptional: it has done so when the respondent State, through the effective control of the relevant territory and its inhabitants abroad as a consequence of military occupation or through the consent, invitation or acquiescence of the Government of that territory, exercises all or some of the public powers normally to be exercised by that Government.[79]

The Court noted in addition that other recognised instances of the extraterritorial exercise of jurisdiction by a State include cases involving the activities of its diplomatic or consular agents abroad and on board craft and vessels registered in, or flying the flag of, that

---

[76] Para 68.
[77] Para 69.
[78] *Bankovic*, para 70.
[79] Para 71. Compare *Coard et al* v. *The United States* Report No 109/99 of the Inter-American Commission on Human Rights, case no. 10.951 (29 September 1999); and see Theodore Meron, "Extraterritoriality of Human Rights Treaties" (1995) 89 *AJIL* 78 at 79.

State. These are specific situations in which customary international law and treaty provisions have recognised the extraterritorial exercise of jurisdiction by a State.[80]

Following this account of the Strasbourg jurisprudence on the jurisdiction question, the Court rejected the applicants' suggestion that the concept of "effective control" could be extended to an obligation upon contracting parties to secure the Convention rights in a manner proportionate to the level of control exercised in any given extraterritorial situation. The applicants argued that the respondents, who were in control of the airspace above Belgrade, could be held accountable for those Convention rights within their control of the situation in question.[81] The Court, however, considered that the obligation imposed by Article 1 could not be divided and tailored in accordance with the particular circumstances of the extraterritorial act in question.[82]

The applicants had submitted in the alternative that the respondents were liable because the strike on the RTS building was the extraterritorial effect of prior decisions taken within the territory of the respondent states.[83] The Court accepted the respondents' argument that the attempted analogy with the *Soering* situation was inapposite and unconvincing – the decision to extradite Soering was taken when he was detained on the territory of the respondent state. It was therefore "a classic exercise of legal authority over an individual to whom the State could secure the full range of Convention rights".[84]

Underlying the Court's analysis of the issues at stake is the understandable anxiety that declaring the claim admissible would mean that "anyone adversely affected by an act imputable to a Contracting State, wherever in the world that act may have been committed or its consequences felt, is thereby brought within the jurisdiction of that State for the purpose of Article 1 of the Convention".[85] In response to the applicants' claim that a denial of jurisdiction would leave a lacuna in the Convention system for the protection of human rights, the Court was therefore at pains to emphasise the essentially regional character of the *ordre public* mission of the Convention:

[80] Para 73.
[81] Paras 46–47, 52, 74–75.
[82] Para 75.
[83] Para 53.
[84] Paras 44 and 77.
[85] Para 75.

The Court's obligation, in this respect, is to have regard to the special character of the Convention as a constitutional instrument of *European public order* for the protection of individual human beings and its role, as set out in Article 19 of the Convention, is to ensure the observance of *the engagements undertaken* by the Contracting Parties. . . . It is therefore difficult to contend that a failure to accept the extra-territorial jurisdiction of the respondent States would fall foul of the Convention's *ordre public* objective, which itself underlines the essentially regional vocation of the Convention system. . . .[86]

The Court distinguished its decision in *Cyprus v. Turkey* in which it had expressed the need to avoid "a regrettable vacuum in the system of human-rights protection" in northern Cyprus. The Court was there concerned with a situation in which the Cypriot Government, a Contracting State, was precluded by Turkey's effective control of the territory from securing to the inhabitants of northern Cyprus the Convention rights and freedoms which they had previously enjoyed:[87]

> In short, the Convention is a multi-lateral treaty operating, subject to Article 56 of the Convention, in an essentially regional context and notably in the legal space (*espace juridique*) of the Contracting States. The FRY clearly does not fall within this legal space. The Convention was not designed to be applied throughout the world, even in respect of the conduct of Contracting States. Accordingly, the desirability of avoiding a gap or vacuum in human rights' protection has so far been relied on by the Court in favour of establishing jurisdiction only when the territory in question was one that, but for the specific circumstances, would normally be covered by the Convention.[88]

BRINGING *BANKOVIC* HOME

Two questions arise in relation to the relevance of *Bankovic*. First, does *Bankovic* delimit the extraterritorial application of the HRA?

[86] Para 80, references omitted.
[87] Para 80.
[88] Para 80. Art 56 of the European Convention makes provision for "any State to declare, by notification addressed to the Secretary General of the Council of Europe that the . . . Convention shall extend to all or any of the territories for whose international relations it is responsible." See the discussion of this provision in *R v. Secretary of State for Foreign and Commonwealth Affairs ex parte Quark Fishing Ltd* [2003] EWHC 1743 at paras 20–26.

Secondly, if it does so, to what extent does the *Bankovic* judgment really constrain the extraterritorial application of the HRA?

As to the first question, *Bankovic* turns on an interpretation of a provision which is not incorporated in the HRA. *Bankovic* is notionally distinguishable on this basis. As pointed out above, however, the very enactment of the HRA is said to give effect to the UK's obligation under Article 1.[89] The relevance of decisions on the scope of Article 1 is therefore undeniable – even if the category of actual or potential victims for the purposes of Article 34 of the Convention is not prescribed by the boundaries of Article 1.[90]

As to the second question, the extent to which *Bankovic* will constrain the extraterritorial application of the HRA will depend largely on what a court considers to constitute "effective control" by the UK over the applicants in the circumstances of a particular case. The concerns which militated against admissibility in the *Bankovic* case would not necessarily extend to all cases in which a public authority, such as the army or a consular official, exercises direct authority over persons on foreign territory. In many such situations, the degree of control may be as extensive and effective as that in the *Loizidou* case. Moreover, it may not be shared to the extent that it was in the *Bankovic* case.[91] This indicates that *Bankovic* has narrowed, but has certainly not closed off the scope of claims arising from acts of public authorities beyond the borders of the United Kingdom.

R v. *Secretary of State for Employment and Pensions ex parte Carson*[92] concerned the claim of a British pensioner living in South Africa to the same uprating of UK state pensions as that received by pensioners living in the United Kingdom. Mrs Carson claimed that the

---

[89] Along similar lines, it could be argued that the HRA was passed in order to "bring rights home"; not to export them. That argument would miss the point. Holding public authorities accountable in the courts of the UK for acts incompatible with the HRA which are performed or have consequences abroad does not export Convention rights and freedoms but brings them home in the fullest sense.

[90] See, eg *R* v. *Secretary of State for Foreign Affairs ex parte Abbasi* [2002] EWCA Civ 1598; [2003] UKHRR 76, at paras 48–50 and 69–79, especially at paras 72–76.

[91] Interestingly, the Court in *Bankovic* did not refer to the extent to which responsibility for the Belgrade bombings was shared by NATO members – including the United States, a non-contracting party; cf *Hess* v. *United Kingdom* Commission Admissibility Decision, 28 May 1975 2 DR 72.

[92] [2002] EWHC 978; upheld on appeal at [2003] EWCA Civ 797.

denial of inflation based uprating to pensioners living in South Africa (and other "old Commonwealth" countries) infringed her rights under Article 1 of Protocol 1 to the Convention (the right to property) read together with Article 14 (the prohibition of discrimination in respect of Convention rights and freedoms) and was therefore unlawful under the HRA.

Before dealing with the substance of the discrimination claim, the Court considered whether the provisions of the Convention applied to the claimant and those in her position, since they resided beyond the territorial jurisdiction of the United Kingdom. The Court noted that Article 1 of the Convention is not incorporated in the HRA,[93] but nevertheless analysed it as being relevant to the reach of the HRA. With reference to the French text of Article 1, as well as the jurisprudence of the ECHR and state practice, the Court concluded that Article 1 does not refer only to the presence of persons within the territory, but to jurisdiction in a legal sense.[94] Mrs Carson's claim was held to fall clearly within the "legal space" of the United Kingdom:

> the object of the application of the Convention is legislation that confers benefits on individuals. It clearly operates in (and only in) the "legal space" of the UK, and is therefore within the scope of the Convention. There is no question of any possible infringement of the sovereignty of another state or the exercise of sovereignty over those present in another state.[95]

More difficult was the claim in *R* v. *Secretary of State for Foreign and Commonwealth Affairs ex parte Abbasi.*[96] The first claimant was a British national captured by United States forces in Afghanistan and held at Guantanamo Bay without recourse to any court or tribunal, or even a lawyer. Abbasi sought to establish a duty on the part of the Foreign and Commonwealth Office to take positive steps to redress his situation, or at least to give a reasoned response to his request for assistance. One of the bases upon which it was sought to establish such a duty was the Human Rights Act. With reference to Article 1 of the European Convention, it was accepted that Mr Abbasi needed

---

[93] *Carson*, paras 17–24.
[94] *Carson*, paras 20–21.
[95] Ibid para 22.
[96] [2002] EWCA Civ 1598; [2003] UKHRR 76.

to establish that he fell within the jurisdiction of the United Kingdom in order to invoke the HRA. He did so, it was argued, because he was a British national in relation to whom the United Kingdom Government had jurisdiction to take measures.[97] It was argued that if Mr Abbasi's continued arbitrary detention resulted from the failure to afford Mr Abbasi diplomatic protection, then such failure violated Article 5 of the Convention and hence section 6 of the HRA.[98]

In considering this argument, the Court remarked that it would be a considerable extension of the causation based theory if the Convention were held to require a state "to take positive action to prevent, or mitigate the effects of, violations of human rights that take place outside the jurisdiction and for which the state has no responsibility".[99]

On the question of jurisdiction, the Court reviewed the decisions of the ECHR in *Al-Adsani*[100] and *Bankovic*.[101] From these it derived the following principles:

1. The jurisdiction referred to in Article 1 of the Convention will normally be a territorial jurisdiction.
2. Where a State enjoys effective control of foreign territory, that territory will fall within its jurisdiction for the purposes of Article 1.
3. Where, under principles of international law, a state enjoys extra-territorial jurisdiction over an individual and acts in the exercise of that jurisdiction, that individual will be deemed to be within the jurisdiction of the state for the purposes of Article 1, insofar as the action in question is concerned.

Under none of these principles, held the Court, could Mr Abbasi, albeit a British national, claim to fall within the jurisdiction of the United Kingdom for the purposes of Article 1 of the Convention. The United Kingdom Government exercised no control or authority over him while he was held by United States forces.[102] With reference

---

[97] The argument was developed on the basis of the *Carson* case.
[98] *Abbasi*, above n 96, at paras 48–50.
[99] Ibid para 71.
[100] (2002) 34 EHRR 11.
[101] (2001) 11 BHRC 435.
[102] *Abbasi*, above n 96 para 77.

to *Bertrand Russell Peace Foundation* v. *United Kingdom,*[103] the Court rejected any suggestion that a right to diplomatic protection could be inferred from a State's obligation under Article 1 of the Convention to "secure" the Convention rights to those within its jurisdiction. Hence the Court rejected Mr Abbasi's claims based on the HRA. It nevertheless accepted that there is, in certain circumstances, scope for judicial review of a refusal to render diplomatic assistance to a British subject who is suffering a violation of a fundamental human right as the result of the conduct of the authorities of a foreign state.[104]

HOME AND AWAY: MUTUALITY AND THE RULE OF LAW

As pointed out above, although the relevance of Strasbourg jurisprudence is inscribed in section 2 of the HRA, it is not the only source of learning on the interpretation and application of the rights and freedoms embodied in the Convention. It is instructive to consider the approach to similar and related questions taken by courts in other jurisdictions. Comparative jurisprudence may assist in charting a principled route through a thicket of competing considerations. It may also illustrate the pitfalls of following a particular approach.

At issue before the Canadian Supreme Court in *R* v. *Cook* [1998] 2 SCR 597[105] was whether a citizen of the United States suspected of having committed a crime in Canada, to be prosecuted in Canada, could invoke Charter rights in respect of his interrogation in the United States by Canadian police. The Court held that the acts of the Canadian detectives fell within the purview of section 32(1) of

---

[103] Commission Admissibility Decision, 2 May 1978, Application 7597/76.

[104] *Abbasi*, above n 96, at paras 80–106. An account of the considerations underlying the Court's acceptance of this proposition falls beyond the purview of this chapter. In *R* v. *The Prime Minister of the United Kingdom ex parte the Campaign for Nuclear Disarmament* [2002] EWHC 2777 QB, the Divisional Court held that the court will not determine an issue if to do so would be damaging to the public interest in the field of international relations, national security or defence. This was one of the grounds for dismissing an application by CND for an advisory declaration on the proper meaning of United Nations Security Council Resolution 1441.

[105] Also reported at 128 CCC (3d) 1, 164 DLR (4th) 1, 55 (2d) 189; 57 BCLR (3d) 215.

the Charter[106] because they were Canadian law enforcement officials acting under powers of investigation derived from Canadian law.[107] The application of the Charter beyond Canadian territory could not, however, be determined with reference to section 32(1) alone. Only if the application of the Charter did not give rise to an objectionable extra-territorial effect by interfering with the sovereign authority of the foreign state in question, could it be held to apply beyond Canadian territory.[108]

In the circumstances of the case, there was no imposition of Canadian criminal law standards upon foreign officials, nor was there any interference with US criminal procedures. It was therefore reasonable to require the Canadian detectives to comply with Charter standards, and to permit the suspect, himself required to adhere to Canadian law and procedure, to claim Canadian constitutional rights in respect of his interrogation in New Orleans.[109] Hence the failure properly to have informed the suspect of his right to counsel prior to his interrogation had breached section 10(b) of the Charter,[110] with the result that the statement he gave in the course of his interrogation should have been excluded under section 24(2).[111]

L'Heureux-Dubé J took a dissenting view of the applicability of section 10(b) to the interrogation of the suspect in the United States. The argument of the majority, she considered, had simply assumed the suspect to be a holder of a right under the Canadian Constitution, whereas that very question was logically anterior to the question as to whether section 32(1) was engaged by state action

---

[106] "This Charter applies:
  (a) to the Parliament and government of Canada in respect of all matters within the authority of Parliament including all matters relating to the Yukon Territory and Northwest Territories; and
  (b) to the legislature and government of each province in respect of all matters within the authority of the legislature of each province."

[107] Paras 25 and 49.

[108] Para 25.

[109] Paras 50–51.

[110] "10. Everyone has the right on arrest or detention . . . (b) to retain and instruct counsel without delay and to be informed of that right".

[111] "Where in proceedings under subsection (1), a court concludes that evidence was obtained in a manner that infringed or denied any rights or freedoms guaranteed by this Charter, the evidence shall be excluded if it is established that, having regard to all the circumstances, the admission of it in the proceedings would bring the administration of justice into disrepute".

which may have infringed the right claimed.[112] L'Heureux-Dubé J reached no conclusion on whether the suspect was a holder of rights under the Charter, since that issue had not been argued before the Court,[113] but she clearly considered that the question should be treated with circumspection should it arise in the future.

In the United States, the courts have generally adopted a parsimonious view of the extra-territorial reach of Constitutional rights.

In *Johnson v. Eisentrager*[114] 21 German nationals were convicted of engaging in continued military activity against the United States after the surrender of Germany and before the surrender of Japan in World War II. The United States Supreme Court rejected their efforts to obtain writs of habeas corpus. It was held that the Constitution did not confer a right of personal security nor an immunity from military trial and punishment upon an alien enemy engaged in the hostile service of a government at war with the United States.

In *United States v. Verdugo-Urquidez*,[115] the Supreme Court held by a majority that the Fourth Amendment to the United States Constitution did not apply to the search and seizure by United States agents of property owned by a non-resident alien and located in a foreign country.[116] This decision was said to follow the approach of the Court in *Johnson v. Eisentrager*, in which, according to the majority, the Court "rejected the claim that aliens were entitled to Fifth Amendment rights outside the sovereign territory of the United States".

In his concurring opinion, Justice Kennedy expressed the view that in cases involving the extraterritorial application of the Constitution, the law of the United States draws a distinction

---

[112] Paras 84–87.

[113] Her dissent on the facts was based on a different point.

[114] 339 US 763 (1950).

[115] 494 US 259 (1990).

[116] The fourth amendment provides: "The right of the people to be secure in their persons, houses, papers, and effects, against unreasonable searches and seizures, shall not be violated, and no Warrants shall issue, but upon probable cause, supported by Oath or affirmation, and particularly describing the place to be searched, and the persons or things to be seized."

between claims brought by citizens,[117] which will be maintained, and those brought by aliens, which will not:[118]

> The distinction between citizens and aliens follows from the undoubted proposition that the Constitution does not create, nor do general principles of law create, any juridical relation between our country and some undefined, limitless class of noncitizens who are beyond our territory.[119]

In his dissenting opinion, in which Justice Marshall joined, Justice Brennan said that the majority had mischaracterised the *Johnson* case – the claims of the German nationals were there rejected, he pointed out, not because they were foreign nationals, but because they were enemy soldiers.[120]

The double standard endorsed by the majority decision is powerfully exposed by the dissenting opinion of Justice Brennan:

> Today the Court holds that although foreign nationals must abide by our laws, even when in their own countries, our Government need not abide by the Fourth Amendment when it investigates them for violations of our laws.[121]

Brennan J pointed out that the juridical nexus between Verdugo-Urquidez and the United States arose because the government was investigating him and attempting to hold him liable under the laws of the United States:

> He has become, quite literally, one of the governed. Fundamental fairness and the ideals underlying our Bill of Rights compel the conclusion that when we impose "societal obligations" . . . such as the obligation to comply with our criminal laws, on foreign nationals, we in turn are obliged to respect certain correlative rights, among them the Fourth Amendment.[122]

---

[117] As in *Reid* v. *Covert* 354 US 1 (1957)

[118] *Johnson* v. *Eisentrager* 339 US 763 (1950).

[119] 494 US 259 at 275.

[120] 494 US 259 at 290–91, referring to *Johnson* v. *Eisentrager* 339 US 763 (1950) at 771–72.

[121] 494 US 259 at 279–80 – Brennan J went on to cite a range of instances of federal laws holding foreign nationals liable for conduct committed entirely beyond the territorial limits of the United States that nevertheless had effects within the United States – these include drug laws, antitrust laws, securities laws and a host of federal criminal statutes.

[122] 494 US 259 at 284.

At the heart of Justice Brennan's approach was the principle of mutuality, according to which those made subject to United States laws, whether at home or abroad, are entitled to claim the protections of those laws.[123] But the parsimonious view of the reach of constitutional rights has prevailed in recent decisions in which individuals captured in Afghanistan and held at the United States Naval Base at Guantanamo Bay have asserted constitutional rights in seeking the assistance of the United States courts.

The claim in *Coalition of Clergy et al* v. *George Walker Bush et al*[124] was dismissed partly on the basis that the 1903 lease in respect of Guantanamo Bay preserved Cuba's ultimate sovereignty over the territory, although it conferred upon the United States the right to exercise "complete jurisdiction and control" over and within Guantanamo Bay. With reference to *Johnson* v. *Eisentrager*,[125] the right of access to the courts of the United States was said to be predicated upon the presence of a person within territory under United States sovereignty. The California Court followed the decision of the Eleventh Circuit of the United States Court of Appeals in *Cuban American Bar Association* v. *Christopher*[126] holding that Cuban and Haitian migrants temporarily detained at Guantanamo Bay could not assert rights under the United States Constitution *inter alia* because Guantanamo Bay was not United States sovereign territory. On appeal, the United States Court of Appeals for the Ninth Circuit dismissed the claim for lack of the petitioner's standing; but found that the district court was without jurisdiction to hold that the habeas corpus rights of all Guantanamo Bay detainees were suspended, regardless of their particular circumstances.

The petition for a writ of habeas corpus in *Rasul et al* v. *Bush et al*, brought by two British and one Australian petitioners in the United States District Court for the District of Columbia, was dismissed for want of jurisdiction because the military base at Guantanamo Bay

---

[123] 494 US 259 at 284–85; compare Lord Scarman's dictum in *R* v. *Home Secretary ex parte Khawaja* [1984] 1 AC 74 at 111.

[124] Decision of the United States District Court of the Central District of California, February 2002, 189 F. Supp 2d 1036, 1039 (C. D. Cal. 2002).

[125] 339 US 763 (1950).

[126] 43 F. 3d 1412, 1425 (*cert. denied* 515 US 1142 and 516 US 913 (1995)).

was beyond the sovereign territory of the United States and because the petitioners were aliens. A similar petition was dismissed on the same bases in *Odah et al* v. *United States of America et al.* These decisions were affirmed by the United States Court of Appeals for the District of Columbia circuit on 11 March 2003 in *Al Odah Khaled A. F. v. USA.*

The American cases are briefly considered by the Court of Appeal in *R* v. *Secretary of State for Foreign and Commonwealth Affairs ex parte Abbasi* at paragraphs 12–15. Noting that the decision in *Rasul* is subject to appeal, their Lordships simply remark that:

> On the face of it we find surprising the proposition that the writ of the United States courts does not run in respect of individuals held by the government on territory that the United States holds as lessee under a long term treaty.[127]

CONCLUSION

If a public authority from one State exercises the police powers of that State in the territory of another, it cannot in good conscience deny correlative constitutional protections to the persons over whom such powers are exercised.[128]

A principled guide to the circumstances in which the HRA should be applied beyond the borders of the United Kingdom is to be found in the concept of mutuality articulated by Brennan J in his dissent in the *Verdugo-Urquidez* case. Its relevance to the international rule of law in the world in which we now live is stark:

> Mutuality . . . serves to inculcate the values of law and order. By respecting the rights of foreign nationals, we encourage other nations to respect the rights of our citizens. Moreover, as our Nation becomes increasingly concerned about the domestic effects of international crime, we cannot forget that the behaviour of our law enforcement agents abroad sends a powerful message about the rule of law to individuals everywhere. As Justice Brandeis warned in *Olmstead* v. *United States* 277 US 438 (1928):

[127] *Abbasi*, above, n 96 para 15.

[128] Different considerations may, however, apply to the exercise of military power over enemy aliens in time of war – in which case the Geneva Conventions would apply.

"If the Government becomes a lawbreaker, it breeds contempt for law; it invites every man to become a law unto himself; it invites anarchy. To declare that in the administration of the civil law the end justifies the means . . . would bring terrible retribution. Against that pernicious doctrine, the Court should resolutely set its face." Id., at 485 (dissenting opinion). This principle is no different when the United States applies its rules of conduct to foreign nationals. If we seek respect for law and order, we must observe these principles ourselves. Lawlessness breeds lawlessness.[129]

---

[129] 494 US 259 at 285.

Interpretation and Incompatibility: Striking the Balance

Dinah Rose* and Claire Weir*

Sections 3 and 4 of the Human Rights Act 1998 ("HRA") strike a delicate constitutional balance between the incorporation of the European Convention on Human Rights ("the Convention") and the protection of parliamentary sovereignty. Section 3 requires courts to construe legislation compatibly with the Convention so far as it is possible to do so. However, if a compatible construction is impossible, courts have no power to strike down the legislation itself, or to prevent its continued application and enforcement. Section 4 merely permits a court[1] to grant a declaration of incompatibility, leaving it to the executive to decide whether to amend the offending provision, with Parliament's approval.

Section 3 is at the heart of the HRA scheme. It applies to legislation whenever enacted, requiring the re-interpretation of pre-HRA legislation where necessary, to achieve a Convention-compliant result. It is enmeshed with the HRA section 6 duty of public authorities not to act incompatibly with Convention rights. Section 6(2)(b) enables a public authority, accused of breaching a Convention right, to rely by way of defence on the fact that it was acting to give effect to primary or secondary legislation, but only where that legislation "cannot be read or given effect in a way which is compatible with Convention rights".

---

* Blackstone Chambers.
[1] S 4(5) limits the courts able to make such a declaration to (a) the House of Lords; (b) the Judicial Committee of the Privy Council; (c) the Courts–Martial Appeal Court; (d) in Scotland, the High Court of Justiciary sitting otherwise than as a trial court or the Court of Session (e) in England and Wales or Northern Ireland, the High Court or the Court of Appeal.

As Lord Woolf said in *Poplar Housing and Regeneration Community Association Ltd* v. *Donoghue*:[2]

It is difficult to overestimate the importance of section 3. It applies to legislation passed both before and after the HRA came into force. Subject to the section not requiring the court to go beyond that which is possible, it is mandatory in its terms. In the case of legislation predating the HRA where the legislation would otherwise conflict with the Convention, section 3 requires the court to now interpret legislation in a manner which it would not have done before the HRA came into force. When the court interprets legislation usually its primary task is to identify the intention of Parliament. Now, when section 3 applies, the courts have to adjust their traditional role in relation to interpretation so as to give effect to the direction contained in section 3. It is as though legislation which predates the HRA and conflicts with the Convention has to be treated as being subsequently amended to incorporate the language of section 3.

There is no doubt that Parliament intended section 3 to be powerful and far-reaching in its effects, and to be of much greater practical importance than section 4. During parliamentary debates on the Human Rights Bill, amendments were moved to water down section 3 by replacing "possible" with "reasonable", or to add the words "where ambiguous". These amendments were rejected, and the stronger form of words prevailed. The Lord Chancellor said that he wanted courts to "strive to find an interpretation of legislation which is consistent with Convention rights so far as the language of the legislation allows, and only in the last resort to conclude that the legislation is simply incompatible with them".[3] He added that "in 99 per cent of the cases that will arise, there will be no need for judicial declarations of incompatibility".[4]

Sections 3 and 4, although concisely and elegantly drafted, create a number of delicate balancing exercises for the courts. In determining whether a statutory provision is "compatible with a Convention

---

[2] [2001] EWCA Civ 595, [2002] QBD 48, para 75. See also *R* v. *A (No 2)* [2001] UKHL 25, [2002] 1 AC 45, *per* Lord Steyn, para 44.

[3] Committee stage, House of Lords, 583 HL Official Report (5th Series) col 535, 18 November 1997.

[4] House of Lords 3rd reading, 585 HL Official Report (5th Series) col 840, 5 February 1998.

right", to what extent should the court defer to Parliament and, where the issue is the application of that provision by a public body, to the Executive? In determining whether a particular interpretation is "possible", to what extent should the court defer to the will of Parliament in enacting the legislation in the terms in which it did? Is it preferable, in any given case, for the court to allow a public authority to rely on the section 6(2)(b) defence and to make a section 4 declaration of incompatibility, or should it instead give the legislation at issue a more generous (and possibly more strained) interpretation to render it compatible with the Convention? Which approach better expresses the will of Parliament?

"ORDINARY" CONSTRUCTION OR SECTION 3: THE PROPER STARTING POINT

Although Parliament's intention was that section 3 be powerful and wide-ranging in its effect, the courts appear to view section 3 as an additional tool of construction in Convention cases, rather than as the starting point for the interpretative process. In *R (Fuller)* v. *Chief Constable of Dorset Constabulary*,[5] for example, in considering whether section 61 of the Criminal Justice and Public Order Act 1994 was compatible with various provisions of the Convention, Stanley Burnton J preferred to start by construing the legislation "without reference to section 3".[6] He noted that he would then consider "whether it is necessary to have recourse to section 3".[7] A similar approach was applied by Jonathan Parker LJ in *International Transport Roth GmbH* v. *Secretary of State for the Home Department*,[8] discussed further below, in which the compatibility of the carriers' liability provisions of the Immigration and Asylum Act 1999 with Article 6 of the Convention was at issue. Jonathan Parker LJ first considered the nature and effect of the statutory scheme "without

---

[5] [2001] EWHC Admin 1057, [2002] 3 WLR 1133. See also *Re B (a minor)* [2001] UKHL 70, [2002], 1 WLR 258, [2002] 1 FLR 196 ("no need to have recourse to section 3 of the Human Rights Act 1998" where section 15(3)(b) of the Adoption Act 1976 could be read compatibly with Art 8 of the Convention applying normal principles of interpretation).

[6] At para 39.

[7] Ibid.

[8] [2002] EWCA Civ 158, [2002] 3 WLR 344.

reference to section 3",[9] and then purported to construe the scheme "in accordance with section 3".[10]

There is nothing in section 3, however, which compels or even endorses this compartmentalised approach. Section 3 simply requires that all legislation be read and given effect compatibly with the Convention, where possible. It is a command to courts, not a separate canon of construction. The fact that courts appear to be seeking to apply "normal" canons of construction to a piece of legislation, and then if a potential breach is applied, to put the legislation through the section 3 "compatibiliser", leads to the use of section 3 being viewed as an extreme step. Section 3, and the generous and purposive construction which it requires, should be seen as integral to the process of construction in any case where it is alleged that a statutory provision, or the exercise of powers pursuant to a statutory provision, is incompatible with the Convention.

"COMPATIBLE WITH THE CONVENTION": STRIKING THE APPROPRIATE BALANCE

This chapter is not the appropriate place for a detailed analysis of the balance to be struck between the actions of the Executive, the will of Parliament, and the rights of the individual in implementing the Convention.[11]

It is obvious, however, that the extent to which the courts will be required to strain the meaning of a legislative provision to make it conform with the Convention will depend on the view which the court has taken of the scope and requirements of the relevant Convention article.[12] As Francis Bennion has indicated,[13] section 3

[9] [2002] EWCA Civ 158, [2002] 3 WLR 344.
[10] Ibid para 149.
[11] These issues are dealt with by Tim Owen QC ch 3 below.
[12] In *Lee* v. *Leeds City Council* [2002] EWCA Civ 6, [2002] 1 WLR 1488 , which concerned the proper scope of the obligation to repair a dwelling house in section 11 Landlord and Tenant Act 1985, the first instance judge found that the right to family life in Art 8 of the Convention did not require a landlord to eliminate damp, mould and condensation from a house. Chadwick LJ, giving the judgment of the Court of Appeal, held, unsurprisingly, that in these circumstances section 3 could not operate to require section 11 of the Act to be read as including this extended repairing obligation, although he accepted that section 11 could be construed in this way.
[13] Bennion, "What Interpretation is 'Possible' under section 3(1) of the Human Rights Act 1998?" [2000] *PL* 77.

requires not only interpretation of the legislative provision at issue, but the interpretation of the Convention right against which it is measured. This in turn requires a balance to be struck between the degree of protection to be afforded to the individual and the degree of deference to be afforded to the Executive or Parliament.[14] This process may be required not only in relation to those Convention rights which allow justification (in particular, the rights at Articles 8 to 11 of the Convention), but in relation to other rights which appear absolute on their face.[15]

The relationship between the proper interpretation of a statutory provision and the proper scope of a Convention right is extremely fluid. In *Roth*,[16] for example, Laws LJ (dissenting) noted that the appeal concerned the effects of the Immigration and Asylum Act 1999 properly construed, but went on to decide the case on the basis that, applying the appropriate degree of deference to the Executive, Article 6 of the Convention was not breached. Simon Brown LJ and Jonathan Parker LJ preferred to decide the case on the basis that the carriers' liability scheme was caught by Article 6 and could not be "saved" by the application of section 3 HRA.

In *Wilson* v. *Secretary of State for Trade and Industry* [2003] UKHL 40, unrep., decision of 10 July 2003 having concluded that section 3 was not retrospective and therefore not applicable, the House of Lords went on to interpret and apply the relevant Convention rights in such a way as to render them inapplicable in any event.

In *R* v. *Lambert*,[17] the House of Lords had no difficulty in reading an apparently clear statutory reversal of the burden of proof in section 28 of the Misuse of Drugs Act 1971 as imposing only an

[14] And also to the decisions of the European Court of Human Rights. By section 2 HRA a court or tribunal determining a question which has arisen in connection with a Convention right must take into account judgments, decisions and opinions of the European Court of Human Rights (ECtHR) and Commission on Human Rights. Although courts are only bound to take account of these texts, and not bound to follow them, the English courts have so far proved themselves extremely willing to treat the word of the ECtHR as the first and last word on the proper interpretation of Convention articles.

[15] *International Transport Roth GmbH & Ors* v. *Secretary of State for the Home Department* [2002] EWCA Civ 158, [2002] 3 WLR 344 per Laws LJ.

[16] Ibid.

[17] [2001] UKHL 37, [2002] 2 AC 545; in fact decided on the ground of the non-retrospectivity of the relevant provisions of the HRA.

evidential burden on a defendant, in order to avoid a violation of Article 6. In *Lynch* v. *Director of Public Prosecutions*,[18] however, the Divisional Court refused to construe a similar provision in section 139 of the Criminal Justice Act 1988 in the same way, and found instead that the reverse onus provision at issue did not breach Article 6(2) of the Convention.[19]

"SO FAR AS IT IS POSSIBLE": THE LIMITS OF SECTION 3

It is clear, as set out above, that Parliament intended section 3 to be powerful and far-reaching. In its application, however, courts are required to tread a narrow path, balancing the will of Parliament as expressed in the HRA, including the section 3 obligation, against the will of Parliament as expressed in the statutory provision being interpreted. As Jonathan Parker LJ noted in *Roth*:[20]

> In one sense the interpretative obligation in section 3 is the corollary of "deference", in that the point at which interpretation shades into legislation will inevitably be affected by the degree of deference which the courts should accord to the legislative body in recognising its discretionary area of judgment.

Lord Woolf, in *Poplar Housing*[21] laid down some general guidelines for the application of section 3 that give an idea as to where the limits of its application might lie. He made the important point that, if a court has to rely on section 3, it should limit the extent of the modified meaning to that which is necessary to achieve compatibility, and commented, at paragraph 76:

> The most difficult task which courts face is distinguishing between legislation and interpretation. Here practical experience of seeking to apply section 3 will provide the best guide. However, if it is necessary in order to obtain compliance to radically alter the effect of the legislation this will be an indication that more than interpretation is involved.

---

[18] See also *R* v. *Matthews* [2003] EWCA Crim 813, unrep., decision of 25 March 2003; *R* v. *Johnstone and ors.* [2003] UKHL 28, unrep., decision of 22 May 2003.
[19] [2001] EWHC Admin 882, [2002] 3 WLR 863 (Div Ct).
[20] Above n 15, para 144.
[21] Ibid para 75.

Lord Hope expressed the view in *R* v. *A (No 2)*[22] that,

> . . . compatibility is to be achieved only so far as this is possible. Plainly this will not be possible if the legislation contains provisions which expressly contradict the meaning which the enactment would have to be given to make it compatible. It seems to me that the same result must follow if they do so by necessary implication, as this too is a means of identifying the plain intention of Parliament.

There is little room for argument about statutory provisions that *expressly* contradict a meaning proposed. For example, it would be impossible to interpret a statutory provision stating that men are entitled to receive a state pension at 65, and women are entitled to receive a state pension at 60, in such a way as to eliminate discrimination between men and women on the grounds of their sex. However, it is not quite so clear whether it is impossible to construe a statute that *by necessary implication* violates a Convention right in such a way as to avoid that incompatibility. Lord Hope pointed out that such a necessary implication was a means of identifying the plain intention of Parliament. But that intention must now be read in the light of Parliament's intention expressed in section 3: that there should be no incompatibility if a compatible construction is possible.[23] The search is for a "possible meaning that would prevent the need for a declaration of incompatibility".[24] Such a meaning may contradict the clear intention of Parliament when enacting the offending provision, yet it is also the intention of Parliament, expressed in section 3, that the Convention-compatible meaning should be adopted unless such a course is impossible.

Courts have not so far found it easy to resolve the conflict between the intention of Parliament when enacting a particular statutory

---

[22] Above n 2, para 108.

[23] In an interesting article David Manknell has suggested that section 19 HRA, which requires a minister in charge of a Bill to make a statement of compatibility in relation to that Bill, creates a rebuttable presumption, in relation to legislation for which such a declaration has been made, that a compatible interpretation, pursuant to s 3, is possible: see "The Interpretative Obligation under the Human Rights Act" [2000] *JR* 109.

[24] Lord Steyn, "Current Topic: Incorporation and Devolution – A Few Reflections on a Changing Scene" [1998] EHRLR 153.

provision that appears to violate the Convention, and the intention of Parliament when enacting section 3.

In *Roth*,[25] a majority of the Court of Appeal[26] adopted a holistic approach to the issue of whether the carriers' liability provisions in sections 32 to 36 of the Immigration Act 1999 were compatible with Article 6 and Article 1 of the First Protocol to the Convention. The majority held that it was not possible to apply section 3 to interpret the scheme compatibly with the Convention, apparently on the basis that, while one or two objectionable features of the scheme might have been capable of consistent interpretation, the scheme viewed in the round,was simply too full of Convention holes to make it capable of remedy.

Simon Brown LJ identified[27] three features of the scheme which concerned him: (i) the fact that the burden of establishing blamelessness was placed on the carrier,[28] (ii) the fact that the penalty imposed was fixed and cumulative,[29] and (iii) the fact that, even where a carrier was ultimately determined not to be liable, his or her vehicle may well have been detained in the intervening period, and no compensation was payable in respect of the detention even where the Secretary of State had acted unreasonably in issuing a penalty notice.

He found, on the basis of concern (ii) above, namely the size and fixed nature of the penalty, that the scheme was contrary to Article 6.[30] He concluded that it would be quite impossible to "recreate" the scheme by section 3 as one compatible with Convention rights, since

> to achieve fairness would require a radically different approach . . . [counsel for the defendant] is necessarily inviting us to turn the scheme inside out, something we cannot do . . . the Court's task is to distinguish between legislation and interpretation, and confine itself to the latter. We cannot create a wholly different scheme . . .[31]

[25] Above n 8.
[26] Simon Brown and Jonathan Parker LJJ. As set out above, Laws LJ found that there was no incompatibility between the scheme and the Convention.
[27] At para 24.
[28] By s 34(1).
[29] Section 32(2); Reg 3 of the Carriers' Liability (Clandestine Entrants and Sale of Transporters) Regulations 2000.
[30] At para 47.
[31] At para 66.

His concerns were echoed by Jonathan Parker LJ, who considered each element of the scheme in turn by reference to section 3, and concluded in each case that its application would involve rewriting the scheme to an impermissible extent.[32]

THE ASSERTIVE APPROACH TO SECTION 3:
R v. *A (No 2)*

The decision of the House of Lords in *R* v. *A (No 2)*[33] is the most radical example so far of the use of section 3 to adopt a construction of a recent statute that appears to fly in the face of Parliament's intention in enacting the provision question. The House of Lords was considering the "rape shield" law in section 41 of the Youth Justice and Criminal Evidence Act 1999. Section 41 prohibits the giving of evidence or cross-examination about any sexual behaviour of the complainant in a rape case, except with the leave of the court. The circumstances in which a court may give leave are narrowly and quite deliberately circumscribed, so as to protect rape victims from intrusive questioning as to their sexual history. The defendant in *R* v. *A (No 2)* argued that section 41 could result in a violation of his right to a fair trial under Article 6 of the Convention, since, on its natural construction, it would prevent him from calling evidence and cross-examining the complainant to the effect that she had been engaged in a consensual sexual relationship with him for some weeks prior to the alleged rape. The House of Lords (with Lord Hope dissenting on

---

[32] At paras 180, 184, 186 and 188. Despite the breadth of this reasoning the declaration of incompatibility made by the Court was quite narrow in its terms, consisting of a declaration that the "penalty scheme" was incompatible with the Convention "in that the amount of the penalty is fixed (and therefore cannot have regard to an individual's circumstances) and is substantial in scale". On one view, this single incompatibility could have been resolved by the application of s 3 to the Act and the Regs. Section 32(2) of the Act provides that "the person (or persons) responsible for a clandestine entrant is (or are together) liable to (a) a penalty of the prescribed amount. . .". By Reg 3 of the Regs "The amount payable for the purposes of section 32(2) of the Act . . . is £2000." Although Jonathan Parker LJ considered this impossible (para 184), on one view the word "maximum" could have been read into the Regs, and, if necessary, into s 32(2), to render it compliant.

[33] Above n 2.

the point)[34] agreed, and relied on section 3 HRA in order to adopt a construction of section 41 that was plainly contrary to Parliament's intention in enacting the 1999 Act.

THE RETREAT FROM *R* v. *A (No 2)*

So far, *R* v. *A (No 2)* appears to mark the high point of the bold approach to section 3. In subsequent cases, the more cautious approach to section 3 adopted by Lord Hope in *R* v. *A (No 2)* has been preferred to the approach of Lord Steyn.[34a]

In *Re S (Care Order: Implementation of Care Plan)*[35] the House of Lords considered an appeal from a decision in which the Court of Appeal had relied on section 3 to insert in the statutory scheme under the Children Act 1989 a range of powers by which courts could supervise and monitor the implementation of care orders by local authorities, so as to protect children and families against violations of their Article 8 rights.

The House of Lords held that the Court of Appeal had stretched section 3 too far. Lord Nicholls of Birkenhead recognised[36] that section 3 was drafted in "forthright, uncompromising language," but stressed that its reach was not unlimited, and that courts must be ever mindful of its outer limit. "Interpretation of statutes is a matter for the courts: the enactment of statutes, and the amendment of statutes, are matters for Parliament."

As Lord Nicholls recognised, the real difficulty lies in identifying the limits of the permissible interpretation of a statute in a particular case, and that this is a particularly acute problem, given the more liberal and purposive approach to construction now adopted by courts. "The greater the latitude with which courts construe documents, the less readily defined is the boundary."

He concluded that:

a meaning which departs substantially from a fundamental feature of an Act of Parliament is likely to have crossed the boundary between inter-

[34] Above n 2 at paras. 108–10.
[34a] See, for example, *Hooper* v. *Secretary of State for Work and Pensions* [2002] EWCA Civ 813, unrep., decision of 18 June 2003, paras. 26–28.
[35] [2002] UKHL 10, [2002] 2 AC 291.
[36] Ibid paras. 37–44.

pretation and amendment. This is especially so where the departure has important practical repercussions which the court is not equipped to evaluate. In such a case the overall contextual setting may leave no scope for rendering the statutory provision Convention compliant by legitimate use of the process of interpretation. The boundary line may be crossed even though a limitation on Convention rights is not stated in express terms. Lord Steyn's observations in *R* v. *A (No 2)*, para 44 are not to be read as meaning that a clear limitation on Convention rights in terms is the only circumstance in which an interpretation incompatible with Convention rights may arise.[37]

Lord Nicholls also stressed the importance of a court clearly identifying the particular statutory provision or provisions whose interpretation led to the result proposed.

It is the approach in *Re S*, and not the more radical approach of Lord Steyn in *R* v. *A (No 2)* that currently appears to be prevailing. In *R (Anderson)* v. *Secretary of State for the Home Department*,[38] the House of Lords approved the passage from Lord Nicholls' opinion set out above. It held that the power granted to the Secretary of State under section 29 of the Crime (Sentences) Act 1997 to fix the tariff of a prisoner serving a mandatory life sentence was incompatible with the Convention, but declined to use section 3 to construe the power away. In the words of Lord Bingham, reading section 29 as precluding participation by the Home Secretary, "would not be judicial interpretation but judicial vandalism". The only relief granted was a declaration of incompatibility.[38a]

Similarly, in *R (D)* v. *Secretary of State for the Home Department*,[39] Stanley Burnton J found it impossible to interpret section 34(5) of the Criminal Justice Act 1991 compatibly with the Convention. He noted that to do so would involve "judicial legislation", and expressly referred to Lord Hope's speech in *R* v. *A (No 2)*.[40]

---

[37] Ibid para 40.

[38] [2002] UKHL 46, [2002] 3 WLR 1800, para 30.

[38a] See also *Wilkinson* v. *Commissioners of Inland Revenue* [2003] EWCA Civ 814, unrep., decision of 18 June 2003, paras 29–49.

[39] [2002] EWHC 2805 Admin, [2003] 1 WLR 1315.

[40] Ibid para 27. He also considered that, in deciding whether an alternative interpretation of legislation was "possible", the court must take account of the practical and negative consequences of that interpretation: para 26.

TECHNIQUES OF INTERPRETATION USING SECTION 3

Notwithstanding the courts' apparent retreat from the liberal approach adopted in *R* v. *A (No 2)*, Lord Steyn's identification of the techniques of interpretation that may be used when section 3 is in play remains valid. Lord Steyn stressed[41] that section 3 required more than the adoption of a "contextual and purposive" interpretation and noted that it would sometimes be necessary to adopt an interpretation which "linguistically may appear strained". He identified two further techniques that could be used by a court:

"*reading in*": implying provisions into statutes that are necessary to safeguard Convention rights;[42]

"*reading down*": restricting the scope and effect of apparently broad and clear statutory language, to ensure that powers can only be exercised consistently with Convention rights.[42a]

"Reading In"[43]

In *R* v. *A (No 2)* itself, the solution was found by "reading in". The House of Lords concluded that it was possible to read section 41(3)(c) of the Act, which enables a judge to admit relevant evidence

---

[41]	*R* v. *A (No 2)*, above n 2, para 44.

[42]	It has also been suggested ("Readings and Remedies: Section 3(1) of the HRA and Rectifying Construction", Andrew Henderson [2000] *JR* 258) that the well-known judicial technique of severance could be applied by the courts pursuant to s 3. This is undoubtedly true in principle, although we have been unable to identify any case on s 3 so far in which severance (rather than reading down or reading in) was the technique adopted by the courts.

[42a]	And see also *Hooper* v. *Secretary of State for Work and Pensions* [2002] EWCA Civ 813, unrep., decision of 18 June 2003, para 136, in which the Court of Appeal applied section 3 in holding that the Secretary of State was obliged to make extra-statutory payments. The Court noted that "Acts of Parliament should be read, in so far as possible, as not precluding common law or prerogative powers of the Crown to take any action that may be necessary to prevent infringement of Convention rights".

[43]	For a good example of readiness on the part of the courts to read words into a statute at common law, see *R (Zenovics)* v. *Secretary of State for the Home Department* [2002] EWCA Civ 273, unrep, decision of 7 March 2002 (CA) (para 9(2) of sch 4 to the Immigration and Asylum Act 1999 redrafted to allow for further appeal on uncertified asylum claims).

about the complainant's prior sexual history in certain circumstances, as subject to the *implied* provision that "evidence or questioning which is required to secure a fair trial under Article 6 of the Convention should not be treated as inadmissible".[44]

According to Lord Steyn, this approach was justifiable on the basis that Parliament, if alerted to the problem, would not have wished when enacting section 41(3)(c) to deny the defendant a fair trial, and must therefore have intended this provision to be construed in such a way as to be compatible with that right.[45]

The fiction that, by using section 3 to read words into a statute courts are correcting Parliament's inadvertent failure to legislate compatibly with the Convention becomes unreal, however, in relation to legislation enacted prior to the HRA or indeed prior to the Convention coming into being. In relation to this legislation, the only justification for the exercise in which a court is engaging when it "reads in" provisions to the legislation, is that they are treating the Parliamentary intention expressed in the HRA as, in effect, "trumping" the intention in the statute under consideration.

R v. *A (No 2)* was a case in which the court was prepared to read words in to circumscribe a statutory discretion.[46] A much more cautious approach to section 3 was taken by the Court of Appeal in *R (H)* v. *Mental Health Review Tribunal, North and East London Region.*[47] The Court considered whether section 73 of the Mental Health Act 1983 was compatible with the right to liberty in Article 5 of the Convention. Section 73(1) read with section 72(1) provides

---

[44] *R* v. *A (No 2)*, above n 2, para 45. This conclusion was criticised by Lord Phillips of Worth Matravers MR, in his 2001 Keating Lecture, "The Interpretation of Contracts and Statutes", delivered on 10 October 2001.

[45] Ibid. See also *Attorney-General of the Gambia* v. *Jobe* [1984] 1 AC 689 at 702B–F, in which the Privy Council adopted a similar approach to the construction of legislation passed by the Parliament of the Gambia that, on its face, appeared to be unconstitutional.

[46] For further examples of the use of s 3 to read words in in this context, see *Goode* v. *Martin* [2001] EWCA Civ 1899, [2002] 1 WLR 1828 (CA) (words read in to CPR r 17.4(2) power to allow the amendment of a statement of claim so that "substantially the same facts as a claim" was amended to read "substantially the same facts as are already in issue on a claim", in line with the enabling legislation); *Cachia* v. *Faluyi*, [2001] EWCA Civ 998, [2001] 1 WLR 1966 (CA) ("action" in s 2(3) Fatal Accidents Act 1976 to be read as "served process").

[47] [2001] EWCA Civ 415, [2002] QB 1 (CA).

that Mental Health Review Tribunal should discharge a patient from hospital "if satisfied", *inter alia*, that he is not suffering from mental illness or another disorder such that it is appropriate for him to be detained. Section 73(1) therefore apparently precludes the release of a mental patient by a review tribunal unless *the patient can satisfy the tribunal* that he is not suffering from a mental disorder. It was accepted before the Court of Appeal that this provision, interpreted in this way, was incompatible with Article 5 of the Convention.

The Court concluded, applying section 3, that there was no possible construction of section 73(1) that would avoid the incompatibility, on the basis that it was not permissible "to interpret a requirement that a tribunal must act if satisfied that a state of affairs does not exist as meaning that it must act if not satisfied that a state of affairs does exist. The two are patently not the same".[48]

The Court of Appeal did not, it would appear, consider the possibility of reading words in to save sections 72 and 73 from incompatibility with the Convention. In fact,[49] it would have been possible to construe the sections, with the aid of section 3 of the HRA, as including a provision to the following effect: "A Mental Health Review tribunal must conclude that it is satisfied that a patient is not suffering from a mental disorder unless it has been reliably shown that he is suffering from such a disorder".[50]

It is notable that, by contrast with *H*, in *R* v. *Lambert*[51] the House of Lords had no difficulty in reading an apparently clear statutory reversal of the burden of proof in section 28 of the Misuse of Drugs Act 1971 as imposing only an evidential burden on a defendant, in order to avoid a violation of Article 6.[52]

---

[48] Ibid para 27.

[49] *Pace* John Wadham in "The Human Rights Act: One Year On" [2001] EHRLR 620 at 637–38.

[50] Adopting the wording of the ECtHR case law in this area: see *Winterwerp* v. *Netherlands* (1978–1980) 2 EHRR 387, paras 39–40; *Johnson* v. *United Kingdom*, (1999) 27 EHRR 296, para 60, cited in *H* at para 28.

[51] above n 17, paras 42, 84, 157.

[52] See also *R* v. *DPP, ex parte Kebilene* [2000] 2 AC 326, in which Lord Cooke in *obiter dicta* before the HRA came into force, argued that when s 3(1) of the HRA was in operation, the provisions of section 16A of the Prevention of Terrorism Act, placing the burden of proof on a defendant, should be read as imposing only an evidential, and not a legal burden. Parliament amended the offending legislation, enacting ss 118(1) and (2) of the Terrorism Act 2000, which expressly place only an evidential burden on the accused.

In *Matthews* v. *Ministry of Defence*,[53] Keith J refused to read words into sections 10(1)(b) and 10(2)(b) Crown Proceedings Act 1947 limiting the scope of the Secretary of State's power to certify that personal injury and death suffered by a member of the armed forces was attributable to his or her service, and therefore not something for which the Crown could be sued in tort. He considered whether the provision might be rendered more proportionate, and therefore compatible with the right of access to a court in Article 6 of the Convention, if a provision was to be implied in to section 10 to the effect that a certificate would only be issued in "exceptional circumstances". He concluded, however, that, this type of provision was not one which could sensibly be read into section 10, and the Government did not seek to persuade him otherwise.

In the Court of Appeal[54] an additional submission to the effect that words should be read into section 10 to prevent such a certificate being issued save where the Secretary of State was satisfied that the circumstances in which the death or personal injury occurred "were those of warlike conditions" was also rejected, on the basis that this course would amount to "legislation".

"Reading Down"

The second technique identified by Lord Steyn in *R* v. *A (No 2)* is "reading down" legislation. As Lord Hope of Craighead explained in *R* v. *Lambert*,[55] this may involve giving the words a narrower construction than their ordinary meaning would bear, saying what the effect of the provision is without altering the ordinary meaning of the words used, or expressing the statutory words in different language, in order to explain how they are to be read in a way that is compatible.[56]

---

[53] [2002] EWHC 13, *The Times*, 30 January 2002 (QBD).

[54] [2002] EWCA Civ 773, [2002] 1 WLR 2621, paras 73–76. When the matter came before the House of Lords ([2003] UKHL 4, [2003] 2 WLR 435) it was common ground that if the claimants succeeded, s 3 HRA could not assist the Secretary of State, and that a declaration of incompatibility would follow. Since their Lordships found no violation of Art 6 of the Convention no declaration was, however, required.

[55] Above n 17, para 81.

[56] See *Vasquez* v. *The Queen* [1994] 1 WLR 1304.

A good example of the way in which a court may "read down" apparently broad and clear powers in legislation that interfere with fundamental rights is provided by the pre-HRA case of *R* v. *Secretary of State for the Home Department, ex parte Simms*.[57] In *Simms* the House of Lords considered the lawfulness of the Home Secretary's policy, maintained pursuant to rules 37 and 37A of the Prison Rules, that journalists were not to be permitted to interview convicted prisoners unless they signed undertakings not to publish any part of the interview. The House of Lords held that rules 37 and 37A must be restrictively construed, even in the absence of any ambiguity, in accordance with the "principle of legality", to avoid disproportionate interference with the prisoner's right to freedom of expression, having regard to the importance of investigations by journalists in identifying miscarriages of justice. Thus, although rule 37A was apparently clear and broad in scope, it could *not* be relied on as permitting a blanket ban on professional visits by journalists.

SECTION 4: THE LAST RESORT

Where a court is unable to construe legislation compatibly with the Convention, it may offer no remedy other than a discretionary declaration of incompatibility, in accordance with section 4 of the HRA.

A declaration of incompatibility has been described as a "booby prize".[58] It is unsatisfactory to a complainant whose Convention rights have been infringed. He cannot recover compensation. The law will remain effective, and can be enforced against him. Only two means of remedying the incompatibility remain. By section 10 of the HRA, a minister of the Crown may by order make such amendments to the legislation as he considers necessary to remove the incompat-

---

[57] [2000] 2 AC 115. The principle in *Simms* was reaffirmed by the House of Lords in *R* v. *Special Commissioner, ex parte Morgan Grenfell & Co Ltd* [2002] UKHL 21, [2002] 2 WLR 1299, in which the Inland Revenue's general statutory power to require the delivery of documents was read down to exclude the power to require delivery of documents subject to legal professional privilege.

[58] Geoffrey Marshall, "Two kinds of compatibility: more about section 3 of the Human Rights Act 1998" [1999] *PL* Autumn, 377.

ibility.[59] Otherwise, the complainant may take his complaint to Strasbourg.[60]

It should not be assumed, however, that a declaration of incompatibility is of no value. In practice, the political pressure created by such a declaration is likely to lead to the amendment of the offending legislation (as has happened in relation to Mental Health Review Tribunals),[61] or, at the very least, careful reconsideration by Parliament as to whether it really is their intention to maintain legislation that is incompatible with the Convention.

In the case of *R (Wilkinson)* v. *Inland Revenue*,[62] Moses J granted a declaration of incompatibility in a case where the primary relief sought was construction of the legislation compatibly with the Convention, and an award of compensation. Moses J awarded 50 per cent of the costs in favour of the claimant, noting that, whether or not it was correct to describe a declaration of incompatibility as a remedy, it was an important way in which a citizen could challenge breaches of the Convention of which the State was guilty.

Parliament is unlikely, in practice, to refuse to amend or annul a significant proportion of legislation declared incompatible by the courts, since to adopt this course of action would be substantially to undermine the legitimacy of the declaration as a remedy, since it is likely that the courts would become less willing to use it.

As already set out above, when it enacted sections 3 and 4 of the HRA, Parliament clearly intended that a section 4 declaration of incompatibility would be a remedy of last resort for the courts. In *R* v. *A (No 2)*[63] Lord Steyn emphasised this point, noting that the

---

[59] Such orders are subject to parliamentary supervision, in accordance with the provisions of sch 2 to the HRA.

[60] In "Is a Declaration of Incompatibility an Effective Remedy" [2000] *JR* 247, Caroline Neenan suggests that it would not be sufficient to comply with the Article 13 ECHR requirement of an effective remedy for a breach of Convention rights. Article 13 is not, of course part of the HRA. She suggests that the Strasbourg court is unlikely to be impressed by the fact that a declaration has been made in any given case, although Strasbourg decisions are not themselves binding on the UK. In *Hobbs* v. *United Kingdom*, App. No 63684/00, decision of 18 June 2002 the ECtHR held that a declaration of incompatibility was not a sufficiently "effective" remedy to require exhaustion under Article 35(1) of the Convention.

[61] Subject, of course, to legislative time.

[62] [2002] EWHC 182 Admin, (2002) STC 347, upheld by the Court of Appeal on 18 June 2003, [2003] EWCA Civ 814.

[63] Above n 2, 1563G, para 44.

making of a declaration "must be avoided unless it is impossible to do so". However, after a slow start, it appears that such declarations are becoming more commonplace than Parliament had anticipated. This is the inevitable result of the more cautious approach to section 3 adopted in *Re S*.

CONCLUSION

By enacting section 3 of the HRA, Parliament radically changed the approach courts must take to statutory interpretation, and handed powers to judges for which they have so far shown varying degrees of enthusiasm. The confidence with which courts exercise the interpretative obligation in section 3 will to a large extent determine how effective the HRA turns out to be in guaranteeing the protection of fundamental rights. Unless courts take seriously the Lord Chancellor's suggestion that section 3 will afford compatibility in "99 per cent" of cases, claimants will still have to take the long road to Strasbourg for an effective remedy. In short, we suggest that the House of Lords got it right in *R* v. *A (No 2)*, and that it would be most unfortunate if the retreat from this approach were to proceed too far.

Fair Trial Rights, Due Deference and the Wider Impact of the Human Rights Act in Administrative Law

Tim Owen QC*[1]

In preparing this chapter I was tempted to be very brief. Is there really any justification for another immensely detailed analysis of the Human Rights Act ("HRA") case law on the subject of due deference and the standard of review under the 1998 Act in comparison with conventional *Wednesbury*[2] (occasionally leavened by a touch of anxious scrutiny)? Surely, it was all correctly foreshadowed in the oft-quoted paras 3.25–3.26 of Lester and Pannick's *Human Rights Law and Practice*,[3] reaffirmed in greater detail by Professor Jowell in his 2000 *Public Law* article[4] and then given its authoritative, final confirmation in Lord Steyn's relatively brief, but incisive, speech in *Daly*[5] with which the remainder of the Committee expressed their full agreement? In law, in the HRA era as before, context really is everything. And, one might add, so is your tribunal. Whichever way you dress up (or down) the elements of the proportionality test, in the end knowledge of which judge (or judges) will decide your case will tell you in advance whether you are likely to win or lose. Why not leave it at that?

---

* Matrix Chambers.

[1] This paper results from discussion and debate with a number of colleagues but in particular to Nicholas Blake QC and Phillippa Kaufmann. But the usual acknowledgement of personal responsibility obviously applies.

[2] *Associated Provincial Picture Houses* v. *Wednesbury Corporation* [1948] 1 KB 223.

[3] (London: Butterworths, 1999).

[4] "Beyond the Rule of Law: Towards Constitutional Judicial Review" (2000) *PL* 671.

[5] *Secretary of State for the Home Department, Ex Parte Daly, R* v. [2001] UKHL 26; [2001] 3 All ER 433; [2001] 2 WLR 1622, para 24.

Tempting though brevity may be, I am acutely conscious that such a brief statement of my views would be unfair. So more will be provided without claiming that there is anything startlingly new to say on the subject. But for the avoidance of doubt, my own view is that despite the undoubted – and wholly welcome – change in the required approach resulting from section 6 of the HRA, context and the identity of the tribunal remain the overriding factors in determining the outcome of individual cases. Everything else may provide excellent material for discussion and academic debate but is ultimately peripheral to an understanding of what actually goes on in the cut and thrust of argument between advocates and the court. Whether this is good, bad or merely inevitable is of course a matter of opinion.

FAIR TRIAL RIGHTS AND DUE DEFERENCE

Unsurprisingly, criminal law cases have been very important in defining how the concept of due deference is to be handled by judges. Three House of Lords decisions and one Privy Council decision, all concerned with fair trial rights, reveal a subtle but significant shift in attitude in relation to the role of due deference in decision making under the HRA.[6]

The first decision was *R* v. *DPP ex parte Kebilene*[7] and was decided before the HRA was fully in force. In 1997, three Algerian men were arrested and charged under section 16A of the Prevention of Terrorism (Temporary Provisions) Act 1989 ("PTA") with possession of articles in circumstances giving rise to a reasonable suspicion that they were possessed for a purpose connected with the commission, preparation or instigation of acts of terrorism in Algeria by the Group Islamique Armee. Conviction on indictment carried a maximum penalty of 10 years' imprisonment. On the Crown's analysis, all it had to prove under the terms of section 16A was a reasonable *suspicion* that the otherwise lawful articles in the defendants' flats in south London were possessed for a terrorist purpose whereupon the burden

---

[6] These are all principally concerned with criminal matters. For a review of due deference in relation to administrative decision-making see *R (Alconbury)* v. *Secretary of State for the Environment, Transport and the Regions* [2001] 2 All ER 929.

[7] [2000] 2 AC 326.

of proof shifted to the defendants to prove on the balance of proba-
bilities that they were not so possessed. Failure by a defendant to
discharge the reasonable suspicion of terrorist purpose meant that the
jury was *obliged* to conclude that he or she had a terrorist purpose
despite the fact that they might have entertained a reasonable doubt
as to the real purpose lying behind the possession of the articles. So
much then for the golden thread, said by Viscount Sankey LC, to run
through the English criminal law.

The legality of the DPP's decision to give his consent to a prosecution on such an understanding of the law in October 1998 (when
the Human Rights Act was about to receive Royal Assent albeit not
destined to be fully in force until 2 October 2000) was challenged by
the defendants via an application for judicial review of the DPP's
consent decision. At the heart of the challenge was the presumption
of innocence as enshrined in Article 6(2) of the Convention.
Notwithstanding the apparently unqualified terms of Article 6(2),
the Strasbourg Court had nonetheless managed to provide some flex-
ibility to Member States in formulating criminal offences based on
presumptions of fact and law which, on their face, significantly derogated from the simple concept that a defendant is presumed innocent
until the prosecution proves his guilt. Fortified by the somewhat
jejeune Strasbourg case law, the Director argued that in the light of
the clear Parliamentary intention to create a reverse legal burden
of proof and the urgent need to take effective action against
international terrorism, it could not be said that a conviction for the
section 16A offence would necessarily result in a successful appeal
once the HRA was fully in force. In other words, so the Director
argued by way of justification for his consent to prosecute, once
seized with full HRA powers the Court of Appeal (Criminal
Division) would defer to Parliament's decision to make inroads on
the presumption of innocence because of the special need to conduct
an effective war on terrorism. And all would be well.

The Director's argument received extremely short shrift in the
Divisional Court. Lord Bingham CJ cited Lord Atkin's statement in
Liversidge v. *Anderson*[8] that "in this country, amid the clash of arms,
the laws are not silent" as well as eloquent South African authority
in support of his conclusion that section 16A undermined the

---

[8] *Liversidge* v. *Anderson* [1942] AC 245.

presumption of innocence in a blatant and obvious way. Laws LJ was even blunter, commenting that "Mr Pannick's plea is not for fair balance" but rather that "for pragmatic reasons Article 6(2) should be disapplied". He described the Director's submission as "an affront to the rule of law". Not much room then, in this analysis, for any deference to Parliament's legislative choice in an area of policy making which could, after all, claim the imprimatur of Lord Lloyd's authoritative report on legislating against terrorism.[9]

In the House of Lords things proceeded rather differently with the Director's appeal ultimately being allowed on jurisdictional grounds rather than an analysis of the merits of the argument that a post-2 October 2000 Court of Appeal would inevitably quash any conviction (on the basis that Article 6(2) had been infringed at trial). Nonetheless Lord Hope's speech contained a section on the discretionary area of judgment which boded ill for those who believed that life would be very different once judges were able to apply section 6 of the HRA to administrative as well as judicial decisions. While distinguishing the domestic law concept of a discretionary area of judgment from the Strasbourg doctrine of the margin of appreciation and stating that "it will be easier for such an area of judgment to be recognised where the Convention itself requires a balance to be struck, much less so where the right is stated in terms which are unqualified", Lord Hope went on to say that, "even where the right is stated in terms which are unqualified the courts will need to bear in mind the jurisprudence of the European Court which recognises that due account should be taken of the special nature of terrorist crime and the threat which it poses to democratic society".

Far from being an affront to the rule of law, Lord Hope considered that in the light of society's strong interest in preventing acts of terrorism before they are perpetrated – the very aim which section 16A sought to achieve – it was "open to argument" that section 16A struck a fair balance between the needs of society and the defendant's individual Convention right to be presumed innocent. The difficulty with this approach was that if the discretionary area of judgment was to be deployed in the way suggested by Lord Hope in relation to a Convention right such as Article 6(2), it was hard to see how the HRA would strengthen constitutional protection of fundamental

---

[9] [2002] 2 AC 326.

rights against the competing demands of the public interest in fighting social evils such as terrorism, drug dealing or other forms of serious crime. If the fair balance principle could, in Lord Hope's view, even possibly rescue section 16A of the PTA from being declared incompatible with Article 6(2) then constitutional protection of the presumption of innocence was almost non-existent.

A similar approach to deference was detectable in the speech of Lord Bingham in *Brown* v. *Stott*,[10] a devolution case from Scotland which raised the issue of the compatibility of a provision of the Road Traffic Act 1988 ("RTA") with the presumption of innocence. Having drawn a clear distinction between absolute and qualified Convention rights and held that the only absolute right in Article 6 was the right to a fair trial, he began his concluding reasons with the following general statement:

> Judicial recognition and assertion of the human rights defined in the Convention is not a substitute for the process of democratic government but a complement to them. While a national court does not accord the margin of appreciation recognised by the European Court as a supranational court, it will give weight to the decisions of a representative legislature and a democratic government within the discretionary area of judgment accorded to those bodies: see Lester & Pannick, *Human Rights Law and Practice* (1999) 73–76.

Lord Steyn's speech, in contrast, contained a more precise exposition of the role of deference. He began by emphasising that "national courts may accord to the decisions of national legislatures some deference *where the context justifies*" and cited the passage in Lester & Pannick in which they assert that national courts will accept that there are some circumstances in which the legislature and the executive are better placed to perform the function of balancing the needs of society against the individual rights of citizens. He then considered the precise factual context of the case at hand, which he expressed as turning on Parliament's effort to respond to the high rate of road accidents by enacting a provision (section 172 RTA 1988) which regulated car owners by in effect compelling them to account for who was driving a car at a material time on pain of imposing a presumption that the owner was in fact the driver. Having held that the

---

[10] [2001] 2 WLR 817.

legislature was in as good a position as a court to assess the gravity of the problem of road traffic accidents and the public interest in addressing it, Lord Steyn pointed out that the proportionality of section 172 was "ultimately a question for the court". Lord Steyn's personal view ("if the matter was not covered by authority, I would have concluded . . .") was that "in the field of the driving of vehicles" Parliament could lawfully have adopted either section 172 of the RTA or a reverse burden technique without infringing Article 6. His emphasis on the particular focus of the RTA – regulating car owners – suggests that a similar technique deployed in relation to "truly" criminal offences would have given rise to real difficulties in terms of compliance with Article 6(2). On this basis, context was all important to Lord Steyn's conclusion.

The next major criminal case to be decided by the House of Lords adopted a very different approach to deference. In chapter two on "Interpretation and Incompatibility" Dinah Rose and Clare Weir rightly talk of the truly radical implications of the decision in *R* v. *A (No 2)*[11] in terms of the reach of section 3 of the HRA. But it was significant also for Lord Steyn's clear assertion of a court's duty to make its *own* judgment of what the requirements are for a fair trial notwithstanding Parliament's clear, unequivocal legislative decision to opt for a particular scheme restrictive of a defendant's right to cross examine his accuser. All members of the House of Lords recognised that section 41 of the Youth Justice and Criminal Evidence Act 1998 ("YJCEA") represented Parliament's considered attempt, in the words of Mr Boateng (then minister of state at the Home Office) "to keep as much evidence of complainants' sexual behaviour out of trials as possible". The justification for the restriction was that it was believed to be the most effective way of countering the twin myths that a woman who has had sexual intercourse in the past is more likely to have consented to intercourse on the occasion in question and that by reason of her behaviour in the past she is less worthy of belief as a witness. No one disputed that this was a laudable aim. The issue was whether the balance between the public interest in affording women greater protection in court proceedings while maintaining a defendant's right to a fair trial had been properly struck and,

---

[11] [2002] 1 AC 45.

more importantly, the extent to which the courts should defer to Parliament's view on *how* this delicate balance should be struck.

The majority (Lord Hope dissenting on this issue) were clear that insofar as the case was solely concerned with the content of the right to a fair trial, little if any deference to Parliament should be given. The key passage in Lord Steyn's speech was para 36:

> Counsel for the Secretary of State further relied on the principle that in certain contexts, the legislature and the executive retain a discretionary area of judgment within which policy choices may legitimately be made: see *Brown* v. *Stott*... Clearly the House must give weight to the decision of Parliament that the mischief encapsulated in the twin myths must be corrected. On the other hand, when the question arises whether in the criminal statute in question Parliament adopted a legislative scheme which makes an excessive inroad into the right to a fair trial the court is qualified to make its own judgment *and must do so.* (emphasis added)

By contrast, and against the background of his analysis that the right to lead evidence and to put questions are not unqualified rights in Article 6, Lord Hope concluded that the circumstances in which section 41 YJCEA was enacted brought it within the discretionary area of judgment which the courts should accord to the legislature and that Parliament's solution was prima facie a proportionate one. In the light of this reasoning, Lord Hope was unwilling to accept that the necessary degree of general incompatibility, such as would justify the majority's resort to a section 3 reading-in of an implied discretion in trial judges to permit cross examination so as to secure a fair trial, had been established.[12]

The House of Lords decision in *R* v. *Lambert*[13] on the issue of the compatibility of the offence of possession of a controlled drug with the presumption of innocence was no less radical than *R* v. *A (No 2)*. Most significantly the majority (this time including Lord Hope with

---

[12] It is clear that in the later case of *In Re S and others* [2002] UKHL 10, the House of Lords rowed back from the radical reading of the scope of s 3 which had emerged in particular in the speech of Lord Steyn in *R* v. *A (No 2)*. But while Lord Nicholls' reminder of the difference between interpretation and amendment was clearly intended to redress the constitutional balance which many felt had been disturbed by the outcome of *R* v. *A (No 2)*, the principle that courts should show far less deference to Parliament where fair trial rights are engaged remains sound.

[13] [2001] 3 WLR 206.

Lord Hutton on this occasion the sole dissenting voice) clearly
departed from the more conservative analysis to be found in Lord
Woolf CJ's judgment in the Court of Appeal. Having held that the
Strasbourg jurisprudence "makes clear [that] the court does not have
to ignore the wider interests of the public in applying those provisions of the Convention which have no express limitation" and
basing himself on Lord Hope's speech in *Kebilene*, Lord Woolf had
held below that:

> It is also important to have in mind that legislation is passed by a demo-
> cratically elected Parliament and therefore the courts under the
> Convention are entitled to and should, as a matter of constitutional prin-
> ciple, pay a degree of deference to the view of Parliament as to what is in
> the interest of the public generally when upholding the rights of the indi-
> vidual under the Convention. The courts are required to balance the
> competing interests involved.[14]

When he turned to consider the compatibility of the relevant provisions of the Misuse of Drugs Act 1971 with Article 6(2), Lord
Woolf said that the Court "could well understand why Parliament
wanted to restrict the extent of the knowledge required for the
commission of the offence" and concluded that "there is an objective
justification in the case of drugs for [Parliament's] choice and it is not
disproportionate". By contrast in the House of Lords, none of the
speeches even mention the concept of the discretionary area of judgment or the principle of due deference to Parliament's legislative
choice in a politically charged area of law enforcement policy. Instead
the language is simply that of justification and proportionality with,

---

[14] Lord Woolf said something very similar in his judgment in *R* v. *Benjafield*
[2001] 3 WLR 75, a case which concerned the compatibility of criminal confiscation law with Art 6. Having found that Arts 6(1) and (2) both applied to the confiscation procedure and that both the drugs and non-drugs confiscation statutes
reversed the burden of proof he considered that when the issue of compatibility was
addressed "it is appropriate to show a degree of deference to the policy which the legislature considered was in the public interest" and cited Lord Hope's speech in
Kebilene in support of this approach. Having then recorded Parliament's efforts to
balance the interest of the defendant against that of the public interest, and in the
context of his finding that the extent of the interference with the normal presumption of innocence was substantial, Lord Woolf commented that "it is very much a
matter of personal judgment as to whether a proper balance has been struck between
the conflicting interests".

in Lord Steyn's words "the burden [being] on the state to show that the legislative means adopted were not greater than necessary".

The majority held that the sophisticated methods adopted by drug smugglers justified some degree of interference with the presumption of innocence but the question was whether this could be achieved by imposing an evidential, rather than a legal, burden of proof on an accused in relation to the issue of knowledge of the nature of the item in a container which was found on analysis to be a controlled drug. As Lord Steyn said, "the principle of proportionality requires the House to consider whether there was a pressing necessity to impose a legal rather than evidential burden on the accused". In the light of the paramount concern that a legal burden risked producing grave miscarriages of justice, the majority decisively held that the State had not established such a pressing necessity and deployed section 3 to read down the relevant statutory words so as to ensure compatibility.

The fair trial case law and the role of deference in HRA decision-making received a comprehensive review in the Court of Appeal in the case of *International Transport Roth GmbH & others* v. *Home Secretary*.[15] Having cited from Lord Bingham's speech in *Brown* v. *Stott*, Simon Brown LJ said that in addressing the question of whether the penalty regime in the Immigration and Asylum Act 1999 was plainly unfair he would recognise a wide discretion in the Home Secretary in his task of devising a suitable scheme and a high degree of deference due by the Court to Parliament when it comes to determining its legality. But that being said, he stated unambiguously that,

> the court's role under the 1998 Act is as the guardian of human rights. It cannot abdicate this responsibility. If ultimately it judges the scheme to be quite simply unfair, then the features that make it so must inevitably breach the Convention.

Even allowing for wide discretion and a high degree of deference, Simon Brown LJ concluded that the scheme was quite simply unfair to carriers and in breach of Article 6(1) – though not 6(2) – because of the inflexibly high penalty which the scheme inflicted regardless of fault or mitigation.

---

[15]   [2002] EWCA Civ 158.

The judgment of Laws LJ contained a more detailed analysis of the issue of deference to the democratic decision-maker. In adopting Simon Brown LJ's description of the court as guardian of human rights, he said that as a domestic tribunal, the court's judgment as to the deference owed to the democratic powers will reflect the culture and conditions of the British state and that the importance of this, in the light of the Strasbourg doctrine of the margin of appreciation, was that "our courts' task is to develop an autonomous, and not merely adjectival, human rights jurisprudence". He then proceeded to identify a hierarchical principle of deference with greater deference being paid to an Act of Parliament than to a decision of the executive or subordinate measure:

> Where the decision-maker is not Parliament but a minister or other pub-lic or governmental authority exercising power conferred by Parliament, a degree of deference will be due on democratic grounds – the decision-maker is Parliament's delegate – within the principles accorded by the cases. But where the decision maker is Parliament itself, speaking through main legislation, the tension of which I have spoken is most acute. In our intermediate constitution the legislature is not subordinate to a sovereign text, as are the legislatures in "constitutional" systems. Parliament remains the sovereign legislator. It, and nor a written constitution, bears the ultimate mantle of democracy in the State.

With this fundamental principle in mind, Laws LJ then identified three further principles to guide the courts. First, as Lord Hope said in *Kebilene* there is more scope for deference where the Convention itself requires a balance to be struck, much less so where the right is stated in terms which are unqualified. Secondly, greater deference will be due to the democratic powers where the subject matter in hand is peculiarly within their constitutional responsibility (eg defence of the realm) and less when it lies within that of the courts (maintenance of the rule of law). And thirdly (and closely linked to the second) greater or lesser deference will be due according to whether the subject matter lies more readily within the actual or potential expertise of the democratic powers or the courts. Thus gov-ernment decisions in the area of macro-economic power will be rela-tively remote from judicial control and so, in Laws LJ's view, would the government's assessment of the social consequences flowing from the entry into the UK of clandestine immigrants. Having concluded that the penalty regime was civil rather than criminal in character (but that the fair trial principles in Article 6(1) nonetheless were engaged) he held that though the scheme possessed harsh features it would not be appropriate to hold that Article 6 was in fact infringed. This conclusion was decisively influenced by Laws LJ's conclusion that the scheme was civil rather than criminal because in his judgment "the issue whether this scheme is to be regarded as effectively imposing criminal liability, and so exacting criminal sanctions, is critical to the extent to which the court will defer to the legislative scheme and decline to confine or reduce it on human rights grounds". On the basis that there was clearly more than one possible or reasonable view as to the balance to be struck between the efficacy of the policy aim in issue and the fair treatment of carriers, he said that "the principles of deference (and its withholding) point to a conclusion in this case whereby the democratic powers' judgment upon the striking of the balance ought to be accepted". But for the duty to defer, then, it would seem that Laws LJ would probably have concluded that the harsh features of the scheme did result in a breach of Article 6(1) even though the scheme was civil rather than criminal.

In his judgment Jonathan Parker LJ pointed out that the case raised both issues involving question of social and economic policy and fair trial issues which the court was especially well placed to assess and agreed with both Simon Brown and Laws LJJs that Parliament's discretionary area of judgment should be regarded as being as wide as possible. This meant that the court should not intervene in the operation of the scheme "save in circumstances where the bedrock of the Article 6 right to a fair trial begins to be eroded" at which point intervention by the courts becomes unavoidable. Having analysed the scheme, Jonathan Parker LJ held that it was to be categorised as criminal in nature, that the reverse burden created by section 343(3) of the 1999 Act violated the right of silence and the presumption of innocence and that the penalty regime was not only absurd but wholly unfair. For good measure, he also held that because the scheme makes the Home Secretary judge in his own cause it was plainly incompatible with the independence requirement in Article 6 (regardless of whether it was to be viewed as criminal or civil in nature).

After a somewhat shaky start, then, in *Kebilene* and, perhaps to a lesser extent, in *Brown* it seems tolerably clear now in the light of

R v. *A (No 2)* and *Lambert* that where fair (criminal) trial rights are engaged, the courts in practice display little, if any, deference to Parliament in the sense of holding back from expressing a personal, judicial view based on principled respect for the legislature's democratic credentials. While noting that respect or weight is to be given to Parliament's legislative choice if, in the court's view, that choice threatens the right to a fair trial, the court simply says so and resorts to its HRA toolkit either to repair the damage or declare the incompatibility. There can, surely, be no objection to this approach. As Lord Steyn clearly implied in *R* v. *A (No 2)*, the judges are eminently qualified to make a judgment on what a fair trial requires both procedurally as well as substantively. Indeed, as was pointed out in *Lambert*, Parliament's lamentable record over the past 50 years in enacting criminal offences which result in multiple breaches of the presumption of innocence shows that it has a less than perfect understanding of the consequences of its actions in this area.[16] The withering away of due deference and the narrowing, to the point of extinction, of the discretionary area of judgment in the fair trial case law has produced real and marked benefits in a relatively short time. In particular, as *Lambert* showed, it has enabled the courts to regulate Parliament's ignorant disregard for the presumption of innocence thereby decreasing the risk of miscarriages of justice in relation to grave criminal offences.

PRIMARY JUDGMENT OR DEFERENTIAL REVIEW: DEVELOPMENTS IN PUBLIC LAW

Away from the criminal law, the focus of the argument in public law has been on the differences and similarities between the traditional grounds of review and the proportionality test. A series of pre-HRA prison law cases had already identified the principle of legality as a

---

[16] See Andrew Ashworth and Meredith Blake, "The Presumption of Innocence in English Criminal Law" [1996] *Crim LR* 306 in which the authors found 219 examples among 540 offences triable in the crown court of legal burdens or presumptions operating against the defendant. They observed that no fewer than 40% of the offences triable in the Crown Court appeared to violate the presumption.

common law basis for protecting fundamental rights.[17] Against the background of the Prison Act 1952 lacking express authority for any interference with the rights of access to the court and to legal advice, the rule making power in section 47(2) had been held to authorise, by necessary implication, a measure of interference with the right to legal professional privilege. But, in determining whether a particular measure is authorised by necessary implication, the Court of Appeal held in *Ex parte Leech (No 2)* that it was insufficient simply to establish that there was a pressing need for some interference. What must be established is a pressing need *for that degree* of interference. And such a need can only be established if the legitimate object cannot be met by a less intrusive measure. Thus did Steyn LJ, in his groundbreaking judgment in *Leech (No 2)*, begin to articulate a common law proportionality principle in the field of basic or constitutional rights such as those of access to the courts and to legal advice. In *Leech (No 2)* the Court of Appeal applied this approach to test the *vires* of a blanket rule authorising the routine reading of all mail passing between prisoners and their legal advisers. Finding that a rule of such breadth must create a considerable disincentive to a prisoner exercising his basic rights of access to the court and to legal advice, the Court held that the legitimate need to establish that privileged legal correspondence was bona fide, could be met by a far less intrusive measure. No pressing need for the blanket rule was established. The legitimate object only authorised a rule that permitted correspondence to be read in exceptional circumstances where the authorities had reasonable cause to believe that the privilege was being abused and then only to the extent necessary to determine the bona fides of the communication.

In *Ex parte Simms* the House of Lords adopted the *Leech (No 2)* approach and held that the Secretary of State had not established a pressing need for the policy of preventing journalists from visiting prisoners in connection with alleged miscarriages of justice. The House did not invoke, in addition, the language of "minimum interference", but it is clear that the policy was found to be unlawful

---

[17] See *Raymond* v. *Honey* [1983] AC 1; *R* v. *Home Secretary ex parte Anderson* [1984] 1 QB 778; *R* v. *Home Secretary ex parte Leech (No 2)* [1994] QB 198; *R* v. *Home Secretary ex parte Pierson* [1998] AC 539 and *R* v. *Home Secretary ex parte Simms and O'Brien* [2000] 2 AC 115.

because no pressing need for the degree of interference was established. In other words, the pressing needs of maintaining order and discipline could be met by a less intrusive measure. Lord Steyn (with whom Lords Browne-Wilkinson and Hoffmann agreed) stated:

> . . . I have taken full account of the essential public interest in maintaining order and discipline in prisons. But, I am satisfied that consistently with order and discipline in prisons it is administratively workable to allow prisoners to be interviewed for the narrow purposes here at stake notably if a proper foundation is laid in correspondence for the requested interview or interviews. One has to recognise that oral interviews with journalists are not in the same category as visits by relatives and friends and require more careful control and regulation. That is achievable. This view is supported by the favourable judgment of past experience. Moreover, in reality an oral interview is simply a necessary and practical extension of the right of a prisoner to correspond with journalists about his conviction.

From this analysis it can be seen that the question whether an interference is authorised according to the principle of legality is, therefore, an objective one with the Court discharging its primary duty to secure and protect fundamental rights. In both *Leech* and *Simms* the importance of the right at stake or the purpose served by its exercise in the particular case, were held to be significant factors in determining the circumstances in which a statute would be held to authorise by necessary implication its abolition or limitation. In neither case were the circumstances such that the court considered it appropriate to afford the Home Secretary an area of judgment within which the judiciary would defer on democratic grounds to his considered opinion. This was so even though the area of expertise engaged was that of prison security and the measures which were reasonably necessary to ensure the maintenance of good order, discipline and safe custody In *R v. SSHD ex parte Mahmood*[18] and *R v. SSHD ex parte Isiko*[19] the Court of Appeal had held that in applying the test of proportionality under the HRA, the court's task is not to exercise a primary judgment as to whether the interference is proportionate and so

---

[18] *R on the application of Mahmood* v. *Secretary of State for the Home Department* [2000] All ER (D) 2191.

[19] *R v. Secretary of State for the Home Department ex parte Peter Isiko; Susan and Shemy Isiko* [2000] EWCA Civ 346.

justified, but only to review the primary decision maker's determination. On this analysis the Court could only intervene where it concludes that the decision maker could not reasonably have concluded that the interference was necessary to achieve one or more of the legitimate aims recognised by the Convention. Even allowing for the fact that both *Mahmood* and *Isiko* concerned the blunt instrument of deportation to achieve the aim of deterring non-nationals from engaging in drug dealing against the background of (from a claimant's perspective) unpromising Article 8 case law, the language adopted by Lord Phillips MR in *Mahmood* to explain the Court's role under the HRA was, to say the least, surprising. It was surely plain from the language of the HRA that the question whether a public authority is acting compatibly with a Convention right is one of law for the primary judgment of the courts. The courts were required to ask for themselves whether each element required to justify an interference has been established. And many eminent and informed observers had made it clear that the HRA was intended to achieve a real change in the role of the courts where Convention rights were engaged.

Thus, in his Tom Sargent Memorial Lecture on 16 December 1997,[20] the Lord Chancellor described the role of the judiciary under the 1998 Act in the following passage:

> The Court's decision [under the HRA] will be based on a more overtly principled, and perhaps moral, basis. The Court will look at the positive right. It will only accept an interference with that right where a justification, allowed under the Convention, is made out. The scrutiny will not be limited to seeing if the words of an exception can be made out. The Court will need to be satisfied that the spirit of this exception is made out. It will need to be satisfied that the interference with the protected right is justified in the public interest in a free democratic society. Moreover, the Courts will in this area have to apply the Convention principle of proportionality. This means the Court will be looking substantively at that question. It will not be limited to a secondary review of the decision making process but at the primary question of the merits of the decision itself.

---

[20] Lord Irvine of Lairg, "The Development of Human Rights in Britain under an Incorporated Convention on Human Rights" [1998] *PL* 221.

In reaching its judgment, therefore, the Court will need to expand and explain its own view of whether the conduct is legitimate. It will produce in short a decision on the *morality* of the conduct and not simply its compliance with the bare letter of the law. Lord Bingham apparently shared this view, when he gave the Earl Grey Memorial Lecture he pointed out:[21]

[W]hen they come to decide whether any restriction relied upon is "necessary in a democratic society", then I think that the judges will be undertaking a task which will be, to some extent at least, novel to them. They will have to decide whether there is a pressing social need for the restriction, and whether the restriction is proportionate to the mischief against which it is directed: both of these are problems which do not ordinarily confront judges in their familiar task of deciding applications for judicial review according to the three-fold tests of illegality, irrationality, and procedural impropriety.

And in *Brown* v. *Stott* Lord Steyn observed:

Under the Convention system the primary duty is placed on domestic courts to secure and protect Convention rights . . . only an entirely neutral, impartial, and independent judiciary can carry out the primary task of securing and enforcing Convention rights.

In requiring the judiciary to be the final arbiter of whether a Convention right is being violated, the HRA does not arrogate to the judges powers that have been democratically conferred on the Executive. Rather it recognises that embedded in the very notion of a democracy is a respect for fundamental human rights and that the protection of these rights creates a fetter or brake upon the exercise of legislative or executive power. It is incompatible with the very principle that there exists an area of inviolability into which public authorities cannot step, to leave to those self-same public authorities the power to determine where the border lies. The constitutional difficulties apparently perceived by Lord Phillips MR and others in *Mahmood* and *Isiko* do not in fact exist for a number of reasons. First, through the principle of legality, the courts have already been exercising a primary judgment whether and when the legislature (in enacting delegated legislation), or the Executive acting under the purported

---

[21] [1998] 1 Web JCLI.

authority of a statutory power, have improperly stepped into the inviolable territory defined by the ambit of the right. In other words, a primary judgment was already being exercised in the very same areas that are the reach of sections 3 and 6 of the 1998 Act. Indeed, perhaps somewhat mischievously, Lord Hoffmann in *Simms* drew no distinction between the approach of the court when applying the principle of legality and that which it would apply under the HRA 1998.

Secondly, there is a fundamental distinction between the jurisdiction conferred by Parliament under the 1998 Act and that which the courts have themselves developed under the common law. It is wrong to apply the principles of judicial review to the completely different functions conferred on the courts under the HRA. In exercising their supervisory jurisdiction prior to the HRA, the courts have had to be acutely sensitive to their own constitutional position and particularly to parliamentary sovereignty. Thus, where Parliament confers a power upon a public authority, it is not for the courts to step into the shoes of that authority and take the decision on its behalf, but only to review that decision to ensure that it is taken lawfully. The development of the principle of irrationality was justified as an expression of the will of Parliament rather than a usurpation of it: while Parliament intended the powers conferred by it to be exercised by the chosen recipient, it did not intend or authorise the recipient to exercise the power in a manner that is perverse, unreasonable or irrational.

There is no reason to take such a self-limiting approach in relation to the test of proportionality for the very reason that Parliament has directly expressed its will on the matter in both sections 3 and 6 of the HRA 1998. Parliament has declared its intention that "so far as is possible" legislation must be construed compatibly with Convention rights, and public authorities act unlawfully if they act incompatibly with Convention rights. The Act makes express Parliament's intention that the primary duty of determining the compatibility with Convention rights of legislation and/or the acts of public authorities rests with the courts. Finally, it is wrong to assume that little turns upon the conceptualisation of the court's function. It matters constitutionally and symbolically. And, it can matter substantively in the individual case. One need look no further than *Ex parte Smith*.[22] When the case came before the European Court

---

[22] [1996] QB 517.

(*Lustig-Prean* v. *UK*)[23] it was held that there had been a violation of the applicants' Convention rights.

The outcome of *Daly* has already been referred to. Lord Bingham said that the new approach under the Human Rights Act means that "domestic courts musts themselves form a judgment whether a Convention right has been breached (conducting such inquiry as is necessary to form that judgment) and, so far as permissible under the Act, grant an effective remedy". Lord Steyn's speech emphasised the differences between this new approach and conventional *Wednesbury* review and thereby "clarified" Lord Phillips' statement in *Mahmood*. He said that the criteria for proportionality were "more precise and more sophisticated" in three ways. Proportionality could require the reviewing court to assess the balance which the decision maker has struck, not merely whether it was within the range of rational or reasonable decisions and may require attention to be directed to the relative weight accorded to interests and considerations. Moreover, and using Article 8 by way of example, he said the reasoning process required by the proportionality test meant that the court had to engage with the twin requirements that the limitation of the right was necessary in a democratic society, in the sense of meeting a pressing social need and the question whether the interference was really proportionate to the legitimate aim being pursued. This was different from the threshold question for anxious scrutiny and though the outcome in many cases would be the same, a different conclusion would sometimes result from the proportionality approach.

In an illuminating article in *Public Law*,[24] Ian Leigh has questioned the extent to which *Daly* has really succeeded in burying *Wednesbury* in Convention cases and cites the later decision of the Court of Appeal in *Samaroo*[25] as evidence of the Lazarus-like qualities of the *Wednesbury* principle. While recognising that the approach of Dyson LJ may be broadly correct insofar as it was being applied in the context of the qualified Article 8 right to respect for family life, Professor Leigh expresses the view that "there are indications in the judgment that 'fair balance' is offered as an overarching formula, with the balance to be struck varying according to the importance of the

---

[23] 29 EHRR 548.
[24] "Taking Rights Proportionately: Judicial Review, the Human Rights Act and Strasbourg" [2002] *PL* 265.
[25] [2001] EWCA Civ 1139.

Convention right in question and the technical expertise of the court in assessing the type of reasons for limitation of the right advanced by the executive". He points out – correctly in my view – that "this approach is wholly inappropriate in the case of unqualified rights".

But, while critical of the actual decision reached, I do not read *Samaroo* as applying the fair balance test in this blanket, one-size-fits-all way. Dyson LJ acknowledged that what Lord Steyn said about proportionality was intended to be of general application but pointed out that *Daly* was a case in which the House of Lords found that the legitimate aim of the cell searching policy could have been achieved by means which were less interfering with the fundamental right of prisoners to preserve legal professional privilege, ie by only excluding from the search those prisoners likely to disrupt the conduct of the search. By contrast, Dyson LJ considered that in a case such as *Samaroo* "where the legitimate aim cannot be achieved by alternative means less interfering with a Convention right, the task for the decision-maker, when deciding whether to interfere with the right, is to strike a fair balance between the legitimate aim on the one hand and the affected person's Convention rights on the other".

On this analysis, the decisive factor was the Court's acceptance of the Home Secretary's argument that a policy of deportation was a valuable deterrent to actual or prospective drug traffickers and that immigration control plays an important part in the fight against drug trafficking. Once that – highly dubious argument – had been accepted then the difference between the blunt instrument of deportation and the cell searching policy in play in *Daly* is clear. You can only deport or not deport whereas there are many ways to skin a cat when it comes to devising a cell searching policy. In a case where it *can* truly be said that the legitimate aim can only be achieved by one particular policy – and so there is no question of considering whether the objective of the measure can be achieved by means which are less interfering of an individual's rights – then it seems to me that Dyson LJ's approach is consistent with *Daly* and the only issue is whether the application of the policy in question to the particular individual has an excessive or disproportionate effect on his Convention rights. In this situation, according to Dyson LJ, "the function of the court is to decide whether the Home Secretary has struck the balance fairly between the conflicting interests of Mr Samaroo's right to respect for his family life on the one hand and the prevention of crime and disorder on the other". And in reaching its decision "the court must recognise and allow to the Secretary of State a discretionary area of judgment". Once this was accepted to be the only live issue, the relatively soft nature of the Article 8 right in issue and a body of Strasbourg case law which indicated a willingness to uphold deportation orders despite the most serious interference with Convention rights meant that the Court's conclusion was more or less inevitable.

Two points are worth making about *Samaroo*. First, it can not be read as creating a uniform test for compatibility in relation to unqualified rights such as Article 3. Secondly, Dyson LJ's ultimate conclusion reflects an acceptance of the court's enhanced role under the HRA even where, as with deportation policy, it may be appropriate to defer significantly to the Home Secretary's allegedly greater expertise. Thus, having noted the obligation on the Home Secretary convincingly to establish a justification for any derogation from Convention rights, Dyson LJ said that:

> The Secretary of State must show that he has struck a fair balance between the individual's right to respect for family life and the prevention of crime and disorder. How much weight he gives to each factor will be the subject of careful scrutiny by the court. The court will interfere with the weight accorded by the decision-maker if, despite an allowance for the appropriate margin of discretion, it concludes that the weight accorded was unfair and unreasonable. In this respect, the level of scrutiny is undoubtedly more intense than it is when a decision is subject to review on traditional *Wednesbury* grounds, where the court usually refuses to examine the weight accorded by the decision-maker to the various relevant factors.

This approach does not, it seems to me, undermine the court's role as guardian of human rights. Had I been deciding the case, I would not, on the basis of the evidence before the court, have accepted the Home Secretary's argument that a policy of deporting class A drug traffickers can be shown to have any deterrent effect whatsoever on potential drug traffickers any more than long prison sentences has any detectable deterrent effect on drug dealers. Accordingly, I would not have accepted that *Samaroo* was a case in which the Home Secretary had convincingly established that the legitimate aim asserted could not be achieved by means less interfering with the relevant Convention right. Having so concluded, I would have con-

cluded that the decision to deport Mr Samaroo was plainly disproportionate in that it would, on the facts, utterly destroy the essence
of his Article 8 right in circumstances where the Home Secretary
accepted that it was unlikely that he personally was likely to re-
offend. Nothing in Dyson LJ's reasoning suggests that this would
have been an impermissible conclusion for me to reach. Indeed,
Dyson LJ ultimately expressed his personal agreement with the
fairness of the Home Secretary's decision to break up Mr Samaroo's
family when he said "in my view this was a fair and reasonable conclusion that he was entitled to reach". In other words, the Court did
not confine itself to stating that the decision fell within a range of reasonable responses open to a Secretary of State but held (ie reached a
primary judgment) that the decision was a fair one to take in the light
of the balancing exercise undoubtedly necessary in an Article 8 case
whether the decision was being taken by the Home Secretary in the
first place or reviewed for legality by the court. In these circumstances, it may be, therefore, that Professor Leigh's critique of
Samaroo is overstated.

The most recent case before the House of Lords to give rise to
detailed consideration of the nature of the proportionality test and
the role of deference was *R* v. *Shayler*,[26] another criminal case, this
time concerning a prosecution of a former intelligence officer under
the broad disclosure provisions of the Official Secrets Act 1989
("OSA"). Interesting because it pitted the high value fundamental
right of freedom of expression against the catch-all demands of
national security, the case contains an exhaustive analysis by Lord
Hope of where precisely we have got to in relation to the role of due
deference to Parliament and the contrast between the proportionality test and *Wednesbury*. Having recalled Lord Steyn's *dictum* in
Lambert as to the burden of justification resting on the State where a
fundamental right is interfered with, Lord Hope went on to say that
concluding that a decision was a reasonable one was not enough.
Rather "a close and penetrating examination of the factual justification for the restriction is needed if the fundamental rights enshrined
in the Convention are to remain practical and effective for everyone
who wishes to exercise them".

---

[26] [2002] 2 WLR 754.

In Lord Hope's view it was because (and only because) the *Daly* test now enabled effective scrutiny of a decision to refuse authorisation to an intelligence officer of a requested disclosure in the public interest that Mr Shayler's argument that a public interest defence should be read into the 1989 Act must be rejected. The safeguard of review under the *Daly* test ensured that the apparently draconian terms of the OSA offence were Convention compliant. Alert to the argument that a general restriction on disclosures by reference to national security considerations would be unlikely to satisfy Article 13 in the light of *Smith and Grady* v. *UK*, Lord Hope made the important point that,

> if they are to be compatible with the Convention right [to freedom of expression], the nature of the restrictions must be sensitive to the facts of each case if they are to satisfy the second and third requirements of proportionality. The restrictions must be rational, fair and not arbitrary, and they must impair the fundamental right no more than is necessary.

It remains to be seen whether the application of the *Daly* test will indeed ensure that Strasbourg will never again find that Article 13 has been breached for want of a sufficiently intense review by the courts of the merits of an individual case. If Lord Hope's approach in *Shayler* is faithfully adopted by courts, and so long as a clear distinction in deploying the concept of deference is maintained as between qualified and unqualified rights, I suspect that another *Smith & Grady* v. *UK* is unlikely.

What is Public Power: The Courts' Approach to the Public Authority Definition Under the Human Rights Act

Kate Markus[*]

INTRODUCTION

Section 6 of the Human Rights Act 1998 ("HRA") imposes a duty on public authorities to act compatibly with Convention rights, subject to the express limitation in section 6(2) where legislation constrains the authority from acting otherwise. By this means, the Act inserts Convention rights into all relationships in the public arena.

One of the most testing features of section 6 is how "public authority" is defined. It has been described as "one of the most significant issues in public law today".[1] The Home Secretary explained the Government's intention as follows:

> Under the Convention, the Government are answerable in Strasbourg for any acts or omissions of the state about which an individual has a complaint under the Convention. The Government has a direct responsibility for core bodies, such as central Government and the police, but they also have a responsibility for other public authorities, in so far as the actions of such authorities impinge on private individuals.
>
> The Bill had to have a definition of public authority that went at least as wide and took account of the fact that, over the past 20 years, an increasingly large number of private bodies, such as companies or charities, have come to exercise public functions that were previously exercised by public authorities. . . . it was not practicable to list all the bodies to which the Bill's provisions should apply. Nor would it have been wise to do so. What was needed instead was a statement of principle to which the

---

* Doughty Street Chambers.
[1] Moses J in *Servite Housing Association and Wandsworth LBC ex p Goldsmith* (2000) 3 CCLR 325.

courts could give effect. [Section 6] therefore adopts a non-exhaustive definition of a public authority. Obvious public authorities, such as central government and the police, are caught in respect of everything they do. Public – but not private – acts of bodies that have a mix of public and private functions are also covered.[2]

In referring to the responsibility of the Government under the Convention, Mr Straw was referring to the jurisprudence of the European Court which makes it clear that states have a duty to put in place a legal framework that secures effective protection for Convention rights. States cannot avoid responsibility under the Convention by delegation to private bodies[3] and they are responsible for acts of private persons where the state has a positive obligation to protect Convention rights.[4] Responsibility cannot be avoided by privatisation of state functions.[5] At a domestic level, the Government's intention was to impose liability on those bodies and persons who act on the State's behalf and, therefore, for whom "the UK Government was answerable in Strasbourg".[6]

It is not easy to transpose these concepts of state responsibility at a supra-national level into the national legal framework. Article 1 of the Convention obliges the State to "secure to everyone within their jurisdiction the rights and freedoms defined in Section I of this Convention". In Strasbourg, therefore, the State is responsible if its own legal system fails to protect the Convention rights of individuals from *any* unlawful interference, whether by state or private bodies or private individuals. As Stanley Burnton J observed in the *Leonard Cheshire*[7] case at first instance (considered in detail later in this chapter):

> The party which would have been liable in *Costello-Roberts* if there had been an infringement of a Convention right was the United Kingdom government. If a State party to the Convention fails to secure such rights,

---

[2] Hansard HC, 16 February 1998 col 775.
[3] *Van der Mussele* v. *Belgium* (1983) 6 EHRR 163.
[4] *Costello-Roberts* v. *UK* (1995) 19 EHRR 112; *A* v. *UK* (1998) 27 EHRR 611; *X and Y* v. *Netherlands* (1985) 8 EHRR 235; *Young James and Webster* v. *UK* (1981) 4 EHRR 38.
[5] *Powell and Rayner* v. *UK* (1990) 12 EHRR 355.
[6] Hansard HC, 17 June 1998 col 406.
[7] *R (Heather)* v. *The Leonard Cheshire Foundation* [2001] EWHC Admin 429, (2001) CCLR 211, paras 78–79.

if necessary by domestic legislation (particularly in the field of education, which, under article 2 of the First Protocol, is the subject of one of the few positive Convention rights), it incurs responsibility to its citizens under the Convention, irrespective of the status of the person or body under its jurisdiction infringing the Convention right in question . . .

In *Costello-Roberts*, the Court held that the United Kingdom would be responsible for any failure to secure rights under Article 3 and Article 8, irrespective of the nature of the body providing education, governmental or otherwise.

The HRA limits the duty to act compatibly with Convention rights as required by section 6 to "public authorities", thus excluding from the ambit of the duty private bodies and persons, at least in respect of their private acts, for whom the government is liable in Strasbourg (save to the extent that the courts' horizontal application of Convention rights might impact on them). In this chapter, it is argued that it is only by adopting a generous interpretation of "public authority" that state responsibility can be effectively transposed to our domestic law.

Although the definition of "public authority" is key to the operation and effectiveness of the Act, there is no definition of this term in the Act. Instead, section 6 states that:

(3) . . . "public authority includes –
a) a court or tribunal, and
b) any person certain of whose functions are functions of a public nature
. . ."
but
(5) In relation to a particular act, a person is not a public authority by virtue only of subsection (3)(b) if the nature of the act is private.

As the above quotation from the Home Secretary's speech to the House of Commons shows, the intention was that responsibility under the Act should be placed on three categories of public authority: "obvious" public authorities, that are caught in respect of everything that they do; those with a mix of public and private functions, that are liable only in respect of their public acts; and courts and tribunals. The terminology of "standard" and "functional" authorities is often used to describe the first two categories.[8]

[8] Clayton and Tomlinson in *The Law of Human Rights* (OUP, 2000, para 5.08) and adopted by Lord Woolf CJ in *Poplar Housing and Regeneration Community Association Ltd* v. *Donoghue* [2002] QB 48, at para [63].

WHAT IS A PUBLIC AUTHORITY?

Clearly it is important to be able to identify a "public authority" as a pre-requisite to bringing proceedings or relying on Convention rights in proceedings under section 7. But identifying which category a body falls into – standard or functional – can also be important, as it is only the standard public authorities which are subject to section 6(1) in respect of *all* their acts, public or private.[9]

THE DISTINCTION BETWEEN STANDARD AND FUNCTIONAL PUBLIC AUTHORITIES

Despite the Home Secretary's certainty that it is possible to identify "obvious" public authorities, the exercise has proved not to be quite so easy in practice. The problem lies, at least in part, in the structure of section 6 and the distinction between standard and functional public authorities. As Lord Woolf CJ pointed out in *Poplar*[10] with regard to functional public authorities: "The purpose of section 6(3)(b) is to deal with hybrid bodies which have both public and private functions". But all bodies, including governmental ones, have private functions in respect of which, for instance, judicial review does not lie (for instance, in employing staff, leasing land or making other commercial arrangements).[11]

It is, moreover, difficult to find a convincing rationale for the distinction and the imposition of Convention responsibility on standard public authorities in respect of their private acts. As has been noted, state responsibility requires all activities, whether carried out by standard or functional public authorities or by private bodies or individuals, to be subject to the requirement of Convention compliance. The State satisfies its Convention obligations in the private sphere because, through the activities of the legislature and the

---

[9] S 6(5).
[10] N 21 post para 59.
[11] See, for instance, *McLaren* v. *Home Office* [1990] ICR 824; *R* v. *National Coal Board ex p NUM* [1986] ICR 791, at 795; *R* v. *Lord Chancellor ex p Hibbit and Saunders* [1993] COD 326; *R* v. *Haringey LBC ex p Lisa Arthurworry and Angella Mairs* [2001] EWHC Admin 698.

courts, domestic law is itself adapted and developed to ensure that private persons respect Convention rights.[12] There is then surely no need for the special responsibilities of public authorities to extend beyond their public activities.

Dawn Oliver has suggested some features to assist in identifying a standard public authority:[13] the existence of authority or coercive power; the provision of public funds; whether the body has a statutory basis; whether it has a role in the public interest or is democratically accountable. As will be seen, however, at least some of those criteria are the same as those that are invoked to assist in characterising functional, and not standard, public authorities. Out of those features, it is the characteristic of democratic accountability which is uniquely defining of pure public authorities and has the effect of narrowly confining the category to embrace only "governmental organisations".

Grosz, Beatson and Duffy[14] suggest that any bodies the source of whose power resides in statute or the prerogative will be standard public authorities within section 6(1). This would therefore include central and local government and inferior courts and tribunals, the police, the immigration service, prisons, health authorities, NHS Trusts, the Legal Services Commission, the Criminal Injuries Compensation Board, the Parliamentary Commissioner, the Local Government Ombudsman, the Data Protection Registrar, the Security Services and Interception and Communications Commissioners, the Planning Inspectorate, English Heritage, executive agencies, and statutory regulatory bodies.

In *Aston Cantlow Parish Church Council* v. *Wallbank*,[15] the House of Lords had to decide whether a parochial church council ("PCC") was a public authority so that its enforcement of a landowner's common law liability to keep the chancels of a parish church in repair had to be exercised compatibly with Convention rights. The House of Lords decided, Lord Scott dissenting, that the PCC was neither a

---

[12] See the Commission in *Earl Spencer* v. *UK* (1998) 25 EHRR CD 105, 117–118.

[13] Dawn Oliver, "The Frontiers of the State; Public Authorities and Public Functions under the Human Rights Act", (2000) *PL* 476.

[14] *Human Rights: the 1998 Act and the European Convention* (London: Sweet & Maxwell, 2000), para 4-07 and 4-13.

[15] [2003] UKHL 37; 26 June 2003.

standard nor a functional public authority. Lord Nicholls held that "public authority" in section 6(1) "is essentially a reference to a body whose nature is governmental in a broad sense of that expression".[16] It should also be taken into account that a standard public authority does not enjoy Convention rights, as a result of section 7(7) HRA and Article 34 of the Convention, and "[I]t must always be relevant to consider whether Parliament can have intended that the body in question should have no Convention rights".[17] He held that the Church of England is essentially a religious organisation. Though some of the emanations of the church discharge functions which may qualify as governmental (eg. church schools, the conduct of marriage services or the legislative powers of the General Synod) this does not infect the Church as a whole, or its emanations in general, with the character of a governmental organisation. PCCs do not have a governmental character, but are engaged in self-governance and the promotion of their affairs.[18] Echoing these comments, Lord Hope said:[19]

> [the PCC] plainly has nothing whatever to do with the process of either central or local government. It is not accountable to the general public for what it does. It receives no public funding, apart from occasional grants from English Heritage for the preservation of its historic buildings. In that respect it is in a position which is no different from that of any private individual.

Although the Court of Appeal had considered that the statutory source of power of the PCC and the special status of the Church in its relationship to the Crown was critical in holding it to be a standard public authority, the House of Lords rejected this approach. Following Strasbourg authorities, such as *Holy Monasteries* v. *Greece*,[20] Lord Hope said that the test of whether a person or body is governmental or not is "whether it was established with a view to public administration as part of the process of government".[20a] The legal framework of the Church of England does not lead to the con-

---

16 Para [7].
17 Para [8].
18 Para [13]–[14].
19 Para [59].
20 (1995) 20 EHRR 1.
20a Para [50].

clusion that it is a public authority. The relationship between Church and State "[i]s one of recognition, not of the devolution to it of any of the functions of government".[20b]

This decision shows that a core public authority must have a governmental character, and that that category of bodies is to be drawn narrowly. In deciding whether a body is governmental, Lord Hope found assistance in the approach of Professor Oliver set out above. The approach of the Court in *Poplar HARCA Ltd* v. *Donoghue*,[21] considered in more detail below, indicates that it is unlikely that, if a body does not pass the "source of power" test, it will be a standard public authority. There, the highly public character of the housing association (including it being publicly funded, subject to the control of a statutory body, and having taken ownership of all the local authority's housing stock available for public allocation) was enough to fit it into the functional category but there was no question of it being a standard public authority. Nor is the existence of coercive authority necessarily sufficient to constitute a standard public authority. There are, for instance, regulatory bodies which can impose sanctions,[22] which are unlikely to be held to be more than functional public authorities.

THE COURTS' APPROACH TO "FUNCTIONAL" PUBLIC AUTHORITIES

The more difficult and significant issue raised by section 6 is whether a body or individual performs "functions of a public nature" so as to be a public authority within section 6(3)(b). The Government gave examples, during the passage of the Bill through Parliament, of the following functional authorities: the Press Complaints Commission, the BBC, the ITC, the British Board of Film Censorship, Railtrack, GPs, privatised utilities, and water companies. The Government declined any attempt to list exhaustively those that would qualify and it is difficult to identify common underlying features or criteria in the examples given.

[20b] Para [61].
[21] [2002] QB 48.
[22] eg, the Independent Committee for the Supervision of Standards in Telephone Information Services.

As will be seen, the few court decisions on this aspect of the Act do not leave us very much clearer as to the scope of the definition but have narrowed its application beyond that anticipated by the Government.

Unfortunately, to date the courts have held that reference to parliamentary material in this respect is not permitted[23] and so have avoided consideration of the most helpful material as to the Government's objectives and examples of the types of bodies to be included in the definition. The exclusion of recourse to parliamentary debates in accordance with *Pepper* v. *Hart*[24] is surprising. The controversy produced by section 6(3)(b), the lack of any clear definition, and the variety of possible approaches to identifying "public function" mean that only one thing is clear about this provision: its ambiguity. Further, the Home Secretary and the Lord Chancellor have made a number of clear statements in parliamentary debate directed to the very issue.[25] In the House of Lords on 27 November 1997[26] there was a lengthy debate about the scope of sections 6(1) and 6(3)(b), including the distinction between public authority and private actor, and the consequences for charities, church bodies and voluntary organisations of being included within the definition of "public authority". The Lord Chancellor expressed his views fully acknowledging that they were intended to be referred to in court in accordance with the rule in *Pepper* v. *Hart*.

Section 6(3)(b) and Judicial Review

The starting point for all four cases that have considered section 6(3)(b) in any detail is that the tests for a functional public authority and for amenability to judicial review are the same.[27] The reasoning is that the Civil Procedure Rules (CPR) 54.2 defines a judicial review claim as a claim to review the lawfulness of an enactment or "a deci-

---

[23] See *Aston Cantlow* v. *Wallbank* para [37] and [162]; *R (Heather)* v. *Leonard Cheshire Foundation* [2001] EWHC Admin 429; (2001) 4 CCLR 211, para [84]. Note that in the Court of Appeal in *Leonard Cheshire*, Lord Woolf CJ did refer to parliamentary debates at para [29] but does not rely on them in his conclusions.

[24] [1993] AC 593.

[25] A selection of these are cited in this chapter.

[26] Hansard HL, 24 November 1997, cols 787–802.

[27] Although it should be noted that Lords Hope and Hobhouse in *Aston Cantlow* said that the judicial review test was not determinative.

sion, action or failure to act in relation to the exercise of a **public function**" (emphasis added). The analysis adopted by the courts is that the use of similar words in the CPR and HRA section 6, both coming into force on the same day, and in a public law context, suggests that they are intended to carry the same meaning.[28]

It is the courts' assimilation of the two tests which lies at the root of the timid approach taken to the definition of "public function" under section 6(3)(b). There are indeed good reasons for keeping the tests separate. Alternatively, if the tests are the same, the judicial review test will require radical amendment. Before considering why, it is helpful to take a short detour into the case law as to amenability to judicial review.

The Test for Amenability to Judicial Review Pre-HRA

The case law as to amenability to judicial review is complex and to a degree inconsistent. The important decision of the Court of Appeal in *R* v. *Panel of Take-overs and Mergers ex p Datafin Ltd*[29] held that no single factor is determinative of jurisdiction. Judicial review is available not only against bodies whose powers are derived from statute or the prerogative but where the body in question is exercising public law functions, or if the exercise of the functions have public law consequences, but is not available against a body whose sole source of power is a consensual submission to its jurisdiction. The Court of Appeal in *R* v. *Disciplinary Committee of the Jockey Club ex p Aga Khan*[30] has clarified the limits of the jurisdiction. A body will be amenable to judicial review where its functions are woven into the fabric of public regulation or a system of governmental control, where it is integrated into a system of statutory regulation or is a surrogate organ of government.[31] Hoffmann LJ observed that in

---

[28]　Stanley Burnton J in *Leonard Cheshire* para 65; Lord Woolf CJ in *Poplar* para [65(i)]; Keith J in *R (A)* v. *Partnerships in Care Ltd* [2002] EWHC 529 Admin, para [9]; Field J in *R (Beer)* v. *Hampshire Farmers Markets Limited* [2002] EWHC 2559 Admin, para [33].

[29]　[1987] QB 815, 838E, 847A–D.

[30]　[1993] 1 WLR 909, 923H.

[31]　See also *R* v. *Insurance Ombudsman ex p Aegon Life Insurance* [1994] COD 426; *R* v. *London Metals Exchange Ltd ex p Albatross Warehousing BV*, Unreported, 30 March 2000, paras [25]–[27]. More recently, see *R (Oxford Study Centre)* v. *British Council* [2001] ELR 803.

Datafin there was a "privatisation of the business of government itself."[32]

Applying those principles, it has been held that a private body may be amenable to judicial review in respect of only some of its functions, where those functions have sufficient statutory or governmental underpinning.[33] In deciding whether a body is public by reason of the nature or consequences of its functions, the courts might take into account whether, if the body did not exist or did not provide the services in question, the State would intervene.[34]

It is doubtful whether it is sufficient for a body merely to be acting in the public interest where there is no statutory or governmental underpinning. Despite the view of De Smith, Woolf and Jowell that the activities of a private body may be governed by the standards of public law when their function or position in the market implies a duty to act in the public interest, giving the example of a private company running a prison,[35] there is no basis for such a conclusion to be found in case law and the example of the private prison can be explained by the fact that prisoners are there under state compulsion and that the prison has statutory powers and obligations and is subject to the control and intervention of the Home Secretary.[36] In *R* v. *East Berkshire Health Authority ex p Walsh*,[37] Donaldson MR said he could not find "any warrant for equating public law with the interest of the public".

What clearly emerges from the case law is that there must be some statutory, prerogative or governmental authority (express or implied)[38] either for a body's existence or for the exercise of the func-

---

[32] At p 931H.

[33] For an example of this see *R* v. *Cobham Hall School ex p G* [1998] ELR 389, where a private school was held to be exercising a public law function in respect of the administration of the assisted places scheme. See also *R* v. *Muntham House School ex p R* (2000) ELR 287.

[34] *R* v. *Advertising Standard Authority ex p The Insurance Services plc* [1990] 2 Admin LR 77, 86C–D; *Aga Khan* at 923G. However, this test has been subject to some criticism: David Pannick QC [1992] *Public Law* 5–6. Where it does apply, it can probably be explained as a form of implied devolution of power, as referred to by Lloyd LJ in *Datafin* at 849C.

[35] De Smith, Woolf and Jowell, *Judicial Review of Administrative Action* (Sweet and Maxwell, 5th edn, 1995), para 3-031.

[36] Stanley Burnton J in *Leonard Cheshire*, para [51].

[37] [1985] QB 152, 164.

[38] See also *R* v. *Chief Rabbi of the United Hebrew Congregation of Great Britain and the Commonwealth ex p Wachman* [1993] 2 All ER 249, at 254d–f.

tions in question if it is to be amenable to judicial review. It was on that basis that Moses J decided in *R* v. *Servite Housing Association and Wandsworth LBC ex p Goldsmith and Chatting*,[39] shortly before the HRA came into force, that a charitable housing association managing a residential home for elderly people was not performing any public law function and therefore not amenable to judicial review. The local authority could not delegate its statutory functions to the housing association.[40] Instead, it discharged its statutory duty by making private arrangements for the provision of residential accommodation by the association,[41] the relationship between the housing authority and the association being purely commercial.[42]

The approach of Moses J has been expressly approved as the correct approach to amenability to judicial review after the passing of the HRA.[43]

Not only must the body in question be amenable to judicial review, but the particular act, decision or omission must itself be amenable to judicial review, in other words the claim must raise an issue of public law rather than private law.[44]

The Difference Between "Functions of a Public Nature" Under Section 6(3)(b) and Amenability to Judicial Review

It can now be seen why the tests for liability under section 6(3)(b) and for amenability to judicial review should not be assimilated:

The HRA aims to ensure that Convention rights are respected throughout our legal system and at all levels of society. It is only by so doing that the state can avoid liability in Strasbourg for permitting such violations, and it explains the non-incorporation of article 13. Unlike judicial review, the purpose is not limited to protecting individuals against abuses of power by the state and governmental bodies. While the presence of a governmental feature is probably conclusive in favour of a body being a public authority within section 6, its absence should not be conclusive against it. A housing associa-

---

[39] (2000) 3 CCLR 325.
[40] At 339H–I.
[41] Ibid p 340D–E.
[42] Ibid p 349B–C.
[43] See Stanley Burnton J in *Leonard Cheshire* at paras [59]–[78].
[44] See the cases cited above at n 11.

tion, for example, can be a functional public authority although, at least before the HRA, it was not amenable to judicial review.[45] For that reason, the HRA applies to all areas of law, and to private as well as public relations. The duties of the courts under sections 2 and 3 apply to all proceedings, and sections 7 and 8 clearly anticipate private law as well as public law proceedings. In comparison, judicial review is a discrete legal process applying to bodies satisfying the amenability tests. Although the rules of procedural exclusivity have been relaxed considerably in recent years,[46] they have not been abandoned.

The courts have eschewed a purely functional test for judicial review. The notes in the White Book indicate that CPR 54.1(2)(a) is intended to reflect the existing law as to the scope of judicial review. Judicial review includes a claim to review "the lawfulness of . . . a decision, action or failure to act", but only in relation to "the exercise of a public function". This simply confirms that the remedy is not available in respect of the private functions of public bodies. Section 6(3)(b) uses "functions of a public nature" as a means of characterising the body in question not the nature of the legal dispute. It focuses attention on the function of the body, and was explained by the Home Secretary as follows:

> As we are dealing with public functions and with an evolving situation, we believe that the test must relate to the substance and nature of the act, not to the form and legal personality.[47]

If the tests are the same, all bodies exercising public functions within section 6(3)(b) would be amenable to judicial review in respect of those functions. Yet section 7 creates independent causes of action for breach of section 6 in respect of which there is a one-year limitation period.

The Strasbourg jurisprudence as to the identity of bodies that engage the responsibility of the State differs materially from the judicial review criteria.[48]

---

[45] Compare *Poplar HARCA* and *Servite Houses*.
[46] Lord Woolf in *Leonard Cheshire* paras [36]–[40]; *Clark* v. *University of Lincolnshire and Humberside* [2000] 1 WLR 1988.
[47] Hansard HC 17 June 1998 vol 314 cols 409–10.
[48] As to this, see Grosz, Beatson and Duffy, above n 15 paras 4–14.

While, therefore, the Government intended that guidance could be gained from the judicial review case law,[49] this should not be taken to mean that the tests are the same.

An alternative approach is to assimilate the two tests, on the basis that it is anomalous for only some public authorities within section 6(3)(b) to be amenable to judicial review with regard to their public functions.[50] But, for the reasons outlined above, in order to give full purposive effect to the HRA, the scope of judicial review test would then require radical change. This is something that, to date, the courts have shown themselves unwilling to countenance.

The Approach of the Courts to Section 6(3)(b) HRA

Five recent decisions of the High Court, Court of Appeal and House of Lords have given some modest assistance in determining the scope and application of section 6(3)(b) HRA. In three of which, as has been seen, the courts confirmed that the test for a public authority subject to judicial review or subject to the duty under section 6 by virtue of section 6(3)(b) is now the same.

The first decision is that of the Court of Appeal in *Poplar HARCA v. Donoghue*.[51] A housing association was seeking possession from a non-secure tenant under the accelerated possession procedure by which the court was bound to order possession if the appropriate notice had been given. The tenant had been a non-secure tenant of the housing authority when the property, along with a large part of the authority's housing stock, was transferred to the association. The tenant claimed that the housing association was a public authority or performing a public function for the purposes of section 6 HRA and that seeking possession under that procedure violated her rights under Article 8(1) of the Convention. The Court of Appeal held that the housing association was not a standard public authority but was a functional one. The Court considered the historic origins of the housing association movement and the functions performed by

---

[49] Hansard HC, 17 June 1998, col 408/9.

[50] But there is no necessity for all public functions to be challenged in judicial review proceedings. See, for instance, the negligence cases such as *Barrett* v. *Enfield LBC* [1999] 3 WLR 79.

[51] [2002] QB 48.

associations today, their funding, the role of the Housing Corporation and the relationship with the local housing authority.

Lord Woolf CJ, delivering the judgment of the Court, set out the following as to the scope of the definition of public authority in section 6(3)(b):[52]

– The definition of who is a public authority and what is a public function, for the purposes of section 6, should be given a generous interpretation.

– Section 6 is inspired by the approach developed by the courts in identifying bodies and activities subject to judicial review and in particular the emphasis on public functions. The emphasis on public functions reflects the approach adopted in judicial review by the courts and textbooks since *Datafin* (the judgment of Lloyd LJ).

– The fact that a body performs an activity which otherwise a public body would be under a duty to perform (for instance, in this case, the provision of social housing) cannot mean that such performance is necessarily a public function. Section 6(3)(b) does not make a body, which does not have responsibilities to the public, a public body merely because it performs acts on behalf of a public body which would constitute public functions if such acts are performed by the public body itself.

– Where a public body uses the services of a private body to perform its public duties, section 6 should not apply to the private body. A private act, such as the renting out of accommodation, remains private in nature even where it is done because another body is under a public duty to ensure that it is done.

– As in *Costello-Roberts* v. *UK*,[53] the state cannot absolve itself of its Convention obligations by delegating their fulfilment to private bodies or individuals so that, if there is a breach of the Convention, it is the state body (the local authority) which remains responsible.

– The fact that a body is a charity or conducted not for profit does not point to it being a public authority.

– The fact that acts are supervised by a public regulatory body does not necessarily indicate they are public.

[52] Paras 58–60 and 65.
[53] Above n 4.

– What can make an act, which would otherwise be private, public "is a feature or combination of features which impose a public character or stamp on the act". Relevant factors are: statutory authority for what is done; extent of control exercised by a public authority over the functions of the other body; and how closely the acts that could be of a private nature are enmeshed in the activities of a public body.

The Court of Appeal concluded that Poplar was a public authority because of the close relationship between Tower Hamlets and Poplar: Poplar was created by Tower Hamlets to take a transfer of local authority housing stock; five of its board members were also members of Tower Hamlets; Poplar was subject to the guidance of Tower Hamlets as to the manner in which it acted towards the defendant. In addition, the tenant had been a tenant of the housing authority at the time of transfer of the housing stock to Poplar, and it was intended at the time of the transfer that she would not be treated differently as a result of the transfer. Poplar therefore "stood in relation to her in very much the position previously occupied by [the housing authority]". However, the Court said that, although the local housing authority had transferred its housing stock to the housing association, it had not transferred its primary public duties. Poplar was merely the means by which the authority sought to perform its public duties. With strong echoes of the judgment in *Servite Houses*, this meant (as Lord Woolf confirmed) that the position would not necessarily be the same with other tenants who were not in the special position of Mrs Donoghue.

Lord Woolf said in conclusion:

> In a borderline case, such as this, the decision is very much one of fact and degree. Taking into account all the circumstances, we have come to the conclusion that while activities of housing associations need not involve the performance of public functions, in this case, in providing accommodation for the defendant and then seeking possession, the role of Poplar is so closely linked to that of Tower Hamlets that it was performing public and not private functions.[54]

The issue was considered again by Stanley Burnton J and by the Court of Appeal in *R (Heather and others)* v. *Leonard Cheshire Foundation*.[55] In that case, residents of a nursing home for the

---

[54] Para 66.
[55] At first instance, [2001] EWHC Admin 429, (2001) CCLR 211; in the Court of Appeal, [2002] EWCA Civ 366, [2002] 2 All ER 936.

disabled applied for judicial review of a decision by LCF to close the home, claiming that LCF was a public authority within the meaning of section 6(3)(b) and that the decision violated the residents' Article 8(1) rights. The claimants were placed in the home by a social services authority pursuant to its duties under section 21(1)(a) National Assistance Act 1948 to provide residential accommodation to those who are in need of care and attention by reason of age, illness or disability. Section 26 of the 1948 Act permitted the authority to make arrangements and pay for such accommodation to be provided by third parties. Others were placed there under similar arrangements made with the health authority.

There was no doubt that, in making arrangements under section 26 with LCF, the local authority was performing a public function.[56] However, both courts held that LCF, in providing accommodation to those to whom the authority owed a statutory duty, was not performing a public function.

Stanley Burnton J's first instance decision is worth setting out in some detail as his reasoning illustrates the effect of applying the judicial review test to section 6(3)(b). Starting from the premise that the judicial review test and the HRA test for public authority are the same, and approving the decision of Moses J in *Servite Houses*, he declined to adopt a purely functional test of public authority. Moreover, he rejected either the presence of state funding, state regulation or the fact that the government would step in if the body in question were not exercising the function, as indicating that the body is exercising a public function,[57] although he did not accept that the existence of contractual relationships or powers derived from contract are necessarily inconsistent with amenability to judicial review.[58]

He then considered whether the introduction of the HRA made any difference to the test for amenability to judicial review, on the basis that this was the same as the test under section 6(3)(b). It was inevitable that he would thereby limit the scope of his inquiry. He rejected a purely functional test which he said would revolutionise

[56] Lord Woolf CJ, para 15.
[57] Paras 47–48.
[58] Para 53. That is perfectly consistent with the judicial review case law which makes it clear that contractual powers can co-exist with governmental functions – see *Aga Khan* and *Albatross Warehousing*, nn. 30 and 34.

the scope of judicial review.[59] Although he set out to achieve a pur-posive interpretation of section 6, in the light of the purpose of the HRA and the ambit of the ECHR,[60] he was clearly influenced by his desire to preserve the concepts inherent in the judicial review test. In the same way that he had concluded that the application of JR norms to purely private persons was counter-intuitive, he concluded that the application of Convention responsibilities to such persons is con-trary to the self-interested character of such persons.[61] Following the reasoning of Lord Woolf in Poplar,[62] Stanley Burnton J said that the case of *Costello Roberts* v. *UK*[63] shows that the party responsible for breach by a non-governmental body of a Convention right which is not part of domestic law is the State and that the Convention was not intended to make non-governmental bodies, acting in accordance with domestic law, directly liable for the breach.[64] The judge then proceeded to distinguish LCF from Poplar HARCA.

The first error in this reasoning is that, while the judicial review jurisdiction has the effect of excluding those private bodies acting in their own economic interests, the same criterion need not apply under the HRA. Respect for Convention rights generally involves a balancing exercise which expressly permits consideration of a range of factors including the rights and freedoms of others. The rights of the contractor (if it is not a governmental organisation within article 34) or others whose rights and freedoms are affected by the activities of the contractor can be accorded due respect in that process.

Second, as already noted, the principle of state responsibility is not capable of direct application in domestic law. *Costello-Roberts* is important precisely because it shows the degree of government responsibility to ensure that Convention rights are respected in all spheres of activity.[65] The HRA is pre-eminently the legislation by which the UK government has chosen to comply with its duty to secure Convention rights by domestic legislation, and it does so by

---

[59] Para 65.
[60] Para 68.
[61] Paras 71–74.
[62] At para 60.
[63] Above n 4.
[64] Paras 75–80.
[65] See para 26 of the judgment of the Court, and para 37 of the opinion of the Commission.

ensuring that those whose actions have an impact on the public are bound to respect Convention rights.

The Court of Appeal dismissed the residents' appeal and, by implication at least, adopted much of the reasoning of Stanley Burnton J. Lord Woolf CJ was of the view that the use by the local authority of LCF as a provider of accommodation would not deprive the residents of protection of their Article 8 rights. The local authority remained subject to its section 21 duty and retained an obligation to the residents under Article 8. Further, the residents had contractual rights against LCF. In future, Lord Woolf said, it would be open to a local authority and a provider such as LCF to enter into a contract to fully protect the resident's Article 8 rights. The Court commented that the residents' arguments in this case would mean that LCF would be subject to obligations under the Convention that had not been contemplated at the time that it contracted with the authority.[66]

Even putting aside such considerations, the Court held that "the role that LCF was performing manifestly did not involve the performance of public functions",[67] taking into account the following:

– There was no material difference between the nature of the services LCF provided to privately funded and local authority funded residents, and yet it was only in relation to the latter that it was contended that LCF was performing public functions.
– While the degree of public funding is relevant, it is not determinative.
– There was no other evidence of a public flavour to the functions of LCF. It was not standing in the shoes of local authorities and was not exercising any statutory powers.
– The argument that, unless LCF is performing a public function, the residents cannot rely upon Article 8 is a circular argument that gets them nowhere. Article 8 cannot change the appropriate classification of a function.
– None of the criteria in *Poplar* applied in this case, save for a degree of regulation by a statutory body.

Although the Court of Appeal did not expressly address whether the test for a public authority under section 6(3)(b) corresponded to the test for amenability to judicial review and, if so, whether that test

---

[66] Paras 33–34.
[67] Para 35.

required any amendment in the light of the Human Rights Act, the reasons given amount to little more than an application of the judicial review test. The decision turned critically on the absence of statutory powers or other delegation by the local authority, and the fact that publicly and privately funded residents received the same services.

In *R (A)* v. *Partnerships in Care Limited*,[68] Keith J also relied on the existence of statutory powers in the search for a public function. The case concerned a patient detained in a private psychiatric hospital under section 3 Mental Health Act 1983, her care and treatment being funded by her health authority. She wished to judicially review a decision by the hospital to change the focus of treatment on her ward so that, according to her, she would no longer receive the specialist care and treatment she needed. Most of the hospital's patients, including the claimant, were placed there pursuant to statutory powers of health authorities to make arrangements for private bodies to provide health services under the National Health Service Act 1977. The hospital was registered as a mental nursing home under the Registered Homes Act 1984 as being entitled to receive patients who were liable to be detained under the Mental Health Act 1983, and was subject to a measure of control and supervision by the health authority by virtue of regulations made under the 1984 Act. The regulations also imposed a duty on the hospital to provide adequate staff and treatment facilities. Admission to hospital and detention and treatment there were governed by the Mental Health Act, and the hospital managers and psychiatrists had statutory responsibility for detention, discharge and treatment of patients admitted to the hospital under the Act. Therefore:

> In its corporate capacity as the body which owns and runs the hospital, the Defendant may be a private company run on commercial lines, free to admit whichever patients it chooses. But in its statutory capacity as manager of the hospital, the Defendant is a body upon whom important statutory functions have devolved, albeit as a result of the contractual arrangements which it has made with the Health Authorities to which the responsibility for the care and treatment of those hospital's patients

---

[68] [2002] EWHC 529 Admin. Although this decision was made after the judgment of the Court of Appeal in *Leonard Cheshire*, the hearing took place beforehand and Keith J refers only to the judgment of Stanley Burnton J. It seems unlikely that, had he considered the judgment of the Court of Appeal, it would have made any difference to the outcome in the light of his finding that the hospital exercised statutory powers.

who are not being treated privately have been delegated by the Secretary of State under . . . Regulations.[69]

Keith J accepted that it might be said that the activities of the hospital and the health authorities are not closely enmeshed in the way that the activities of Poplar and the Tower Hamlets were, given that the statutory obligations of the health authorities ended when they made arrangements for the hospital to provide care and treatment to mentally disordered patients and the hospital did not assume the Health Authorities' statutory obligations. However, the decision complained of by hospital managers to change the focus of the ward was an act of a public nature. There were free-standing obligations imposed on the managers, not derivative from those of the health authorities: the statutory duty to provide adequate staff and facilities was cast directly on the hospital.[70]

Although Keith J also took into account that there was a "public interest" in the hospital's care and management of its patients just as there was in the purpose and nature of the detention of prisoners in a privatised prison,[71] and that patients were admitted by compulsion rather than choice, this does not appear to have been decisive.

In *Aston Cantlow* v. *Wallbank*,[71a] the House of Lords, having decided that the PCC was not a core public authority, also decided by a majority that it was not a public authority within section 6(3)(b). Interestingly, none of their Lordships considered any of the three cases just discussed. Their approach is however informative. The following considerations guided their approach:

– The purpose of section 6(1) is that those bodies for whose acts the state is answerable before the European Court of Human Rights shall be subject to a domestic law obligation not to act incompatibly with Convention rights.[71b]

– Section 6(3)(b) is intended to embrace the numerous functions of a governmental nature that in a modern developed state are frequently discharged by non-governmental bodies.[71c]

[69] Para 17.
[70] Paras 23–24.
[71] Para 25, referring to a passage from De Smith, Woolf and Jowell at 3–031. See n 100 below.
[71a] [2003] UKHL 37; [2003] 3 WLR 283.
[71b] Lord Nicholls para [6].
[71c] Lord Nicholls para [9].

– The expression "public function" in section 6(3)(b) should be given a generously wide scope.[71d]

– There is no single test for a public function but relevant factors include the extent to which in carrying out the relevant function the body is publicly funded, or is exercising statutory powers, or is taking the place of central government or local authorities, or is providing a public service.[71e]

– In determining whether a body in general or a specific function is a public one, their Lordships considered Strasbourg jurisprudence rather than that of domestic administrative law to provide the necessary guidance. It was not necessary, however, to explore this broadly as there were two cases in which the position of churches had been addressed.[71f]

More recently the Court of Appeal in *Hampshire County Council v. Graham Beer*[71g] held that HFML, a private company set up by but independent of the county council to manage and regulate farmers markets in the county, was both amenable to judicial review and a public authority in deciding to exclude a particular farmer from participation in the markets. Although HFML was a private body with no statutory underpinning nor weaving into any system of governmental control, it was a not-for-profit organisation engaged in promoting the public interest by facilitating access to trading outlets, it acquired the good will and assets of the business from the county council for no charge, the markets were held on public sites owned by the local councils who gave permission for such use, so that HFML were engaged in running what were in substance public markets to which the public have a common law right of access. Regulation and organisation of that right was a public function. Dyson LJ held that this conclusion was difficult to avoid in the light of a number of decisions holding that licensing decisions by local authorities regulating public markets were public functions that were amenable to judicial review.[72] In this case, HFML

[71d] Lord Nicholls para [11].

[71e] Lord Nicholls para [12].

[71f] *Holy Monasteries v. Greece* (1994) 20 EHRR 1; *Hautanemi v. Sweden* (1996) 22 EHRR CD 155.

[71g] [2003] EWCA Civ 1056.

[72] *R v. Barnsley MBC ex p Hook* [1976] 3 All ER 452; *R v. Basildon DC ex p Brown* [1981] 79 LGR 655; *R v. Wear Valley DC ex p Binks* [1985] 2 All ER 699; *R v. Durham CC ex p Robinson, The Times*, 31.1.92; *R v. Birmingham CC ex p Dredger* [1994] 6 Admin LR 553.

had stepped straight into the county council's shoes and so it too was exercising a public function.[73] The court followed the decision in *Leonard Cheshire* and *Donoghue* in concluding that there is an extremely close relationship between the test for judicial review and public authority. Dyson LJ held that there was nothing in the speeches in *Aston Cantlow* which suggests that what was said in those two cases is not a useful guide to amenability to judicial review, and that provided it is borne in mind that regard should be had to any relevant Strasbourg jurisprudence, then those cases will continue to be a source of valuable guidance as to the nature of "public authority" under section 6(3)(b).[73a] Indeed, while Strasbourg jurisprudence is especially likely to be helpful in determining whether a body is a standard public authority, "it is likely to be less helpful in relation to the fact-sensitive question of whether in an individual case a hybrid body is exercising a public function".[73b]

Summary of Decisions

It is difficult to extrapolate from the decisions in these cases clear guidance of general application in identifying a functional public authority. Although the Court in *Poplar* excluded certain factors as "necessarily" indicating that a body was public, the presence of such factors may nonetheless assist in determining the question in a particular case. It is suggested that the following propositions can be derived from the case law to date:

There will be a public function where there is:

- statutory authority for what is done;
- statutory responsibility imposed on the body in question in respect of the core functions;[74]
- true delegation or sharing of powers or functions by the public body;

---

[73]   Para 37.
[73a] Para [15] and [25].
[73b] Para [28].
[74]   In *Poplar* there was evidence of the statutory duties of registered social land-lords (RSLs) to co-operate with local housing authorities, and the existence of nomination arrangements between the housing authority and RSLs. In *A* the statutory capacity of the hospital manager was conclusive.

– close proximity between the body in question and the public body including a degree of control over the functions of the body in question by the public body;
– public funding for the activity in question.[75]

The fact that a body is subject to statutory regulation in the performance of its functions does not necessarily indicate a public function and may, in some circumstances, militate against it.[76] The inference to be drawn from regulation is likely to depend upon its nature and purpose in any particular case. Where regulation forms part of a framework for the delivery of a public service, such as social housing, it may indicate that the regulated functions are public. It will be different where regulation exists to enforce minimum standards upon private activities. Thus, for example, regulation of the media does not render the media activities public.

COMPARATIVE MATERIALS

It is instructive to consider the approaches of the courts to this problem in other Commonwealth and European jurisdictions.

Jurisdictions with strong constitutional horizontality

In some jurisdictions, the strong horizontality provided by the relevant Charter or Bill of Rights means that there has been less need for the courts to identify public bodies upon whom human rights responsibilities fall. The following are a few examples.

South Africa

The South African Constitution of 1996 expressly[77] binds not only all organs of the state, but "a natural or juristic person if, and to the extent that, it is applicable, taking into account the nature of the rights and of any duty imposed by the right" and enjoins the courts to apply or, if necessary, to develop the common law to give effect to

---

[75] Though Stanley Burnton J in *Leonard Cheshire* doubted it – para 48(i).
[76] *Poplar*, para 65(v); *Leonard Cheshire*, QBD, para 48(ii); CA, para 21.
[77] Section 8.

the Bill of Rights. The Constitution moreover expressly applies some rights to private bodies.[78]

Ireland

Irish law accepts full horizontal application of constitutional rights between private parties, derived from Article 40(3.1) of the Constitution which states that "the State guarantees in its laws to respect, and, as far as practicable, to defend and vindicate, the constitutional rights of the citizen". This obligation applies to the courts as well as to the executive and legislature, and the courts will make a remedy available under the Constitution where the common or statutory law do not provide one, and have created torts arising directly from the Constitution against private persons where necessary.[79]

Germany

The doctrine of *Drittwurking* provides indirect horizontal effect to the Constitution, though only state institutions are directly subject to the basic constitutional rights.

Jurisdictions with no or weak constitutional horizontality

In other systems, where there is no or only weak constitutional horizontality, the courts have developed their own means of interpreting legislation and applying and developing the common law so as to ensure compliance with fundamental rights. Again, a few examples illustrate this:

---

[78] Section 9(4) states "no person " may unfairly discriminate; s 12(1)(c) gives a right to be free from all forms of violence from public or private sources; s 15(2) imposes obligations on "state-aided institutions" in relation to religious observances.

[79] *Crowley* v. *Ireland* [1990] IR 103: a cause of action against a teachers' trade union whose strike had kept children out of school; *Lovett* v. *Grogan* [1995] IR 132: a private coach operator was in breach of the plaintiff's constitutional right to earn a livelihood, where the private operator ran without a licence and the plaintiff was licensed to run a service on the same route; see also *Hanrahan* v. *Mereck Sharpe and Dohme* [1988] ILRM 629.

Canada

The Canadian Charter of Rights and Freedoms states, in section 32:

(1) This Charter applies
to the Parliament and government of Canada in respect of all matters
within the authority of Parliament . . .
to the legislature and government of each province in respect of all matters within the authority of the legislature of each province.

The Canadian Charter has no horizontal effect.[80] However, it is
established that the Charter may apply to a private entity in two
ways, similar to the "standard" and "functional" categories under the
HRA. First, the private entity may be found to be in reality "government", because of its nature or the degree of governmental control.
In such cases, all of its actions will be subject to the Charter. Second,
the private entity may be found to be exercising certain functions, the
nature of which is public. It will then be bound by the Charter only
in respect of those functions.

Much of the case law on the first, "governmental" category
concerns organisations where private employment functions were
in issue. In a series of cases on mandatory retirement policies of
universities, colleges and hospitals,[81] the Court held that section 32 did
not apply, because the institutions concerned were not part of the appa-
ratus of government, and because the mandatory retirement polices did
not implement a government programme, nor were the bodies acting
in a governmental capacity in implementing these programmes.
However, in a similar case on retirement polices,[82] the Court found
that the Charter did apply, since the college, because of its constituent
Act, could be considered an emanation of government.[83]

[80] *Retail, Wholesale and Department Store Union* v. *Dolphin Delivery* (1987) 33
DLR (4th) 174.
[81] *Stoffman* v. *Vancouver General Hospital* [1990] 3 SCR 483. *McKinney* v.
University of Guelph [1990] 3 SCR 229; *Harrison* v. *University of British Columbia*
[1990] 3 SCR 451.
[82] *Douglas/Kwantlen Faculty Assn.* v. *Douglas College* [1990] 3 SCR 570.
[83] See also *Lavigne* v. *Ontario Public Service Employees Union* [1991] 2 SCR 211,
in which the Ontario Council of Regents for Colleges of Applied Arts and
Technology, was found to be an emanation of government, under the terms of its
empowering Act, which gave the Minister for Education routine and regular control
over its administration.

In *Eldridge* v. *Attorney General for British Columbia*[84] La Forest J formulated the principles determining whether a body is liable in the second category. He set out a number of principles in determining whether the charter applies:

- The Charter applies to all government[85] activities, whether or not they are commercial.
- The Charter applies to private bodies where:
    - the body "is government" because of the degree of governmental control exercised over it, or
    - the activity is something that can be ascribed to government, for instance because it is implementing a specific government policy or program.

La Forest J stated that there must be "an investigation not into the nature of the entity whose activity is impugned but rather into the nature of the activity itself. . . . one must scrutinise the quality of the act at issue, rather than the quality of the actor". The rationale is explained as follows: "while it is a private actor that actually implements the program, it is government that retains responsibility for it. Just as governments are not permitted to escape Charter scrutiny by entering into commercial contracts or other "private" arrangements, they should not be allowed to evade their constitutional responsibilities by delegating the implementation of their policies and programs to private entities.[86]

Thus in *Eldridge* a private hospital was subject to Charter obligations in respect of the provision of medical services under the Hospital Insurance Act. Although hospitals are not governmental, in providing medically necessary services it was carrying out a specific government objective as part of a comprehensive social programme.

New Zealand

The Bill of Rights Act ("BORA") applies only to "acts done (a) by the legislative, executive, or judicial branches of the government of New

---

[84] [1997] 3 SCR 624.
[85] "Government" is somewhat narrower in its scope than those bodies subject to judicial review.
[86] Para 42.

Zealand; or (b) by any person or body in the performance of any public function, power, or duty conferred or imposed on that person or body by or pursuant to law".

Although the New Zealand courts have held that the Act has a degree of indirect horizontal effect,[87] they have also held that there are circumstances in which private persons might fall within category (b). Thus, in *TV3 Network Ltd* v. *Eveready New Zealand Ltd*,[88] Cook P in the Court of Appeal suggested that the obligation to comply with the Bill of Rights could extend to a licensed TV broadcaster so that "it is a tenable view that, if the plaintiffs establish malicious falsehood or unlawful defamation, the Bill of Rights may provide a basis for an order that corrective information be broadcast to the viewing public".

In *R* v. *H*,[89] the Court of Appeal applied the definition of a public authority to a private accountant who had, after an interview with the police and with police encouragement, searched a company's files and provided the police with documents, where the searches were alleged to be illegal, and in breach of the Bill of Rights. However, the definition did not extend to an earlier search carried out privately even though he then volunteered them to the police. Richardson J noted that section 3 of BORA,

> is directed to the exercise of the powers of the state and the conduct of governmental agencies. Wholly private conduct is left to be controlled by the general law of the land. Thus the Bill of Rights does not extend to any search or seizure undertaken privately by a private individual. But if there is governmental involvement in a search and seizure actually carried out by an informer or other private individual, that may attract the Bill of Rights protections.

He observed that, while the dividing line between governmental and public actions would be difficult to draw, action by private persons would fall within section 3 where a public official "instigated" a search or seizure, or where the private person could be seen as the agent of the government. To do otherwise would frustrate the objects of BORA.[90]

[89] [1994] 2 NZLR 143.
[90] At p 147.

Hong Kong

The Hong Kong Bill of Rights Ordinance 1991 ("BORO"), section 7, states:

(1) This Ordinance binds only –
  (a) the government and all public authorities; and
  (b) any person acting on behalf of the Government or a public authority.

The Bill of Rights has been held not to have strong horizontal effect.[91] Against that background, In *Hong Kong Polytechnic University* v. *Next Magazine Publishing Ltd*,[92] Keith J held at first instance (and not reconsidered by the Court of Appeal) that Hong Kong Polytechnic University was not under governmental control, even though some members of the university's governing body were appointed by government. Nonetheless, it could be considered a public authority within the meaning of section 7, because it was a statutory corporation, it had a public purpose not performed for profit, it conferred degrees recognised by the government, and it was largely publicly funded. The judge stated:

> In my view, for a body to be a public authority within the meaning of section 7(1) of the BORO, it is not sufficient for it to be entrusted with functions to perform for the benefit of the public and not for private profit: there must be something in its nature or constitution, or in the way in which it is run, apart from its functions, which brings it into the public domain. . . . it may take the form of public funding, of a measure of governmental control or monitoring of its performance, or some form of public accountability.

India

Article 12 of the Indian Constitution states:

> In this Part, unless the context otherwise requires, "The State" includes the Government and Parliament of India and the Government and the

---

[91] *Tam Hing-yee* v. *Wu Tai-wai* [1992] 1 HKLR 185.

[92] [1996] 2 HKLR 260 (High Court); [1997] HKCA 207 (8 May 1997) (Court of Appeal).

Legislature of each of the States and all local or other authorities within the territory of India or under the control of the Government of India.

MC Mehta v. *Union of India*[93] established that, in certain defined circumstances, "other authorities" can include non-state bodies to which state functions have been delegated. There, the Supreme Court was asked to order the closure of a chemical and fertiliser factory, and for compensation in respect of an oleum gas leak from it, on the basis of the constitutional right to life under Article 21. In assessing the applicability of Article 12, the court considered it significant that: (i) government policy was that the production of chemicals and fertilisers was an industry of vital public interest, which the State intended to carry out itself in due course, but which for an interim period was to be carried out by private corporations with state financial support and state control; (ii) the factory's activities were subject to extensive and detailed control, through a legislative licensing regime: (iii) it received government loans; and (iv) it was engaged in an industry with potential to affect the life and health of large sections of the people.

Bhagwati CJ considered that it was "prima facie arguable that" a corporation in the position of Shiram should be subject to the same constraints as the State and to Article 12. However, the Court did not consider it necessary to decide the question for the purposes of the case. Bhagwati J did, however, note with approval the fact that the Court had "expanded the horizon of Article 12 primarily to inject respect for human rights and social conscience in our corporate structure".

Nonetheless, the Court's conception of the circumstances in which a corporation could fall within Article 12 remained relatively limited, and appears to require some state control. It referred with approval to *Ramanna Shetty* v. *International Airport Authority*,[94] where five factors were enumerated: state financial assistance; other forms of assistance; state control of management and policies; state controlled or state conferred monopoly status; whether the corporation's functions were public in nature.

---

[93] The *Oleum Gas Leak* case, SC 1986.
[94] [1979] 3 SCR 1014.

CRITIQUE

The Court of Appeal to date has spurned the opportunity to develop a functional approach to the definition of "public authority", seeking instead a "public character or stamp" derived either from statutory authority or proximity to a public authority, akin to the pre-HRA test for amenability to judicial review, and expressly concluding that a function may have a different character depending on the nature of the body performing it. This is a very surprising result which is inconsistent with the stated objectives of the Government and with the language of section 6 itself, which suggests that it is the nature of the act, not the status of the body, which ought to determine the application of the section.[95]

The result of the current approach of the courts is that, whether or not a person can effectively enforce their Article 8 rights against a service provider depends upon decisions made by local authorities over which a service user has little or no influence. It ignores the reality of increased reliance by local authorities upon private contractors to discharge their statutory duties[96] and allows state bodies to avoid responsibility, deprives individuals of their ability effectively to enforce their human rights, introducing a randomness to their efficacy depending upon the arrangements in any particular geographical area. The problem, of course, has many dimensions beyond the delivery of public services, and extends to all areas of state functions which are delegated, devolved or contracted to private bodies, but this chapter focusses on the former because of the clear human rights implications.

The courts' position is to be contrasted with the stated intentions of the Government which are illustrated by the following:

In identifying Railtrack as a public authority, the Home Secretary said:

> Railtrack acts privately in its functions as a commercial property developer. We were anxious . . . that we should not catch the commercial activities of Railtrack – or, for example, of water companies – which were

---

[95] See also Claire McDougall, "The Alchemists Search for the Philosopher's Stone: Public Authorities and the Human Rights Act (One Year On), [2002] *JR* 23.

[96] *R* v. *Wandsworth LBC ex p Beckwith* [1996] 1 WLR 60.

nothing whatever to do with its exercise of public functions. Private security firms contract to run prisons: what Group 4, for example, does as a plc with other bodies is nothing whatever to do with the state, but plainly where it runs a prison, it may be acting in the shoes of the state.[97]

The Lord Chancellor stated:

> If a court were to hold that a hospice, because it provided a medical service, was exercising a public function, what on earth would be wrong with that? Is it not perfectly true that schools, although underpinned by a religious foundation or a trust deed, may well be carrying out public functions? If we take, for example, a charity whose charitable aims include the advancement of a religion, the answer must depend upon the nature of the functions of the charity. For example, charities that operate . . . in the area of homelessness, no doubt do exercise public functions. The NSPCC, for example, exercises statutory functions which are of a public nature, although it is a charity, . . .[98]

Later, the Lord Chancellor said:

> A private security company would be exercising public functions in relation to the management of a contracted-out prison but would be acting privately when, for example, guarding commercial premises. Doctors in general practice would be public authorities in relation to their National Health Service functions, but not in relation to their private patients.[99]

Even before the HRA, the scope of the judicial review test was subject to some criticism, precisely because of the developing relationship between the State and the private sector in areas of public service and provision. For instance, de Smith, Woolf and Jowell[100] have said:

> Public functions need not be the exclusive domain of the State. Charities, self-regulatory organisations and other nominally private institutions . . . may in reality also perform some types of public function. As Sir John Donaldson MR urged, it is important for courts to "recognise the realities of executive power" and not allow "their vision to be clouded by the subtlety and sometimes complexity of the way in which it can be

---

[97] Hansard HC, 17 June 1998, cols 409–410.
[98] Hansard HL, 24 November 1997, col 800.
[99] Ibid col 811. Contrast this with the Court of Appeal's reasoning in *Leonard Cheshire*.
[100] *Judicial Review of Administrative Action* (Sweet and Maxwell, 1995, 5th ed).

exerted". Non governmental bodies such as these are just as capable of abusing their powers as is Government.[101]

. . . not all activities of private bodies (such as private companies) are subject only to private law. For example, the activities of a private body (such as a recently privatised company) may be governed by the standards of public law when its decisions are subject to duties conferred by statute or when, by virtue of the function it is performing or possibly its dominant position in the market, it is under an implied duty to act in the public interest. A private company selected to run a prison, for example, although motivated by considerations of commercial profit should be regarded, at least in relation to some of its activities, as subject to public law because of the nature of the function it is performing. This is because the prisoners, for whose custody and care it is responsible, are in the prison in consequence of an order of the court, and the purpose and nature of their detention is a matter of public concern and interest.[102]

Murray Hunt has argued:[103]

The test for whether a body is "public", and therefore whether administrative law principles presumptively apply to its decision-making, should not depend on the fictional attribution of derivative status to the body's powers. The relevant factors should include the nature of the interests affected by the body's decisions, the seriousness of the impact of those decisions on those interests, whether the affected interests have any real choice but to submit to the body's jurisdiction, and the nature of the context in which the body operates. Parliament's non-involvement or would be involvement, or whether the body is woven into a network of regulation with state underpinning, ought not to be relevant to answering these questions. The very existence of institutional power capable of affecting rights and interests should itself be sufficient reason for subjecting exercises of that power to the supervisory jurisdiction of the High Court, regardless of its actual or would-be source.

Lord Steyn endorsed those comments, in his paper "The Constitutionalisation of Public Law",[104] saying:

---

[101] Para 3–025.

[102] Para 3–031.

[103] M. Hunt, "Constitutionalism and the Contractualisation of Government in the United Kingdom" in M. Taggart (ed) *The Province of Administrative Law* (Oxford: Hart, 1997), 32–33.

[104] May 1999.

In my view this is the true basis of the court's jurisdiction over the exercise of non-statutory powers. If this reasoning is correct, it calls into question the decision of the Court of Appeal that the Jockey Club is not amenable to judicial review . . . In an era when government policy is to privatise public services, to contract out activities formerly carried out by public bodies and to put its faith in self-regulation, it is essential that the courts should apply a functional test of reviewability.

In *Servite Houses* Moses J was strongly attracted to those arguments as a basis for imposing public law standards on Servite Houses. However, he found that he could not do so because he was constrained by previous decisions to seek, in vain, a governmental quality to Servite's functions. Given the nature of his court, as one of first instance, he said,

> any advance can, in my judgment, only be made by those courts which have the power to reject the previous approach enshrined in past authority,[105] but that once the [Human Rights] Act has come into force, it may be, and I put it no higher, that the courts will have to reconsider the obligations of a provider of a home by a private person under arrangements made with a public body.[106]

In *Leonard Cheshire* Stanley Burnton J followed Moses J's analysis of the authorities as to the law existing prior to the HRA, and as for the law after the HRA. He distanced himself from the latter's regret, stating:

> Privatisation means, in general, that functions formerly exercised by public authorities are now carried out by non-public entities, often for profit. It has inevitable consequences for the applicability of judicial review, which the courts are not free to avoid.[107]

It is unfortunate that the courts have not in this regard embraced the new regime introduced by the HRA, which was intended to have a profound impact on the recognition and enforcement of fundamental human rights and, indeed, fundamentally to challenge many existing legal notions or concepts.

There are in particular very powerful arguments that private contractors upon whom public authorities rely for the discharge of their

---

[105] At p 349J.
[106] At p 352C.
[107] (2001) 4 CCLR 211, 237C–D.

public functions should be bound to respect the Convention rights of those who are affected by the discharge of those functions.

First, the fact that a function is performed by a private body under arrangements made with a state body is itself a consequence of the exercise of state power. The service user (the individual whose Convention rights are exposed to the activities of the contractor) has no say in the decision by the public provider to contract out its services nor any choice as to their dependency on those services. It is the existence of the public function in the hands of the public authority and that authority's decision (pursuant to statutory powers) to contract out the function to a private body, which results in the service user's relationship with the contractor.

Secondly, unless the contractor is liable under section 6, there is a risk that affected individuals will have no effective remedy for breach of a Convention right by the contractor and will, where the State relies on mixed private and public sector provision, suffer discrimination so that they could complain of breaches of either Articles 13 or 14 of the ECHR. It is no answer that the public authority would remain subject to the section 6 duty: in many instances, as in the case of *Leonard Cheshire*, the public authority will be unable to remedy the Convention violations complained of.

Nor does the contractual route proposed by Lord Woolf[108] necessarily achieve an effective remedy. It is not clear how an authority could ensure that the contractual obligations would entrench Convention rights with regard to unforeseen contingencies that might arise very much later. Anyway, the service user has no knowledge of or influence over the contractual arrangements entered into between a local authority and a private contractor which may well have been concluded long before the user requires services. In reality, it is unlikely that an individual would be able to query the contents of a contract or demand modification to the terms, and is unlikely to have the services of a lawyer to enable this. If a contract did not adequately provide for the respect for the Convention rights of service users, the right to damages from the local authority for breach of section 6 would do little to realise their Convention rights in practice.

If contracts do effectively provide for the protection of the Convention rights of users such that users could enforce them,[109]

---

[108] *Leonard Cheshire*, para [34].
[109] Contracts (Rights of Third Parties) Act 1999.

then providers assume the responsibilities of public authorities and so the objections to so classifying them fall away.[110] It has also been suggested that the proper approach to filling the "gap" created by the privatisation of public functions is for the courts to discharge their functions as public authorities under the HRA by developing the common law so as to provide remedies for those whose Convention rights have been interfered with.[111] But this is of little practical benefit where a body performing privatised functions is neither a public authority nor amenable to judicial review. In the absence of judicial review or an action under section 7 for breach by a public authority of its duty under section 6, the jurisdiction of the court will depend on there being some other cause of action upon which the court's role as a public authority can bite. While in *Leonard Cheshire* the claimants did have the option of charity proceedings, that will frequently not be the case. Even in charity proceedings, the scope for intervention where the charity is not a public authority is limited and it is not clear that such proceedings would enable the court to secure protection for Convention rights.

Another argument that has been deployed against the broad approach to section 6 is to the effect that the scope of "public authority" should be restricted to governmental bodies because to do otherwise would deprive public authorities of rights under the HRA,[112] on the grounds that such a body could not then claim to be a victim under Article 34 of the Convention and, by virtue of section 7(7) of the Act, could not bring proceedings under the Act. But this is not a sound argument. Article 34 denies victim status to governmental bodies but not to others exercising a public function. Those bodies that are included within the category of "public authority" by virtue of the broad approach to functional public authority would not thereby be deprived of their rights, and no functional public authority would be affected with regard to its private activities. Moreover, even governmental bodies have rights under the HRA because the courts' role as public authorities will still benefit them in any legal

---

[110] In a paper given at a recent Justice conference, Thomas De La Mare has also proposed that an implied term as to compliance with the Human Rights Act is a possible source of assistance, but as he acknowledges this is entirely undeveloped in existing case law: "Corporate Responsibility: Extending the Boundaries of Rights", March 2002.

[111] Stanley Burnton J, para 106. Dawn Oliver, above n 14, pp 492–3.

[112] Stanley Burnton J, para 105, Dawn Oliver above n 14 at p 491.

proceedings in which they are engaged as will the duties of the courts under sections 2 and 3. Finally, it is important to bear in mind that the HRA is primarily intended to protect the human rights of individuals, and it would be wrong to relegate their rights in order to secure the rights of bodies exercising authority or power over them.

It is far more consistent with the objectives of the HRA and with Strasbourg jurisprudence that the courts, acting in accordance with their duty as public authorities under section 6(1) and applying the interpretative obligation under section 3(1), should extend the ambit of "public authority" so as to ensure that the State's Convention obligations can be enforced effectively in the domestic courts.

Of course there must be a means of defining the limits to the application of section 6(3)(b). As was pointed out by Lord Woolf in *Leonard Cheshire* and in *Poplar*, not all those private bodies and individuals who contract with public authorities in the discharge of their functions can be public authorities within section 6.

The principles adopted by courts in other jurisdictions provide some assistance in achieving the required balance. For instance, we have seen that the Indian Supreme Court places considerable emphasis on the capacity of a private organisation to interfere with human rights. The function of the body in question is given considerably more emphasis in some other jurisdictions, such as Canada, than our own. In others, for instance Hong Kong, the courts have adopted the notion of "public domain" rather than "governmental" as the defining characteristic.

The starting point for deciding which bodies or persons ought to be subject to the duty to act compatibly with Convention rights is to consider the purpose of the HRA in ensuring that, as far as possible and respecting parliamentary sovereignty, the Convention rights of all persons are respected. To the extent that the domestic legal system fails to achieve that end, the UK government will be in breach of its Article 1 duty under the Convention. Section 6 HRA therefore has a pivotal role in securing the state's compliance with Article 1.

The fact that the Government is liable for all Convention violations, including those committed by purely private individuals and bodies, does not mean that all persons in domestic law should be classified as public authorities. The wording of section 6, which anticipates private persons who are not liable, precludes such a classification. Nor is it necessary to do so. True private relationships do not require the application of the section 6 duty in order to secure state compliance with Article 1 of the Convention. The existing criminal and civil law is, or is capable of being made, sufficient to protect Convention rights within those relationships. Where the rights involved in those relationships are qualified within the Convention, selective state intervention is justifiable. Where relationships affect absolute Convention rights, the State comes in wearing the heavy boots of the criminal law.

On the other hand, where persons exercise power in a more structured environment, afforded to them either by the State or by the system of domestic governance, which enables them to interfere with the Convention rights of individuals, and in particular where the individual decisions and activities that can have such an impact are not amenable to detailed control by the state but instead involve the exercise of judgments and discretions, it is right that those bodies should be held responsible for ensuring respect for Convention rights. Applying the approach of Laws LJ in *Smart* v. *Sheffield City Council*,[113] "The court has to arrive at a judicial choice between two possibilities, a choice which transcends the business of finding out what the legislation's words mean". This involves applying domestic law standards which most effectively achieve a "vindication and fulfilment of the Convention rights, for which the HRA was enacted". The courts should give section 6 a generous interpretation. Any limitation upon the liabilities of public authorities for interfering in Convention rights should take place through striking a fair balance between relevant interests, at least where prima facie interferences with rights are capable of being justified by reference to necessity and proportionality, rather than liability being excluded by defining such bodies out of the scope of the section 6 duty.

In order to achieve this, it is suggested that whether a body performs a function of a public nature within section 6(3)(b) is indicated first by the nature of the function in question: whether the function is a means by which the state discharges its responsibilities, or is one that the state recognises as being in the public interest. There are a variety of factors that can assist in applying this test: whether the state has provided for the performance of the function by law; whether there are public policy objectives for the

---

[113] [2002] EWCA Civ 04, (2002) HLR 34.

performance of the function; and whether the function in question is designed to promote or enhance the public interest.

The second indicator is the remit and functionality of the body in question: whether it is in a position to evaluate the fair balance that must be struck by the State when interfering with Convention rights.[114] This test would embrace a very wide range of bodies in respect of at least some of their functions. It would properly exclude bodies operating in the purely private sphere.[115] But there is no escaping responsibility where the public interest is engaged. The definition would catch those bodies that Stanley Burnton J in *Leonard Cheshire*[116] believed ought not to be caught, such as private schools and hospitals. It is possible, even, that certain providers of bed and breakfast accommodation to the homeless might be liable. It is hard to justify their not being liable. They deliver important services to the public, forming part of a framework of provision which the State has determined should exist; in the course of doing so they have the potential to violate fundamental rights; they undertake the activities freely and for their own profit or self-interest; they are capable of assessing whether they can deliver services in a Convention compliant manner. If entrepreneurs choose to enter the field of public provision, why should they not be liable if they violate Convention rights in doing so?

---

[114] This second factor reflects the analysis advanced on behalf of the residents of LCF which was rejected by Stanley Burnton J and the Court of Appeal.

[115] Note that in *RSPCA* v. *Attorney General* [2001] 3 All ER 530, Lightman J was clear that the RSPCA was not a "public authority" within section 6(3)(b), at least with regard to its membership functions.

[116] See para [66].

Access to the Court Under the Human Rights Act: Standing, Third Party Intervenors and Legal Assistance

Nathalie Lieven* and Charlotte Kilroy†

INTRODUCTION

Prior to the passage of and coming into force of the Human Rights Act 1998 ("HRA") there was much debate about whether the HRA facilitated a full and proper consideration of and application of the rights contained in the European Convention on Human Rights ("ECHR") (the "Convention rights"), or whether in fact certain provisions of the HRA hampered the courts' ability to apply those rights.

A crucial aspect of that debate concerned the right of access to court under the HRA and the barriers which existed to that right. One of the barriers which most exercised commentators on the HRA was the "victim" requirement in section 7, by which only those who would be victims for the purposes of bringing proceedings in the European Court of Human Rights had standing to rely on Convention rights. This requirement narrowed considerably the test of sufficient interest in judicial review proceedings. Consequently many commentators felt this narrow test would have a restrictive and detrimental effect on the development of domestic jurisprudence[1] and would make it more difficult for the courts to consider properly the public interest in human rights challenges.

---

* Landmark Chambers.
† Matrix Chambers.
[1] See eg Michael Fordham, "Human Rights Act Escapology" [2000] *JR* 262; Joanna Miles, "Standing under the Human Rights Act 1998: Theories of Rights Enforcement and the Nature of Public Law Adjudication" (2000) *CLJ* 133 at 157; Jane Marriott and Danny Nicol, "The Human Rights Act, Representative Standing and the Victim Culture" (1998) *EHRLR* Issue 6 at 730.

In this chapter we consider the degree to which these concerns have proved to have substance following the coming into force of the HRA in October 2000. We look at how the courts have responded so far and what issues continue to arise. As part of that debate we consider the degree to which the limitations imposed by the victim test can and have been overcome by the courts' approach to third party intervenors in human rights challenges.

The other principal barrier to access to the court is clearly financial. Potential claimants are undoubtedly deterred by lack of funds and the fear of large costs awards. We consider how the rules and practice on legal aid and the awarding of costs affects access to the courts for human rights challenges.

THE "VICTIM" TEST

By section 7(1) HRA:

> A person who claims that a public authority has acted (or proposes to act) in a way which is made unlawful by section 6(1) may:
> bring proceedings against the Authority under this Act in the appropriate court or tribunal, or
> rely on the Convention right or rights concerned in any legal proceedings
> but only if he is (or would be a victim) of the unlawful act.

Section 7(3) introduces the "victim" test into judicial review proceedings. It provides:

> If the proceedings are brought on an application for judicial review, the applicant is to be taken to have a sufficient interest, in relation to the unlawful act only if he is, or would be a victim of that act.

By section 7(7) the Strasbourg concept of "victim" is applied:

> For the purposes of this section, a person is a victim of an unlawful act only if he would be a victim for the purposes of Article 34 of the Convention if proceedings were brought in the European Court of Human Rights in respect of that Act.

Article 34 of the Convention provides:

> The Court may receive applications from any person, non-governmental organisation or group of individuals claiming to be the victim of a viola-

tion by one of the High Contracting Parties of the rights set forth in the Convention and the protocols thereto.

Convention jurisprudence establishes that a victim of a violation of the Convention is a person who is "*directly affected*" by the act or omission being complained of.[2] Complainants do not need to show that their rights have in fact been violated by any particular act, as long as they can show that they "run the risk of being directly affected" by it[3] or that they are part of a class of those at risk.[4] Equally, a complainant remains a victim even if the act or omission has caused no prejudice or detriment.

The Convention jurisprudence makes it clear, however, that interested parties making representative or public interest challenges are not regarded as victims for the purposes of Article 34.[5] Even trade unions cannot claim to be victims on the basis that they represent the interests of their members, although a trade union may itself be a victim of a breach of its own rights.[6] It is this aspect of the "victim" test which is the most controversial. As Supperstone and Coppel put it, it excludes from the effect of the HRA a range of persons and bodies which are entitled to bring judicial review proceedings[7] under the current judicial review test of standing and which may have a considerable interest in so doing. The consequence of this is both that potential claims may not be brought, but also that the courts may be less well informed about human rights' arguments than would otherwise be the case.

Judicial Review Test of Standing

Over the years the courts have developed a liberal test of standing from the requirement to show "sufficient interest" (Supreme Court

---

[2] *Corigliano* v. *Italy* Series A No 57 (1983) 5 EHRR 334.

[3] See *Marckx* v. *Belgium* (1979) 2 EHRR 330; *Norris* v. *Ireland* (1988) 13 EHRR 18; *Campbell and Cosans* v. *United Kingdom* (1980) 3 EHRR 531.

[4] *Open Door Counselling and Dublin Well Woman* v. *Ireland* (1992) 15 EHRR 244.

[5] *Purcell* v. *Ireland* 70 DR 262, App No 15404/89 (1991); *Lindsay* v. *United Kingdom* App No 31699/96 (1997) 23 EHRR CD 199.

[6] See, eg *Council of Civil Services Unions* v. *United Kingdom* 50 DR 228 (1987) EComHR.

[7] See Supperstone and Coppel, "Judicial Review after the Human Rights Act" [1999] *EHRLR* Issue 3.

Act 1981, section 31(3)).[8] In *R* v. *Secretary of State for Foreign and Commonwealth Affairs ex p World Development Movement Ltd*[9] the court held that the merits of the challenge were an important if not dominant factor when considering standing. Significant factors in support of the conclusion that WDM had sufficient interest were the,

> importance of vindicating the rule of law, . . . the importance of the issue raised, . . . the likely absence of any other responsible challenger, . . . the nature of the breach of duty against which relief was sought . . . and the prominent role of the applicants in giving advice, guidance and assistance with regard to the subject matter.[9a]

In *R* v. *Secretary of State for Social Services ex p Child Poverty Action Group*,[10] Woolf LJ noted that CPAG and the National Association of Citizens Advice Bureaux had made their application for judicial review because the issues raised were important in the field of social welfare and were not ones which could necessarily be expected to be raised by individual benefit claimants. Both these organisations played "a prominent role in giving advice, guidance and assistance to such claimants".[10a]

The courts have in recent years allowed cases to be brought by non-victims in the form of public interest groups and representative bodies such as Greenpeace,[11] the Immigration Law Practitioners Association[12] and Help the Aged.[13] In *R* v. *Secretary of State for Social Security ex p Joint Council for the Welfare of Immigrants*[14] the Court of Appeal emphasised the basic nature of the rights in issue and allowed a challenge by JCWI to the lawfulness of the regulations which denied asylum seekers welfare benefits pending the outcome of asylum applications.

---

[8] See Michael Fordham, "Human Rights Act Escapology" (2000) *JR* 262 for an overview of important cases.

[9] [1995] 1 WLR 386.

[9a] Ibid at pp 395–6.

[10] [1990] 2 QB 540.

[10a] [Ibid at p 546.

[11] *R* v. *Her Majesty's Inspectorate of Pollution ex p Greenpeace Ltd* [1994] 4 All ER 329.

[12] *R* v. *Secretary of State for the Home Department ex p Immigration Law Practitioners Association* [1997] Imm AR 189.

[13] *R* v. *Sefton Metropolitan Borough Council ex p Help the Aged* [1997] 4 All ER 532.

[14] [1997] 1 WLR 275.

In *R* v. *Secretary of State for Employment ex p Equal Opportunities Commission*[15] the Equal Opportunities Commission was granted standing by the House of Lords on the basis of the Commission's functions as a specialist statutory body charged with working towards the elimination of discrimination and promoting equality of opportunity between the sexes. The Court stated,

> it would be a very retrograde step now to hold that the EOC has no *locus standi* to agitate in judicial review proceedings questions related to sex discrimination which are of public importance and affect a large section of the population.[16]

And in *ex parte Greenpeace*[17] Otton J stated that denying standing to the organisation might mean that

> a less well-informed challenge might be mounted which would stretch unnecessarily the court's resources and which would not afford the court the assistance it requires in order to do justice between the parties.

It is clear from the above examples that the courts' approach has been motivated by a perception that there is considerable benefit to the development of public law in allowing public interest groups and representative bodies to bring actions. As Sedley J put it in *R* v. *Somerset CC ex parte Dixon*:[18]

> Public law is not at base about rights, even though abuses of power may and often do invade private rights; it is about wrongs – that is to say misuses of public power; and the courts have always been alive to the fact that a person or organisation with no particular stake in the issue or outcome may without any sense being a mere meddler, wish and be well placed to call the attention of the court to an apparent abuse of public power.

The evolution of the standing test in judicial review demonstrates the courts' view that in public law the "emphasis is less on the vindication of particular victim's rights than on the constitutional importance of public authorities complying with the law".[19]

---

[15] [1995] 1 AC 1.

[16] At 26D–E.

[17] *R* v. *Her Majesty's Inspectorate of Pollution ex p Greenpeace Ltd* [1994] 4 All ER 329.

[18] (1998) 75 P & CR 175.

[19] Joanna Miles, "Standing under the Human Rights Act 1998: Theories of Rights Enforcement and the Nature of Public Law Adjudication" above n 1 at 157.

The "victim" requirement in the HRA by contrast ensures that the focus in the development of domestic human rights jurisprudence remains squarely on protecting the rights of the individual victim, rather than on the need to ensure that the public body acts compatibly with the Convention rights. What was the rationale behind this choice?

Reason for "Victim" Test

In the debates on the Human Rights Bill the Lord Chancellor stated:

> I acknowledge that . . . a narrower test will be applied for bringing applications by judicial review on Convention grounds than will continue to apply in applications for judicial review on other grounds. But interest groups will still be able to provide assistance to victims who bring cases under the Bill and to bring cases directly where they themselves are victims of an unlawful act.[20]

He continued:

> Essentially we believe the victim/ potential victim test to be right. If there is unlawful action or if unlawful action is threatened, then there will be victims or potential victims who will complain and who will in practice be supported by interest groups. If there are no victims, the issue is probably academic and the courts should not be troubled.[21]

The Government's choice of the victim test appeared to rest on two bases. The first was that:

> The purpose of the Bill is to give greater effect in our domestic law to the Convention rights. It is in keeping with this approach that persons should be able to rely on the Convention rights before our domestic courts in precisely the same circumstances as they can rely upon them before the Strasbourg institutions.[22]

The second was that to allow a wider test of standing would generate a backlog of cases as interest groups would seek to challenge all sus-

---

[20] Hansard HL, 24 November 1997, col 831.
[21] Hansard HL, 24 November 1997, col 832.
[22] Ibid at col 831.

pected human rights violations thereby preventing victims from bringing cases themselves.[23]

Many critics have found it difficult to see why the imposition of the "victim" test of standing on those applying to the Strasbourg court should necessitate the same test being applied domestically, where there were strong arguments to the contrary and where the pre-existing mechanisms for challenging unlawful action on the part of public authorities posited a different test.[24] This is particularly the case where the standing test is perceived to have worked well and not to have led to a flood of cases, nor to have wasted the courts' time with unmeritorious claims.

The question is: if the courts in judicial review proceedings have come to the conclusion that public interest groups and representative bodies, far from bringing academic cases to the court and far from clogging up the court process, are actually in a position to challenge the very real effect of legislation and administrative action on wide groups of vulnerable people, often more effectively than individual claimants, then why would the position be any different under the HRA?

As it currently stands the test of standing in judicial review allows the courts to distinguish between the busybody and the responsible public interest litigant. If the courts have not been swamped with a deluge of cases as a result of the liberal interpretation of the "sufficient interest" standing test, what is there to fear from allowing the same test to apply to judicial review actions brought under the HRA?

Concerns About the "Deterrent" Effect of the "Victim" Test

Prior to the coming into force of the HRA numerous commentators expressed strong concerns about the effect of the "victim" test. Most notably Lord Lester of Herne Hill in the debates in the House of Lords stated,

> . . . enacting Clause 7(3) as it stands risks preventing some human rights cases from being brought that ought to be brought in the public interest. Public interest groups face losing standing to raise convention human

---

[23] Hansard, 24 June 1998, vol 314 cols 1083–86; Joanna Miles, "Standing Under the Human Rights Act 1998" above n 1 at 144.

[24] Ibid at 143 for discussion on this point.

rights points in circumstances in which otherwise they would have standing, even over fundamental rights points rooted in the common law.

Enacting Clause 7 as it stands would produce discrepancies over standing to bring judicial review proceedings between: (a) purely domestic law cases; (b) domestic law cases under the Human Rights Act; and (c) domestic law cases under directly effective European Community law with a human rights element.[25]

It has been pointed out that JCWI would not have been granted standing to bring their challenge on the basis of Convention rights in *ex parte JCWI*, even though that case involved the most fundamental of rights.[26]

Although some interest groups and representative bodies such as trade unions would be able to identify among their members victims who consent to the bringing of legal proceedings, other less directly representative groups such as Amnesty International, CPAG, Greenpeace and JCWI would have to trawl through cases to identify a victim who can "best illustrate the point at issue and provide an adjudication capable of being relied on in a multiplicity of cases"[27] and to persuade that victim to front one of their cases. There may be some types of cases, particularly those involving pre-emptive challenges to decisions or policy, where it will be difficult to identify the claimant at the stage the action is commenced.

The "victim" test also relies for its effectiveness as a tool of protecting the public interest in general on individuals recognising that their fundamental rights are being, or are likely to be, infringed. It is frequently the case, however, that victims are by reason of poverty, socio-economic position, lack of awareness, assertiveness or resources, unlikely to approach either the court or the potential representative.[28] A specialist body with litigation experience will often be more likely to be able to present a case and assist the court, and to

---

[25] Hansard HL, 24 November 1997, col 827.

[26] See eg Karen Steyn and David Wolfe, "Judicial Review and the Human Rights Act: some practical considerations" (1999) *EHRLR* 6, 615 at 618.

[27] See Sedley J in Leyland and Woods, *Administrative Law* (London: Blackstone Press, 1997), p 344.

[28] See Jane Marriott and Danny Nicol, above n 1 at 737; also Joanna Miles above n 1 at 147.

represent the interests of absent members of a class of victims, than would an individual victim.[29]

An area where the need for a victim, rather than the possibility of an interest group bringing an action, may cause particular difficulties is in environmental challenges under Articles 3 or 8. Where the challenge is to a decision to proceed with some policy that affects the environment it may be very difficult to identify a victim at the stage the challenge needs to be brought. If the challenge waits until a true "victim" arises it may in practice be far too late to do anything about the matter in issue. The potential victims may be too ill defined a group, or difficult to predict, to satisfy the court. Equally, it may be that some or even all of the potential victims are outside the UK, for instance through air or sea pollution, and thereby further complicating the victim requirement. This is a type of challenge to which the environmental interest group is perfectly suited, but which may be frustrated by the operation of section 7.

The issue of no claimant or disappearing claimant is also relevant. In judicial review an individual claimant may, and often is, "bought off" – granted exceptional leave in asylum cases; given the benefit in question in social security cases; found a school place; given a special reconsideration, for example in a planning or housing case; or simply given money to go away. In these circumstances it may be very difficult to challenge the underlying illegality if only an individual victim can bring the case, because that particular claimant will constantly "disappear" from the action. If the challenge is a non-human rights judicial review, then the interest group can bring the challenge, and the fact that a particular individual no longer has an actionable claim will generally not matter. The position is different under the HRA where only the victim can bring the action. Critics pointed to the benefits of representative and/or interest bodies being able to bring proceedings as set out in the judicial review cases on standing set out above. Far from resulting in a backlog of cases, it was felt that interest groups might in fact provide a valuable service by performing a "sifting" function, identifying cases which stood a chance of success, presenting them effectively and thereby preventing a flood of ill-informed applications. One early well-focused case brought by a

---

[29] See Joanna Miles ibid at 147.

specialist group might actually save court time and help contribute to the rational development of the law.[30] We feel that the criticisms of the victim test are largely justified. There seems to us no good reason why the judicial review "sufficient interest" test could not have been applied to standing in judicial review proceedings in the HRA. However, in order to decide whether any real obstacles to justice have been caused by the test it is important to examine to what extent the fears of the critics were justified and to what extent they have been mitigated by the court's approach to the test and more particularly to third party intervenors.

The Courts' Approach to the "Victim" Test

It is true to say that there has not so far been extensive consideration of the victim test and the need or otherwise to expand it. However, as might have been expected the courts appear to have been prepared to take a fairly pragmatic approach, by which they have sought not to reject cases on the apparent technicality of lack of a victim, but rather have looked at the merits of the challenge and then made assumptions about the victim. Most importantly the courts have clearly taken a "liberal" approach to allowing third parties to intervene in cases, thereby in the short run at least avoiding the need to grapple with whether or not to expand the victim test.

In *HM Advocate* v. *R* (2001) SLT 1366, the court rejected an argument that a person who was challenging proceedings brought against him on the grounds that they violated Article 6 ECHR by reason of delay, was not a victim because the proceedings against him had not yet been concluded. The court held that a person directly affected by a violation of his Convention rights must be regarded as a victim unless and until he is granted an effective remedy. This would appear to follow closely the ECtHR approach. The potentially most interesting case in terms of re-visiting the meaning of "victim" is *In re Medicaments and Related Classes of Goods* (No 4) [2001] EWCA Civ 1217. The court was asked to conclude that the situation of the Property Association of Great Britain (PAGB) could be distinguished from the trade unions and representative bodies held not to be victims in *Ahmed* v. *United Kingdom* 20 EHRR CD 72, *Hodgson* v.

---

[30] See Joanna Miles, above n 1 at 145 and Hansard HL, vol 585 cols 807–08.

United Kingdom 10 EHRR 503 and *Bowman* v. *United Kingdom* 4 December 1995. It was argued that PAGB was a public interest group which was really an association of interested individuals who may be regarded as a group of persons each of whom may be regarded as a victim.

The Court of Appeal declined to consider the point, stating that each case had to be decided in its own context. In the context of this case because there was a route in the Restrictive Practices Court (Resale Prices) Rules 1976 whereby the individual parties who made up the membership of PAGB could have been formally represented by them, and that route had not been followed, PAGB could not be regarded as a victim. However, Brooke LJ very much left it open to argument that bodies like PAGB could be victims because of the make up of their membership. The argument failed because of the alternative route which had not been followed, rather than the more absolute argument that PAGB was in a similar position to trade unions and therefore caught by the Strasbourg case law.

In our view there is real scope to argue that a body whose members can be shown to be victims within the test, whether a trade union or a representative body such as the PAGB, should itself fall within the definition of "victim". Strasbourg case law is of course not binding, and there are strong arguments that in the light of the judicial review standing test the position in English law should be somewhat different from that adopted by the European Court of Human Rights. *Re Medicaments* gives a slight indication that the English courts may be sympathetic to such an argument, in an appropriate case.

In marginal cases the courts have shown themselves to be prepared to assume that a claimant satisfies the "victim" test, and then dismiss the claim on substantive grounds (see Buxton LJ in *R* v. *Bow County Court ex p Pelling* [2001] UKHRR 165) This is merely one example of a generally familiar approach by the courts to such theoretical difficulties, but it is an indication that in a strong case the courts are likely to find ways to overcome the potential limitations of the victim test.

Another example of the court not wishing to become enmeshed in whether the claimant was a victim is *R* v. *Secretary of State for the Home Department ex p Holub* [2001] 1 WLR 1359. The Court of Appeal stated that, although the point was not fully argued, if they had had to decide it they thought that the parents of a minor whose human rights had been breached did have the "standing to complain" under section 7. It is far from clear what the Court meant by this, given the fact that only those who are victims have standing under section 7.

DISAPPEARING CLAIMANTS

The problem of the "disappearing" claimant which we outlined above does seem to have been at least partly addressed in the case of *R* v. *Secretary of State For the Home Department ex parte Salem* [1999] 1 AC 450. By the time the case got to the House of Lords Mr Salem had been granted refugee status and therefore had no further direct interest in the case. It was argued that since the claimant was no longer directly affected by the decision the courts should refuse to hear the action; the offending measure having been withdrawn or redetermined and as a result there being no live issue on the claimant's position. In *ex parte Salem*, however, the court stated per Lord Slynn[31] that it accepted "in a cause where there is an issue involving a public authority as to a question of public law, your Lordships have a discretion to hear the appeal, even if by the time the appeal reaches the House there is no longer a lis to be decided which will directly affect the rights and obligations of the parties inter se".

Lord Slynn then set out the circumstances in which that discretion could be exercised. He stated:

> The discretion to hear disputes, even in the area of public law, must, however, be exercised with caution and appeals which are academic between the parties should not be heard unless there is a good reason in the public interest for doing so, as for example (but only by way of example) when a discrete point of statutory construction arises which does not involve detailed consideration of facts and where a large number of similar cases exist or are anticipated so that the issue will most likely need to be resolved in the near future.[32]

Therefore it should be the case that the courts' general approach to considering academic issues, if there remains an important public

---

[31] At 456 G–H.
[32] Ibid at 457 A.

interest in doing so, can extend to human rights arguments if the circumstances so justify. This is potentially an important point, because it means that there does not have to be a "live" or "directly affected" victim at the time the case is considered. Such an approach fits in well with the domestic courts general consideration of what may be termed "academic" issues, but could lessen the rigidity of the requirement for a victim in section 7.

While the existence of this power to hear academic issue goes some way towards solving the problem, it does not wholly do so. First, the House of Lords makes it clear that it is only in limited circumstances that the discretion should be exercised. There remains therefore a clear incentive for a public body to "buy off" a claimant in the hope that the action will cease. In immigration cases where a challenge succeeds at the permission stage, the Home Office will often prefer to reconsider the application for asylum or grant exceptional leave to remain, rather than have the underlying policy or practice challenged in court. If they do so, the onus will be on the claimant's advisors to justify continuing the action both to the court and usually to the Legal Services Commission. In many cases it will be very difficult to convince the court to do so. An interest group could perform an important function in situations like this. They may have a good overview as to whether there is a general problem in issue, which arises in a number of other instances, or whether the issue does not raise a public interest point. For the individual claimant and his or her solicitor the likelihood is that once she or he is given the "benefit" sought, the litigation will cease.

The very fact that Parliament imposed the "victim" test may encourage the courts to say that there needs to be a continuing victim, except in the most exceptional cases. It is important to note that *ex parte Salem* was considered before the HRA came into force and it therefore remains to be seen whether the court would apply the same principles to HRA challenges. This is somewhat difficult to predict. There is an attractive simplicity in the Lord Chancellor's argument that if there are no victims the point is probably academic and the court should not waste its time upon it. However, in cases such as *Salem*, or the local education authority which consistently finds school places for the children who apply for judicial review, but not for many others, it should not be so hard to convince the courts that there is a serious issue which must be considered, even if the actual victims continually drop out of the picture. The burden will undoubtedly be on the claimant to show that this is what is happening, but the courts are usually very quick to see a defendant who is trying to avoid litigation in this way. The undoubted problem is that if the interest group can only be an intervenor, rather than a claimant, it will have to work closely with the claimant to ensure the court is fully informed of the wider position. There is some European Convention support for the courts considering such cases, by analogy with previous case law,[33] but this has been inconsistently applied. However, even if the court is prepared to consider the "academic" case, it is still essential to have a claimant. Therefore the individual claimant must consent to continue with the action, or there will be no choice but for the action to be withdrawn. This is an example of the benefit of a "representative" action, where the individual claimant's position is not determinative.

The problem of the disappearing or non-existent claimant assumes particular importance where there is a "victim" test of standing. It gives defendant public authorities considerable control over which cases are to be litigated and which not. If representative actions, such as that by JCWI can be brought this can of course be overcome. Third party interventions, on the other hand, leave the conduct of the litigation primarily under the control of the principal parties.

STATUTORY BODIES

As is clear from the above the victim test excludes from bringing an action interest groups such as JCWI and CPAG which have become fairly regular attenders in judicial review proceedings. However, perhaps the most troubling groups which have been excluded are those bodies with statutory functions partially involving the effects of the HRA. Bodies such as the EOC and the CRE are subject to the "victim test" with no special provisions. Even if they believe there is

---

[33] There have also been examples of the ECtHR considering cases despite the applicant's desire to withdraw; see *Gericke* v. *FRG* (1966) 20 Coll. 86, 99 and Joanna Miles, above n 1 at 140.

a breach impacting directly on those groups they were created to support they are unable to bring an action. Even if there may be some justification for the exclusion of the wider interest groups it seems illogical that public bodies with human rights related statutory functions cannot take proceedings to right perceived human rights abuses.

For this reason, if and, or, when a UK Human Rights Commission is established, in our view it should have the power both to intervene and to bring cases under the HRA in its own name.

ROLE OF INTERVENORS

A considerable part, although not all, of the problems of the victim test can be overcome if the court is prepared to allow third party interest groups to make submissions as to public interest matters in human rights challenges. This should at least ensure that the court is aware of the public interest considerations, and sees the wider picture.

The Public Law Project in their report[34] on third party interventions point out that judicial review cases increasingly raise fundamental social, moral and economic issues and require competing rights and interests to be finely balanced or difficult policy questions to be addressed. Often such cases raise issues of more general significance beyond the interests of parties to the litigation. PLP observe that the advent of the HRA only strengthens the need for specialist information. Not only are previously untested issues of fundamental and competing rights now coming before the courts which must be decided within complex social contexts, but in addition the courts are now required to apply the doctrine of proportionality when determining whether any interference with qualified rights is justified, and in doing so may need to weigh the impact upon other groups who are not represented by the litigants. The notion that the issues are merely between the parties will often not be correct. For this reason and particularly in the light of the constraints of the "victim" test as highlighted above, third party interventions assume a heightened importance.

One of the concerns expressed during the debates on the HRA was that there was no provision in the HRA to mirror that in the

---

[34] Third Party Interventions in judicial review – an action research study, May 2001.

Convention which explicitly provides for third party interventions.[35] Article 36 sub-section 2 provides:

> The President of the Court may, in the interests of the proper administration of justice, invite any High Contracting Party which is not a party to the proceedings or any person concerned who is not the applicant to submit written comments or take part in hearings.

The Court has interpreted "person concerned" in such a way as to allow groups such as Amnesty, Liberty and JUSTICE to make written submissions in a number of cases.[36]

In response to these concerns the Lord Chancellor stated[37] that as third parties were already allowed to intervene in public law cases, and as non-governmental organisations had been permitted to intervene and file *amicus* briefs by the House of Lords, he expected the courts would be ready to permit *amicus* written briefs in cases concerning Convention rights.

Perhaps unsurprisingly this has in fact proved to be the case. The courts have been welcoming to a range of intervenors in human rights challenges,[38] perhaps because the Act is still in its infancy and the courts are still feeling the need for a wide range of assistance. It is difficult to predict the degree to which this liberal approach will continue when Convention arguments become an entirely familiar part of the judicial landscape. In evidence given to the Joint Committee on Human Rights on 26 March 2001[39] Lord Bingham of Cornhill agreed that the House of Lords was generous in allowing third party interventions by NGOs.

In its report on Third Party Interventions the Public Law Project identified four situations where third party intervention was considered desirable:

1. Where the court would be assisted by background information on how many others have been affected by a decision and examples of its impact upon members of this group.

[35] Hansard HL, 24 November 1997, Lord Lester of Herne Hill at cols 825–6.

[36] Eg, JUSTICE'S application to intervene in *Monnell & Morris* v. *UK* (1987) 10 EHRR 205 and Amnesty's intervention in *Soering* v. *UK* (1989) 11 EHRR 439.

[37] Hansard HL, 24 November 1997, cols 832–3.

[38] See, eg JUSTICE's intervention in *R (on the application of Heather)* v. *Leonard Cheshire Foundation* [2002] EWCA Civ 366; [2002] 2 All ER 936.

[39] Minutes of Evidence taken before the Joint Committee on Human Rights, 26 March 2001, at para 115.

2. Where the interests of a vulnerable or disadvantaged group would otherwise be unrepresented in the proceedings.
3. Where the court would be assisted by expertise in specialist areas of law.
4. Where there was some uncertainty about whether further information or expertise might be necessary, in cases involving fundamental rights of general public significance even if the issue raised might not have a direct impact upon a particularly large group, and a group with specialist expertise might be able to identify a need to present a particular perspective on the issue raised.

There is little doubt that the courts have accepted that interventions can serve a crucial function in certain cases. It is equally clear that intervenors can make up for some of the narrowness of the victim test.

In allowing two parties to intervene in a case concerning data on GPs' prescribing habits, *R* v. *Department of Health ex p Source Informatics Ltd* (No 1),[40] Lord Justice Simon Brown stated:

> It is . . . plain, however, that the Court of Appeal ought not to decide this appeal on so narrowly circumscribed a basis as the judge below. Clearly, they should be properly informed of the difficulties created by the decision and of the various public interest considerations arising. It is in nobody's interest to obtain from the Court of Appeal a judgment leaving as many unanswered questions and as great a degree of uncertainty as the judgment below.

The PLP report notes that some potential intervenors choose to put in evidence in a witness statement in support of the claimant rather than make a formal intervention, perhaps because of fears about costs. There are clearly cases, however, where the interests of the interest group differ from the claimant and it is more appropriate that their intervention should be independent. Indeed it is arguably in those cases where there is a different perspective that the need for third party intervention is greatest.

One example of where an intervenor may raise a somewhat different issue from the principal parties was a case concerning the

---

[40] [2001] QB 424.

National Assistance Act and asylum seekers between Westminster City Council and the National Asylum Seekers Service,[41] where the argument was over who funds asylum seekers. On appeal to the House of Lords various intervenors raised the possibility of being joined on the grounds that the parties were focusing on the narrow issue of who pays for the service, but neither were arguably really focusing on the interests of the users, ie the asylum seekers themselves in a general sense, rather on one particular individual. The House of Lords refused the application to intervene (see *Westminster City Council v. National Asylum Support Service* [2002] 1 WLR 2956) which was submitted by Black Women's Rape Action Project and Legal Action for Women, and Women Against Rape.

Another example of where the intervenor may have a different, or at least a wider perspective, is in *R (Smeaton on behalf of the Society for the Protection of Unborn Children) v. Secretary of State for Health*,[42] a case about the legality of emergency contraception. In that case the Family Planning Association raised the wider social consequences of criminalizing hormonal contraception and the effect that that would have on a very large sector of the population, and were accepted to have had a particular expertise in the field which the court found helpful.

Regulating Interventions

If the problems inherent in the victim test are in practice to be overcome by allowing a broad range of intervenors, then there is considerable need for those interventions to be regulated by the courts, both in terms of their process and their origin. Without such regulation the system becomes entirely ad hoc, and depends on the views of particular judges and the "standing" of the intervenor in question.[43]

As it stands there are no clear criteria in England for the courts to apply in deciding whether to permit third party interventions. In Scotland, by contrast, there are rules on third party interventions.[44]

---

[41] *Westminster City Council v. National Asylum Support Service, R (on the application of Westminster City Council) v. Secretary of State for the Home Department* (2001) 33 HLR 83.

[42] [2002] EWHC 610 (Admin) Judgment of 18 April 2002.

[43] See "Third Party Intervention: In the Public Interest"?, Sarah Hannett, [2003] PL 128 at 146–147.

[44] Scottish Statutory Instrument 2000 No 317.

These state that:

1. An application to intervene must be lodged in the court and served on the parties to the proceedings.
2. The application should state briefly the name and a description of the intervenor, the issue(s) which raise a matter of public interest, the issue(s) to be addressed by the intervenor, and the propositions to be advanced with reasons for believing that they will assist the court.
3. The court may grant leave only if it is satisfied that the proceedings raise a matter of public interest, the intervention is likely to assist the court and the intervention will not unduly delay or prejudice the rights of the parties, including their potential liability for costs.

The Scottish Rules also limit the length of submissions to 5000 words including appendices, unless the Court allows otherwise.

The PLP in its conclusions and recommendations[45] identify the lack of any rules and guidelines together with fears about liability on costs as factors which deter potential intervenors. Clearly if third party intervention in the public interest is perceived to perform an important function in litigation under the HRA, then it is crucial to ensure that those who can assist the court are not deterred from providing it to the court because of ignorance of procedures or fears about costs.

COSTS

PLP's report makes it clear that fears about being penalised in costs are a major factor in preventing less well-resourced groups from intervening.[46] If those seeking to intervene in human rights cases are faced both with the non-availability of public funding and particularly the threat of costs awards against them, it is inevitable that many potential intervenors will be deterred, and therefore arguments not put. In our view, unless the costs and/or funding issue is addressed, the courts will not reap the full benefit of third party interventions

---

[45] Ibid p 29.
[46] Scottish Statutory Instrument 2000 No 317, p 27.

and the consideration and application of Convention rights will suffer accordingly.

One solution to this problem is for the courts to make pre-emptive costs orders in favour of intervenors. In *R* v. *Lord Chancellor ex p Child Poverty Action Group and R* v. *DPP ex p Amnesty and Redress Trust*,[47] however, Dyson J displayed some reluctance to make such an order. Having reviewed the rules and case law, Dyson J came to the conclusion that it was only in the most exceptional circumstances that pre-emptive costs orders should be made even in public interest challenges.[48]

Dyson J was particularly concerned that,

> the court is being asked by the applicants to . . . say, in advance, that a public body should subsidise proceedings that have been brought against it, and to do so even at a time when the court has an incomplete appreciation of the merits of the claim, and when it may also be unable to assess properly the extent of the general public importance of the issues raised by the proceedings.[49]

As a result he set out the following test:

> . . . the necessary conditions for the making of a pre-emptive costs order in public interest challenge cases are that the court is satisfied that the issues raised are truly ones of general public importance, and that it has a sufficient appreciation of the merits of the claim that it can conclude that it is in the public interest to make the order. . . . These necessary conditions are not, however, sufficient for the making of an order. The court must also have regard to the financial resources of the applicant and respondent, and the amount of costs likely to be in issue. It will be more likely to make an order where the respondent clearly has a superior capacity to bear the costs of the proceedings than the applicant, and where it is satisfied that, unless the order is made, the applicant will probably discontinue the proceedings, and will be acting reasonably in so doing.[50]

The result of this ruling is that pre-emptive costs orders are rarely made in favour of public interest challengers. It is strongly arguable, however, that the rationale he gives for his conclusions makes it clear that they should not apply with similar rigour to intervenors.

---

[47] [1999] 1 WLR 347.
[48] See p 355.
[49] At p 358B.
[50] At p 358C–D.

Counsel for CPAG argued that there was an important distinction to be made between the merits of the claim and the merits of bringing the claim: while the merits of the claim might not be clear at an early stage, the merits of *bringing* the claim would be. Dyson J disagreed with this analysis on the basis that the criteria for granting leave to apply for judicial review were so loose that it might ultimately transpire that the application was hopeless. Clearly this logic does not apply to interventions. If groups are given permission to intervene, it is likely to be precisely on the basis that there is merit in them simply putting forward the arguments or perspectives which they are uniquely able to present, so that the court is better able to decide on the merits of the claim itself. To require the court to assess the merits of the claim itself means pre-emptive orders are highly unlikely, and is in our view unduly restrictive.

We accept that it will still normally be necessary for the court to examine whether the point raised in the proceedings is one of general public importance before making a pre-emptive costs order. Although Dyson J expressed doubts about whether the question of public importance could be decided before the case was heard, this is the exercise which the Legal Services Commission Public Advisory Panel has to decide when considering whether to grant legal assistance on public interest grounds. Further, in our view, the level of importance required by Dyson J[51] for the making of a pre-emptive costs order is too high.

The purpose of pre-emptive costs orders is to allow claims to be brought or, in the case of intervenors, arguments to be put forward which would otherwise be unlikely to be heard. If it is accepted that a case raises a point of public importance and that an intervention would assist the court to make a fully informed decision then it is surely in the interests of justice to make a pre-emptive costs order where it seems possible that without one the argument would not be put.

Inevitably, however, the court's decision on an application for a pre-emptive costs order will be influenced by a number of factors, including the resources of the intervenor and the interest that intervenor has in the outcome of the proceedings, the resources of

---

[51] See Dyson's example of *New Zealand Maori Council v. AG of New Zealand* [1994] 1 AC 466.

the parties to the claim, and the extent to which the intervention will raise the costs of the proceedings.

PLP state that there is a strong argument for a presumption that intervenors assisting the court in the public interest should not be liable for other parties' costs, rebuttable on grounds of abuse and misconduct by the intervenor. However, in our view even where the intervenor can be classified as a public interest intervenor (as opposed to an intervenor who has a more direct interest in the proceedings) a pre-emptive costs order may not always be appropriate. To make such a presumption could give significant power in litigation to certain groups who could then intervene with impunity. Given the range of intervenors who may be given permission to intervene, and the varying levels of intervention which may be permitted, in our view the court should retain its wide discretion on costs, but with a less restrictive test than that set out by Dyson J.

In the case of *Campaign for Nuclear Disarmament* v. *Prime Minister and Others*,[52] the Divisional Court made an order limiting the Claimant's costs in the proceedings in the High Court to £25,000. Simon Brown LJ referred to the "exceptional circumstances" test in *CPAG* and stated at paragraph 4 of his judgment:

> The applicants contend that this is a truly exceptional case in which the order should be made. The central arguments they advance in support of the argument are these. First, they are a private company limited by guarantee of modest resources, which, in the event of a large adverse costs order, would be at risk either of going into liquidation or of having to curtail severely their activities; these, in essence, are campaigning against nuclear weapons and other weapons of mass destruction, and in favour of a peaceful resolution of conflict. They state that, unless the court provides them with the certainty of a costs cap as now sought, they will not be able to proceed with the challenge. The time-frame for the challenge, moreover, is necessarily so short that it affords them no opportunity to seek to raise funds elsewhere. Secondly, CND points to the obvious public importance of the issues they seek to bring before the court. This hardly needs emphasis or explanation. Thirdly, and in response to the defendant's argument that the challenge is and will be found to be clearly without merit and, indeed, non-justiciable, CND, whilst contesting that assertion, point out that, if it be right, then the proceedings may be

[52] [2002] EWHC 2712.

expected to end next Tuesday at the preliminary hearing, in which event £25,000 will surely meet the defendant's entitlement to costs in any case. Fourthly, if CND's challenge were to end for want of the pre-emptive costs order now sought, in all likelihood some substitute applicant would be found, perhaps legally assisted, perhaps an unassisted person of limited means, with or without some private funding, in which event, the Crown, supposing it successfully resists the challenge, could not hope to recover even the £25,000 now offered. For my part, I find these arguments compelling, in particular the first three.

Simon Brown LJ went on to conclude that this was an exceptional case in which a pre-emptive costs order should be made. Although the court in this case applied the "exceptional circumstances" test, its reasoning indicates that this test might in future be interpreted more loosely than had previously been supposed. First, the Court did not consider it necessary to assess the merits of the claim, concluding that if the claim were to fail after the preliminary hearing, the costs cap of £25,000 would be sufficient to cover any costs incurred by the defendant. Secondly, the Court accepted the claimant's argument that the urgency of the case was such that it would not have time to raise sufficient funds for the challenge. Thirdly, the Court was prepared to accept that the case raised issues of public importance without a detailed appraisal of the case.

The case may be of some assistance to potential intervenors, because the court side-stepped the assessment of merits in the *CPAG* case. The logic is that as long as the intervenor is in a position to pay some measure of costs for the permission stage, if permission is granted then the court can assume that the merits test is met. If permission is refused then the defendant will receive at least a proportion of their costs. Public interest intervenors may be able to take advantage of this approach particularly if they are able to offer to pay at the outset a fixed amount towards the costs incurred as a result of their intervention, in the event that a costs award is ultimately made against them. For most intervenors it is the risk of unlimited costs which is the deterrent rather than exposure to a fixed, and relatively limited sum.

Whichever approach the court takes, however, it is essential in order to provide a degree of certainty for third party intervenors, that, once the court has identified those intervenors who ought to be heard in some form,[53] and a decision has been taken on whether written or oral submissions will be made, the court then considers the issue of costs in relation to the intervenors. Where possible the court should make it clear at the outset what the costs position will be. Maurice Kay J in his concurring judgment in the *CND* case,[54] advocated applications for pre-emptive costs orders being made at the earliest possible stage in the proceedings, preferably in the claim form, on the basis that "generally, a defendant should be informed at the earliest stage that such an exceptional order will be sought".[55]

Maurice Kay J's judgment makes it clear that there is an advantage to both claimant and defendant in the court deciding whether there is to be no order as to costs or a limited order as to costs at the earliest possible stage.

BALANCING INTERVENORS

Third party intervention is a relatively new phenomenon in English courts and currently relatively few organisations take advantage of the opportunity. These organisations, for instance JUSTICE, Liberty, CPAG, Amnesty, tend to be familiar and trusted and usually have little trouble in obtaining leave to intervene. However, the effect of these interventions may lead to the court hearing a range of arguments on one side of the case, but not other perspectives.[56] As intervening becomes more commonplace the courts may have to consider the need to "balance" interventions, and proactively seek intervenors to present the full range of issues. The alternative in some cases is to appoint an *amicus* to assist the court, but this is unlikely to fully address the problem in cases concerning policy issues, rather than pure legal analysis.

Canada

It is instructive to cast a cursory glance at the Canadian rules on interventions. Both the Federal Court Rules 1998 (FCR) and the

---

[53] See public interest checklist at p 4 of PLP report.
[54] Ibid.
[55] At para 7 of the judgment.
[56] For a full discussion of this problem see Third Party Intervention: In the Public Interest? Ibid at 135–141.

Rules of the Supreme Court (RSCC) of Canada have clear provisions on interventions. Rule 109 of the FCR states that any notice of motion seeking leave to intervene must "describe how the proposed intervenor wishes to participate in the proceeding and how that participation will assist the determination of a factual or legal issue related to the proceeding". On granting a motion the Court must give directions on the role of the intervenor including costs and rights of appeal.

Rule 18 RSCC has more detailed provisions. It states:

(1) Any person interested in an appeal or reference may, by motion made in accordance with Rule 22, apply to a judge for leave to intervene upon such terms and conditions as the judge may determine.

(2) A motion for intervention shall be filed and served within 60 days after the filing of the notice of appeal or the reference.

(3) A motion for intervention shall briefly

(*a*) describe the intervenor and the intervenor's interest in the appeal or reference;

(*b*) identify the position to be taken by the intervenor on the appeal or reference; and

(*c*) set out the submissions to be advanced by the intervenor, their relevancy to the appeal or reference and the reasons for believing that the submissions will be useful to the Court and different from those of the other parties.

(4) An intervenor has the right to file a factum.

(5) Unless otherwise ordered by a Judge, an intervenor

(*a*) shall not file a factum that exceeds 20 pages;

(*b*) shall be bound by the case on appeal and may not add to it; and

(*c*) shall not present oral argument.

(6) In the order granting leave to intervene, the judge may specify the filing date for the factum of the intervenor but shall, unless there are exceptional circumstances, make provisions as to additional disbursements incurred by the appellant or respondent as a result of the intervention.

Professor Patrick Monahan in a study on constitutional cases in the Supreme Court in 2000[57] observed that intervenors appeared in 11 out of the total of 13 constitutional cases with 75 different entities appearing as intervenors 107 times. In 99 of those appearances intervenors were given the right to make oral argument. Governments

---

[57] *Supreme Court Law Review* (2001) 14 SCLR 1.

were the most common intervenors, accounting for just over half of all the intervenors. Apart from governments the largest category of intervenors was non-profit organisations including registered charities, political advocacy groups and industry associations, with the Canadian Civil Liberties Association and the Women's Legal Education and Action Fund the most frequent intervenors of all.

After comparing the success rates of non-government intervenors with Charter claimants[58] Professor Monahan concluded that over the past two years the Court had been significantly more likely to accept the position taken by a non-government intervenor than that of a Charter claimant. A number of points are apparent from Professor Monahan's study. First, that numerous interventions are a common feature of important constitutional cases. Secondly, that despite strict rules, the Supreme Court welcomes interventions from NGOs, with a preference for oral interventions. Thirdly that the submissions made by intervenors do appear to be influential with the court.

There are signs, as Professor Monahan points out, that the Supreme Court perceives that there is a need to exercise firmer control of interventions. A Notice to the Profession published in September 1999[59] reminded advocates of the rules in Rule 18, and concluded "The strict enforcement of Rule 18 will ensure that the interests of both parties and intervenors are safeguarded." Indeed questions do arise as to the fairness to the parties where an array of intervenors is arranged against them. In two constitutional cases cited by Professor Monahan[60] both of which were brought by men accused of sexual offences, more than eight intervenors opposed the position taken by the claimant, and none supported it. Similarly in *R* v. *A*[61] the House of Lords permitted written interventions from the Rape Crisis Federation of England and Wales, the Campaign to End Rape, the Child and Women Abuse Studies Unit and Justice for Women.

---

[58] In 1999–2000 the position taken by non-government intervenors was accepted by the court 58% of the time, whereas the overall success rate for claimants under the Canadian Charter was 33%.

[59] In the *Supreme Court Bulletin*, September 1999.

[60] *R* v. *Darrach* 2000 SCC 46; 11 BHRC 157 where the claimant argued that a law preventing him from adducing the sexual history of the complainant was incompatible with his right to a fair trial; *R* v. *Blencoe* 2000 SCC 44.

[61] [2002] 1 AC 45.

The Canadian experience illustrates the usefulness of interventions, but also their potential to grow in number. The lesson is perhaps the need for clear rules and a method of ensuring that interventions are useful and do not take over the litigation.

To What Degree does Intervention Solve the Problems of the "Victim" Test?

Intervenors are not the claimant so they are not there as of right. This gives a very wide discretion to the court. It may mean that in practice the decision to allow a group to intervene depends on the views of judge as to the merits of the case, and on the public "standing" or reputation of the intervenor. Although the exercise of such discretion may be unavoidable it is one that puts the potential intervenor in a very uncertain position, and may lead to considerable discrepancies between different members of the judiciary.

Another problem which may arise is conflict between the intervenor and the claimant. The public interest arguments may be not just different from, but potentially adverse to, the interests of the claimant. This puts the court in a very difficult position. The court has to consider what is the nature of the court's role – is it to decide the individual dispute or to determine the wider public interest. Surely the right answer is that in determining the legal issue the court should take into account all the relevant information, which includes that pertaining to the public interest, even if this is adverse in some respects to the individual claimant. Therefore the interest group should be allowed in on public interest grounds, even if this is adverse to the particular claimant.

Finally, the intervenor's role in the action is heavily dependent on the claimant's and defendant's conduct of the action. The intervenor will always be an "add on" and consequently its time and evidence will be limited. Furthermore, oral interventions are likely to be far from the norm. If the intervenor is merely making written submissions then this gives him even less control over the outcome of the case.

All these factors mean that intervention by third parties can only ever be a partial solution to the problems raised by the "victim" test.

LEGAL ASSISTANCE

Probably the most significant barrier to the bringing of human rights challenges is the cost likely to be incurred and the availability, or otherwise, of legal assistance, although this is not a problem unique to human rights litigation. Much of this chapter has dealt with the effect the standing test under the HRA will have on challenges by public interest groups. As indicated above these challenges have assumed particular importance in the context of judicial review in large part because public funding for individual claimants is limited. With the standing test narrowed it is therefore crucial that those claimants who do have standing in cases raising human rights issues should not be prevented from bringing their claim because of lack of funding.[62] Otherwise the combination of poorly funded public interest groups fearing adverse costs awards, limited legal aid, and restrictive standing provisions will certainly ensure that important human rights cases do not reach the courts.

Ironically the ECHR itself provides little assistance to those seeking to assert a right to legal aid. The degree to which there is a right to legal assistance in civil proceedings, by reason of Article 6, has been considered by the European Court of Human Rights and is heavily circumscribed. Only if the applicant can show that legal assistance was "indispensable for effective access to court",[63] because it was "most improbable "that they could effectively present their own case, can they argue that their right of access to a court requires the provision of legal assistance.[64]

---

[62] For requirements for claimants to make contributions, see David Wolfe, Phil Shiner and Murray Hunt, "Alternative Funding in Public Interest Cases" (2001) *JR* 227.

[63] *McVicar* v. *UK* App 46311/99.

[64] *Airey* v. *Ireland* (1979–80) 2 EHRR 305. But see *P, C and S* v. *United Kingdom*, judgment of 16 July 2002, App 56547/00 where the European Court of Human Rights held that the applicants had been deprived of fair and effective access to a court when they were denied an adjournment in order to obtain legal representation. The applicants were parents involved in care proceedings. The court referred to the complexity of the case, the importance of what was at stake and the highly emotive nature of the subject matter. Assistance from counsel for the other parties, and latitude provided by the judge was no substitute for competent legal representation. Importantly the court stated that there was no requirement to show actual prejudice

In *Airey* v. *Ireland* it was the combination of the complexity of the law and process, and the emotional issue which arose in the proceedings, which led the Court to the conclusion that Article 6 required the provision of legal assistance. Since *Airey* the Commission and Court have rejected a number of cases where it has been argued that the nature of the proceedings require the provision of legal assistance.[65] It is noteworthy that in *McVicar* the Court took into account not only the nature of the proceedings and the issues raised, but the claimant's own education and experience in determining the issue.

The European Court of Human Rights has also held that a requirement for the grant of legal assistance so that the application should have a reasonable prospect of success does not itself constitute a breach of Article 6.

As at the date of the passing of the HRA there was a potential problem with the compatibility of the legal aid scheme with the Convention case law referred to above. This is because categories of case were excluded from legal aid, regardless of the issues raised and the tests outlined in *Airey*. Such cases would include cases before the social security commissioners which could involve extremely complex law in appeals made by claimants with no legal knowledge or experience, and claims in the employment tribunal and employment appeal tribunal which could involve factual disputes on which it would be very difficult for a claimant to represent him/herself, eg sexual harassment claims.

However, by section 6(8) of the Access to Justice Act 1999 ("AJA"):

The Lord Chancellor
may by direction require the[Legal Services] Commission to fund the provision of any of the services specified in Schedule 2 in circumstances specified in the direction, and may authorise the Commission to fund the provision of any of those services in specified circumstances or, if the Commission request him to do so, in an individual case.

---

from a lack of legal representation in order to be able to rely on Article 6 (para 96). The procedures adopted not only gave the appearance of unfairness but prevented the applicants from putting forward their case in a proper and effective manner on issues that were important to them.

[65] *Winer* v. *UK* (1986) 48 DR 154; *Andronicu* v. *Cyprus* (1998) 25 EHRR 491; *P, C and S* v. *United Kingdom*, judgment of 16 July 2002, App 56547/00.

The Lord Chancellor has issued directions to the Commission which authorise the funding of legal representation in cases that have a significant wider public interest or allege serious wrongdoing, abuse of power or position, or significant breach of human rights against a public body.

The Guidance to the Funding Code issued under the AJA defines the significant wider public interest as "The potential of the proceedings to produce real benefits for individuals other than the client (other than benefits which normally flow from the proceedings of the type in question)". At 5.2 (2) the Guidance suggests four categories of public interest:

1. Protection of life or other basic human rights (eg a challenge to a government immigration policy concerning a class of asylum seekers).
2. Direct financial benefit (eg a challenge to a welfare benefit).
3. Potential financial benefit (eg group actions against manufacturers).
4. Intangible benefit (eg safety and quality of life issues).

Paragraph 5.3(3) states

> if the benefits alleged are general considerations of health, safety or quality of life, the number of persons affected must be very substantial before a significant wider public interest can be established . . . As a general guideline, it would be unusual to regard a case as having a significant wider public interest if fewer than 100 people would benefit from its outcome.

Advising the Legal Services Commission on whether a case raises sufficient public interest is the Public Interest Advisory Panel which classifies cases into those of exceptional public interest, high public interest, significant public interest and no public interest.[66]

In *R (Jarrett)* v. *Legal Services Commission*[67] the Court considered the Lord Chancellor's Guidance in the light of the test in *Airey* of whether the withholding of legal assistance would make the prosecution of Ms Jarrett's defence "practically impossible" and found that the Guidance did not accord with the test. The LSC had however accepted that it needed to reconsider the application under the *Airey*

---

[66] See Guidance at para 5.6.
[67] [2001] EWHC Admin 389.

test and there was therefore no consideration by the Court of whether that particular case did or did not require legal assistance to conform with the Convention.

In practice it seems probable that it will only be the very exceptional case where the courts will interfere with the actual exercise of discretion under section 6(8), given the trend of the European Court of Human Right's jurisprudence. The existence of the public interest category gives the potential for important human rights challenges to be funded. However, doubts have been raised about whether this system is effective in ensuring assistance for all the most appropriate cases.[68]

The current rules on the grant of legal assistance will inevitably restrict access to the courts in human rights challenges, and will prevent some cases being brought. There is little evidence however, that the restrictions affect cases under the HRA more than in other fields of legal challenge. Nor that there are large numbers of significant infringements of human rights which are going unchallenged because of a lack of funding.

It might be argued that there will be difficulties in gaining legal services funding for a challenge which seeks a declaration of incompatibility, because there is no direct benefit to the claimant. However, in our view this is unlikely to be a real rather than a theoretical issue. First, it is difficult to conceive of a claim for a declaration of incompatibility which does not also include an argument under section 3. Therefore it would be difficult for the LSC to decide that only a declaration could be granted. Secondly, even in cases where the remedy is a declaration of incompatibility, such as *R (on the application of H)* v. *Mental Health Review Tribunal for North and East London Region*,[69] there is likely to be a benefit to the claimant. In that case a remedial order was made, reversing the burden of proof before mental health review tribunals, which clearly was a great benefit to the claimant. Thirdly, such cases are likely, although not certain, to raise public interest issues beyond those of the individual claimant. The Lord Chancellor's Guidance now expressly allows the funding of such challenges on public interest issues even when there may be limited

---

[68] See Louise Christian, "Legal Funding for Public Interest Cases: Reality or Illusion" (2002) *JR* 82.
[69] [2002] QB 1.

benefit to the individual claimant and possibly limited chances of success.

CONCLUSION

As is apparent from the above, there was a great deal of debate before the HRA came into force about the constraining effect of the "victim" test, and the impact this would have on potential challenges. So far those fears do not seem to have been realised. In our view there was little justification for the imposition of the "victim" test in section 7. However, there is little evidence whether through case law or academic papers, that challenges have been excluded by the need to find a victim. It is noteworthy that the senior members of the judiciary giving evidence to the Select Committee did not perceive there to be a problem in practice once the Act came into force.

These are very early days and few relevant cases have yet come forward. It would therefore be dangerous to reach any firm conclusions. However, so far the approach of the courts seems to be to try not to exclude cases because there may be said to be no victim and further to take a relaxed attitude to third party intervenors, thereby allowing the public interest to be raised as appropriate. Although these strategies by no means overcome all the problems which were raised by section 7, they have provided a typically English pragmatic solution in the short term. It will probably take some years before one can tell whether this approach allows the public interest to be fully considered and whether there are in fact important challenges which cannot be brought, or which are less completely argued and considered because of the need for a victim.

If, however, interventions are felt to provide valuable assistance to the court then it is essential that intervenors have certainty about when they will be allowed to intervene and what the costs consequences will be. We therefore take the view that there is a pressing need for clear rules on interventions for the benefit of the courts and the parties involved.

Remedies for Breach of Human Rights: Does the Human Rights Act Guarantee Effective Remedies?

Richard Clayton QC[1]

> Most foreign constitution makers have begun with declarations of rights. For this they have often been in no way to blame. . . . On the other hand, there remains through the English constitution that inseparable connection between the means of enforcing a right and the right to be enforced which is the strength of judicial legislation. The law *ubi jus ubi remendium* . . . means that the Englishmen whose labours gradually framed the completed set of laws and institutions which we call the Constitution, fixed their minds more intently on providing the remedies for the enforcement of particular rights . . . than upon any declaration of the Rights of Man or of Englishmen.
>
> Dicey, *The Law of the Constitution*[2]

INTRODUCTION

English law has historically developed out of a remedial conception of the law, the principle that a right entails a remedy.[3] Dicey argued

---

[1] Visiting Fellow, Centre for Public Law, University of Cambridge, *39 Essex Street*. Co-author of *The Law of Human Rights* (Oxford University Press, 2000).

[2] A. Dicey, *The Law and the Constitution* (10th ed) (Macmillan, 1965), pp 198–99.

[3] Thus, Austin took the view that requiring a sanction to be annexed to a command is necessary for "law properly so-called": see J. Austin *Lecture on Jurisprudence or The Philosophy of Positive Law* (5th edn, 1885) I, p 71. For instance, in the famous case of *Ashby* v. *White* 92 Eng Rep 126 (KB, 1703) (subsequently upheld by the House of Lords at (1703) 2 Ld Raym 938), damages were awarded for wrongfully depriving an elector of a vote in parliamentary elections; and Holt CJ proclaimed:

> If the plaintiff has a right, he must of necessity have a means to vindicate and maintain it, and a remedy if he is injured in the enjoyment of it; and indeed it is

that rights could be derived from the rule of law (by examining the right to personal freedom,[4] freedom of discussion[5] and the right to assembly[6]) and that:[7]

> The "rule of law" lastly may be used as a formula expressing the fact that with us the law of the constitution, the rules which in foreign countries naturally form part of a constitutional code, are not the source but the consequence of the rights of individuals as defined and enforced by the courts; that in short, the principles of private law have with us been the action of the courts and Parliament so extended as to determine the position of the Crown and of its servants; thus, the constitution is the result of the ordinary law of the land.

Dicey's idealised private law model of rights is very different from the way in which the Human Rights Act gives effect to Convention rights.[8] There are features of the Act which mean that breaches of Convention rights can occur where a claimant will nevertheless fail; and there are important shortcomings in the drafting of the remedies provision in the Act, which also deprives a claimant of a remedy as of right.

This chapter examines some of the deficiencies in the Human Rights Act. Before embarking on this exercise three points should be made. First, although there have been numerous Human Rights Act points argued since October 2000,[9] the inability of the courts to

a vain thing to imagine a right without a remedy; for . . . want of a right and want of a remedy are reciprocal.

[4] "The right not to be subjected to imprisonment, arrest or other physical coercion in a way which does not admit of legal justification", A. Dicey, *The Law and the Constitution*, above n 1, ch 5, p 208.

[5] Ibid ch 6, ("little else than the right to write or say anything which a jury consisting of twelve shopkeepers thinks expedient and should be said or written", p 246).

[6] Ibid p 271.

[7] Ibid p 203.

[8] Lord Bingham has suggested that Dicey would have had a mixed reaction to the Human Rights Act and would very likely have opposed the Act. Dicey would have been reassured that the Act gave Parliament the last word but would have needed more persuasion that the rights of the citizen required more protection than the ordinary law of the land; and would have opposed the fast track procedure under s 10 for amending legislation: see Lord Bingham, "Dicey Revisited" (2002) *PL* 39.

[9] There are no overall figures for assessing the number of cases which have raised Human Rights Act points. However, in the *Practice Statement (Administrative Court: annual statement)* [2002] 1 All ER 633, it is said that they were raised in 19% of the 5,298 cases received.

provide an effective remedy has been discussed in very few cases. Secondly, it is, perhaps, impracticable to judge the Act in terms of whether it guarantees effective remedies since it is difficult to imagine that any human rights instrument could succeed in measuring up to such a formidable yardstick. Thirdly, the extent to which the Act provides effective remedies might be seen as no more than a subjective evaluation. I shall, however, approach this issue by looking at whether the Act gives effective remedies either by assessing it against domestic •standards or those imposed by international human rights law.

The particular problems I shall consider are:

1. The conflict between Parliamentary sovereignty and human rights protection.
2. The retrospective provisions of the Act.
3. The failure to incorporate the right to an effective remedy under the Convention.
4. The discretionary nature of relief under the Act; and
5. The drafting weaknesses of the provision entitling a court to award damages.

I shall not, however, comment on the well recognised problem created by the very narrow definition of standing under section 7 since this is considered in Natalie Lieven and Charlotte Kilroy's chapter.

My somewhat predictable conclusion is that the Human Rights Act fails to provide effective remedies in several significant respects. Such a perspective has a wider significance than saying that the Government has disappointed a few human rights enthusiasts. The Government presented its case for incorporating the European Convention law in its White Paper, *Rights brought Home: the Human Rights Bill*[10] in terms of the cost[11] and time taken[12] in waiting for adjudication from the European Court of Human Rights, against a background where the UK has been one of the states most frequently charged with Convention violations.

---

[10] CM 3782 published when the Human Rights Bill was introduced in October 1997.

[11] In *Rights brought Home: The Human Rights Bill* (1997) ibid it is estimated that the average case costs £30,000.

[12] The Council of Europe has said that it takes five years before a case is finally decided before the European Court or Council of Ministers: see Council of Europe

The failure to provide effective remedies will require disappointed litigants to bring applications to the European Court of Human Rights; and, now that the expansion of the Council of Europe has led to an explosion of cases,[13] face even greater delays in hearing cases before the Court.[14] The inadequacies of the Act therefore undermine the Government's rationale for enacting it in the first place.

THE CONFLICT BETWEEN PARLIAMENTARY SOVEREIGNTY AND HUMAN RIGHTS PROTECTION

Lord Irvine had originally believed that the Human Rights Act should allow the courts to strike down legislation along the lines of the Canadian Charter of Rights and Freedoms.[15] But the Government chose another route in order to maintain the doctrine of parliamentary sovereignty; and section 3 of the Act provides: "So far as possible to do so, primary legislation and secondary legislation should be read and given effect in a way which is compatible with Convention rights". If such a construction is not possible, then the court has the power to grant a declaration of incompatibility under section 4.

The scheme of the Act therefore permits breaches of Convention rights if legislation cannot possibly be construed in a Convention compliant way. There are difficulties in defining the limits of a

---

"Protocol 11 to the European Convention on Human Rights and Explanatory Report" May 1994 (H (94 5) p 19, para 21).

[13] In the first 20 years of its existence the European Court decided an average of just over two cases a year. In the next decade the figure rose to nearly 23 per annum. In 2001 the Court made final rulings in 888 cases: see *European Court Survey of Activities for 2001.*

[14] The fast increasing case load has meant that the reforms made to Court procedures in November 1998 under the 11th Protocol have failed and are now to be revised: see A. Mowbray, "Proposals for reform of the European Court of Human Rights" [2001] *PL* 252.

[15] Lord Irvine, "The Legal System and Law Reform under Labour" in D. Bean (ed), *Law Reform for all* (London: Blackstone, 1996).

"possible" construction.[16] In the rape shield case, *R v. A (No 2)*[17] divergent views were expressed by Lord Steyn and Lord Hope. Lord Steyn[18] appeared to suggest that a section 3 construction could only be defeated if a statute imposed express restrictions on Convention rights; he took the view that section 3 operated as a rule of priority, ie that Convention rights would prevail unless legislation expressly derogated from them. Lord Hope,[19] on the other hand, emphasised that section 3 was a rule of interpretation and did not entitle judges to act as legislators; and that it would not be possible to construe legislation compatibly with Convention rights if legislation expressly contradicted that meaning or did so by necessary implication.

Lord Hope's approach was adopted by the House of Lords in *In Re S (Care Order: Implementation of Care Plan).*[20] Importantly, this analysis of section 3 has widened the scope for breaches of Convention rights to be overridden by legislation; and has created uncertainty for the future as the courts explore its boundaries.

The fact that the express language of statutory language will defeat Convention rights might suggest that the position in domestic law had not changed since the enactment of the Human Rights Act. However, that conclusion would not be justified: because the Human Rights Act gives a much stronger steer in favour of human rights than traditional canons of construction such as the principle that fundamental rights cannot be overridden by general words;[21] or the presumption that if statutory words authorising an act are ambiguous or obscure, then a construction least restrictive of individual rights should be placed upon them.[22]

---

[16] See generally, D. Rose and C. Weir, "Interpretation and Incompatibility: striking the balance"; my own views are set out in "The limit of what's possible: statutory construction under the Human Rights Act" (2002) *EHRLR* 559.

[17] [2002] 1 AC 45.

[18] Ibid at 69, para 46.

[19] Ibid at 86, para 108.

[20] [2002] 2 AC 291.

[21] See, eg *R v. Secretary of State for the Home Department ex p Simms* [2000] 2 AC 115 in relation to freedom of expression of prisoners; and more recently in relation to legal professional privilege, eg *R (Daly)* v. *Secretary of State for the Home Department* [2001] 2 AC 532 and *R (Morgan Grenfell)* v. *Inland Revenue Commissioners* [2002] 2 WLR 1299.

[22] See, eg *Inland Revenue Commissioners* v. *Rossminster* [1980] AC 952, 1008 per Lord Diplock; *Hill* v. *Chief Constable of South Yorkshire* [1990] 1 WLR 946, 952 per Purchas LJ.

By contrast, the obligation under section 3 to give a possible construction is radical in its effect[23] and is quite unlike any previous rule of statutory interpretation; there is no need to identify an ambiguity or absurdity. Compatibility with Convention rights is the sole guiding principle.[24] Whether a section 3 interpretation is contradicted by necessary implication in a statute is not a straightforward question.[25] As Lord Nicholls emphasised in *In Re S (Care Order: Implementation of Care Plan)*:[26]

In applying section 3 courts must be ever mindful of this outer limit. The Human Rights Act reserves the amendment of primary legislation to Parliament. By this means the Act seeks to preserve parliamentary sovereignty. The Act maintains the constitutional boundary. Interpretation of statutes is a matter for the courts; the enactment of statutes, and the amendment of statutes, are matters for Parliament.

Up to this point there is no difficulty. The area of real difficulty lies in identifying the limits of interpretation in a particular case. This is not a novel problem. If anything, the problem is more acute today than in past times. Nowadays courts are more "liberal" in the interpretation of all manner of documents. The greater the latitude with which courts construe documents, the less readily defined is the boundary. What one person regards as sensible, if robust, interpretation, another regards as impermissibly creative. For present purposes it is sufficient to say that a meaning which departs substantially from a fundamental feature of an Act of Parliament is likely to have crossed the boundary between interpretation and amendment. This is especially so where the departure has important practical repercussions which the court is not equipped to evaluate. In such a case the overall contextual setting may leave no scope for rendering the statutory provision Convention compliant by legitimate use of the process of interpretation. The boundary line may be

---

[23] *R* v. *A (No 2)* above n 18 per Lord Steyn at 69 para 46.
[24] Ibid at 86, para 108 per Lord Hope.
[25] Ibid at 87 para 108 per Lord Hope.
[26] Above n 20 at 731, paras 39, 30. In that case the House of Lords rejected as a legitimate interpretation under s 3 the formulation of a new procedure under the Children Act by the Court of Appeal at (2001) 2 FLR 582, requiring the local authority to notify the child's guardian if a child failed to achieve a starred milestone within a reasonable time; and entitling the local authority or guardian to apply to the court for directions once it did so.

crossed even though a limitation on Convention rights is not stated in express terms.

The dangers involved in widening the limits on a section 3 construction are exemplified by *Adan* v. *Newham LBC*.[27] A local authority had breached Article 6 in handling a homelessness claim because its review officer was not independent and impartial. An appeal was then made to the county court which exercised powers akin to judicial review under section 204 of the Housing Act 1996; and the critical issue was whether this jurisdiction was sufficient to cure a breach of Article 6 where the primary facts were disputed.[28]

Even though section 204 is confined to a "point of law", it was argued that it was possible to interpret the provision so that the county court could decide disputed issues of fact, making the procedure Article 6 compliant. Brooke LJ reviewed the authorities but concluded that this approach would blur the distinction between the judicial role and the legislative one,[29] stating[30] that:

> I do not consider it constitutionally open to us to do it. It would involve a judicial sleight of hand to enlarge the jurisdiction of the county court beyond that given to it by Parliament. Parliament has decided that the local authority should be the final arbiter on the facts, not the courts, and the courts do not, in my judgment, have the power to put these arrangements into reverse.

Hale LJ and David Steel J agreed. However, Hale LJ went on to hold that it was possible to construe section 204 more narrowly under section 3, by conferring jurisdiction on the county court to decide if the decision process as a whole complied with Article 6 in the particular circumstances of the case.[31] Brooke LJ[32] and David Steel J[33] again

---

[27] [2002] 1 WLR 2120.

[28] Note that in *Tower Hamlets LBC* v. *Begum* [2002] 2 All ER 668 the Court of Appeal declined to follow *Adan* and held that the judicial review jurisdiction under s 204 was sufficient to satisfy Art 6.

[29] [2002] 1 WLR 2491. The approach of the Court of Appeal in *Begum* was applied by the House of Lords: see [2003] 2 WLR 388.

[30] Ibid at 946, para 49.

[31] Ibid at 954, 955, paras 75, 77–79.

[32] Ibid at 947, para 50.

[33] Ibid at 958, para 94.

rejected this construction, stating that Parliament had decided that local authorities, not the courts should be the final arbiter of the facts. The reasoning of Brooke LJ and David Steel J in *Adan* is open to question. They rejected a construction which made it possible to achieve compatibility with Article 6 on the basis that it would be constitutionally improper to do so, perhaps because the local authority had the power to contract out its review process so that the court was not boxed into the corner of either giving such an interpretation or making a declaration of incompatibility.[34]

Nonetheless, their approach is problematic. *Adan* was not a case where a section 3 interpretation was contradicted by necessary implication. And the constitutional objection to interpreting legislation in a Convention compliant manner does *not* take its root from the Human Rights Act itself. *Adan* shows that as the reasons for disavowing section 3 interpretations increase, the human rights protection afforded by the Act will diminish.

THE RETROSPECTIVE PROVISIONS OF THE ACT

The Act came into force on 2 October 2000; and the courts have experienced considerable difficulties in deciding whether the Act extends to Convention breaches which take place before it came into effect. In general, the Act applies to any acts committed after the relevant provisions of the legislation have come into force. However, section 22(4) has introduced an element of retrospectivity in relation to proceedings brought by a victim under section 7(1)(a) of the Act; section 7(1)(a) does not apply to acts which took place before October 2000.

However, in *R* v. *DPP, ex p Kebilene*[35] Lord Steyn expressly rejected the argument put forward by the Director of Public Prosecutions that section 22(4) only extended the Act retrospectively to trials, but not to appeals:

> a construction which treats the trial and the appeal as parts of one process is more in keeping with the purpose of the Convention and the Act of 1998. It is a sensible and just construction.

[34] Above n 27 at 958, para 94.
[35] [2000] AC 326 at 398.

In *R* v. *Lambert*[36] the House of Lords took a radically different approach, adopting the reasoning of the Court of Appeal in *Wilson* v. *First County Trust (No 2)*.[37] It held that the Human Rights Act did *not* apply retrospectively to the summing up of a trial heard before the Act came into force. Section 6 of the Act did not deal specifically with acts which took place before October 2000 whereas section 22(4) did so. The House of Lords therefore decided that section 22(4) does not apply to an appeal in relation to court decisions taken prior to October 2000.

The issue was once again considered by the House of Lords in *R* v. *Kansal (No 2)*.[38] This time the majority took the view that *R* v. *Lambert* had not been correctly decided on the question of the retrospective effect of the Human Rights Act.[39] Nevertheless, a differently constituted majority decided (with only Lord Hope dissenting), that there was no compelling reason to depart from the majority view in *Lambert*. That conclusion is a surprising and unsatisfactory one. It required the House of Lords to hold in *R* v. *Lyons*,[40] that convictions which the Court of Human Rights had decided were unfair in breach of Article 6[41] were nonetheless safe under section 2 of the Criminal Appeals Act 1995. They took the view that a statutory procedure could not be overridden by giving direct effect to the Convention as an international convention.

Judicial interpretation has resulted in the conclusion that the Human Rights Act does not apply to Convention breaches occurring before October 2000. This means that frustrated victims of Convention violations must still apply to Strasbourg – which is a particularly disappointing outcome because the rationale for excluding these claims is so unconvincing.

---

[36] [2001] 3 WLR 206.
[37] [2002] QB 74.
[38] [2002] 3 WLR 1562.
[39] See Lord Lloyd para 17, Lord Steyn para 26 and Lord Hope, para 72.
[40] [2002] 3 WLR 1562.
[41] *Saunders* v. *United Kingdom* (1996) 23 EHRR 313 and *IJL* v. *United Kingdom* (2000) 33 EHRR 11.

THE DEFICIENCIES OF THE DECLARATION OF INCOMPATIBILITY PROCEDURE

A declaration of incompatibility is granted if a breach of Convention rights cannot be remedied by a section 3 construction, entitling the Government to initiate the fast track procedure to amend the legislation under section 10. A number of declarations have been made since the Act has been in force.[42]

In *Wilson* v. *First County (No 2)*[43] the Court of Appeal held that the absolute bar on enforcing a credit agreement which did not contain the prescribed terms under section 127(3) of the Consumer Credit Act was a disproportionate interference with the right of access to the court and made a declaration. It also granted a declaration in *R (H)* v. *N & E London Mental Health Review Tribunal*[44] that sections 72 and 73 of the Mental Health Act were incompatible with Articles 5(1)(4) because they imposed the burden of proof on a mental patient to establish that one of the criteria for lawfully continuing his detention is no longer satisfied. In *R (International Transport Roth)* v. *Secretary of State for the Home Department*[45] the Court of Appeal held that the statutory scheme which penalised carriers of illegal immigrants into the UK under the Immigration and Asylum Act breached Article 6 and made a declaration of incompatibility.

The House of Lords in *R (Anderson)* v. *Secretary of State for the Home Department*[46] held that the setting of the tariff in the case of a mandatory life prisoner was a sentencing exercise and therefore

---

[42] The declaration of incompatibility in *R* v. *Secretary of State for the Environment ex p Alconbury* made by the Divisional Court (see *The Times*, 24 January 2001) that the planning system breached Article 6 was reversed by the House of Lords (see [2001] 3 WLR 1389). Similarly, the decision of Keith J in *Matthews* v. *Ministry of Defence* (see *The Times*, 30 January 2002) that the bar on taking proceedings against the Crown under s 10 of the Crown Proceedings Act breached the right of access to the court under Art 6 was reversed by the Court of Appeal (see [2002] 3 WLR 2621).

[43] [2002] QB 74 following the adjourned hearing in *Wilson* v. *First County* [2001] QB 407. The Court of Appeal decision was reversed by the House of Lords: see [2003] 3 WLR 568.

[44] [2002] 1 QB 1.

[45] [2003] QB 728.

[46] [2003] 1 AC 837.

should be subject to the constraints of Article 6 following the decision of the European Court in *Stafford* v. *United Kingdom* Judgment of 28 May 2002.[47] The House of Lords went on to grant a declaration of incompatibility.

Moses J decided that sections 36–38 of the Social Security Contributions Act were discriminatory against widowers and therefore with Article 14 read together with Article 1 of the First Protocol in *Hooper* v. *Secretary of State for Work & Pensions*;[48] and granted a declaration. He again made a declaration in *Wilkinson* v. *Inland Revenue Commissioners*,[49] holding that section 262 of the Income and Corporations Taxes Act discriminated against widowers.

There are obvious and serious problems for a claimant if the only remedy he can obtain is a declaration. Before considering these I would like to address a drafting problem concerning section 4 which arguably prevents the grant of a declaration despite a contravention of Convention rights. It has been suggested *obiter* that the procedure cannot extend to breaches of positive rights.

DECLARATIONS OF INCOMPATIBILITY AND BREACHES OF POSITIVE RIGHTS

In *In Re S (Care Order: Implementation of Care Plan)*[50] Lord Nicholls considered a potential breach of the right of access to the court under Article 6 under the Children Act where, for example, a child was unable to bring proceedings because there was no parent or guardian willing and able to question the local authority's care decision. He pointed out:[51]

> The Convention violation now under consideration consists of a failure to provide access to a court as guaranteed by article 6(1). The absence of such provision means that English law may be incompatible with article 6(1). The United Kingdom may be in breach of its treaty obligations regarding this article. But the absence of such provision from a particular

---

[47] Judgment of 28 May 2002.
[48] (2002) UKHRR 785.
[49] (2002) STC 347.
[50] Above n 20 at 740, para 82.
[51] Ibid at paras 85, 86.

statute does not, in itself, mean that the statute is incompatible with article 6(1). Rather, this signifies at most the existence of a lacuna in the statute.

> This is the position so far as the failure to comply with article 6(1) lies in the absence of effective machinery for protecting the civil rights of young children who have no parent or guardian able and willing to act for them. In such cases there is a statutory *lacuna,* not a statutory incompatibility.
>
> [emphasis added]

In *R (J)* v. *Enfield LBC*[52] Elias J also took the view *obiter* that the declaration of incompatibility procedure could not be invoked where there was a breach of a positive right. In that case the claimant proved that the failure of a local authority to accommodate herself and her child breached Article 8. The family was subject to immigration control and the local authority had no power to provide accommodation.[53]

The difficulty about the declaration procedure in relation to primary legislation[54] (as opposed to secondary legislation)[55] is that section 4 is framed on the basis that a particular provision of primary legislation is incompatible with Convention rights. Elias J therefore concluded[56] that it would be inappropriate to grant a declaration because it was a body of legislation taken together which is incompatible with Article 8; and also rejected the argument that the court ought to identify the particular statutory provision which is most closely linked to the Convention right infringed so that the fast track procedure could be utilised.

There are, however, counter arguments which indicate that the declaration of incompatibility procedure can cover breaches of positive rights. Section 4(2) should be read and given effect so far as it is possible to make it compatible with Convention rights.[57]

---

[52] (2002) 2 FLR 1.

[53] As a result of s 21(1A) of the National Assistance Act 1948 and the interpretation of s 17 of the Children Act by the Court of Appeal in *R (A)* v. *Lambeth LBC* (2002) 1 FLR 353 (which was itself held to be *per incuriam* by the Court of Appeal in *R (W)* v. *Lambeth LBC* [2002] 2 All ER 901).

[54] S 4(1)(2).

[55] S 4(3)(4).

[56] Above n 44 at paras 67 to 71.

[57] In *R* v. *Lambert* [2001] 3 WLR 206, 242 para 110 Lord Hope indicated that the interpretative obligation under s 3 applied to the Human Rights Act just as much as to any other statute.

Furthermore, the Human Rights Act should be interpreted in a broad and generous way to give effect to fundamental rights.[58]

THE INADEQUACIES OF THE DECLARATION OF INCOMPATIBILITY PROCEDURE

Leaving to one side this problem, there are a number of practical complications which arise where a claimant is forced to invoke the declaration of incompatibility procedure. First, the power to make a declaration of incompatibility under section 4 is discretionary although there are strong reasons why a court should make an order. Secondly, while a declaration may prompt the Government to rectify the position under section 10 of the Act, it is under no obligation to do so;[59] and the failure to make a remedial order cannot be challenged under the Act.[60] Thirdly, a declaration of incompatibility is not binding on the parties.[61] Although the Government has the power to make a retrospective remedial order, it is difficult to identify the circumstances in which the power would be exercised. A declaration of incompatibility would, on the other hand, obviously provide important support in proceedings brought before the European Court of Human Rights.

These features of the procedure mean that litigation is unlikely to provide a substantial benefit to a claimant. There is a real risk that the costs of the proceedings will be awarded against him;[62] and some claimants experience considerable difficulties in obtaining public funding from the Legal Services Commission. The procedure has been fairly described as a "booby prize".[63]

---

[58] See *R* v. *DPP ex p Kebilene* [2000] AC 326 at 381 per Lord Hope.

[59] The declaration of incompatibility made in *R (H)* v. *N & E London Mental Health Review Tribunal,* above n 44, led the Government to make a remedial order: see the Mental Health Act 1983 (Remedial Order) 2001 SI 2001/3712.

[60] S 6(6).

[61] S 4(6)(b).

[62] However, in *Wilkinson* v. *Inland Revenue Commissioners,* above n 49, the claimant was ordered to pay 50% of the costs of the proceedings.

[63] G. Marshall, "Two kinds of incompatibility: more about section 3 of the Human Rights Act 1998" (1999) PL 377.

THE WIDE DISCRETION THE GOVERNMENT HAS WHEN TAKING REMEDIAL ACTION

If a declaration of incompatibility is made, the Government has an unchallengeable discretion[64] about whether or not to use the fast track procedure to remove the incompatibility by laying a draft remedial order before Parliament under the affirmative resolution procedure. Thus, the Government might, for example, decline to take remedial action if it rejected the interpretation of the domestic courts about the human rights compatibility of new legislation and wish to argue its position before the European Court of Human Rights. More cynically, it might decide to force a litigant to proceed to Strasbourg in the hope that he or she would not necessarily do so.

When the Human Rights Act was being enacted, the fast track procedure attracted substantial criticism from the Select Committee of Delegated Powers and Deregulation of the House of Lords.[65] The Committee, in particular, expressed concern that orders could be made which change sensitive and important areas of existing law. It also drew attention to the fact that the affirmative resolution procedure did not allow Parliament to amend an order, suggesting that it might be appropriate to develop a new procedure which allowed the opportunity for amendments to be proposed.

Schedule 2, paragraph 1 of the Human Rights Act confers very broad powers on the Minister in making a remedial order.[66] It could enable the Government, for instance, to provide for selective retrospectivity along the lines suggested in European Community cases.[67]

[64] See s 6(6).

[65] Sixth Report, 5 Nov 1997.

[66] (1) A remedial order may –
(a) contain such incidental, supplemental, consequential or transitional provision as the person making it considers appropriate;
(b) be made so as to have effect from a date earlier than that on which it is made;
(c) make provision for the delegation of specific functions;
(d) make different provision for different cases.
(2) The power conferred by sub-paragraph (1)(a) includes –
(a) power to amend or repeal primary legislation (including primary legislation other than that which contains the incompatible provision); and
(b) power to amend or repeal subordinate legislation (including subordinate legislation other than that which contains the incompatible provision).

[67] See Peter Roth's chapter.

In fact, only one remedial order has so far been made. Following the Court of Appeal decision in *R (H)* v. *N & E London Mental Health Review Tribunal*,[68] the Government enacted the Mental Health Act (Remedial)Order.[69] The order made was much less generous than that recommended by the Parliamentary Joint Committee on Human Rights; they had suggested the possibility of compensation for those affected by the incompatibility.[70]

The difference between the Parliamentary Joint Committee and the Minister concerning the terms of the Mental Health Remedial Order underline a fundamental difficulty, the remedial procedure basically confers an unlimited discretion on the Executive to secure compliance with human rights. Although this approach is consistent with the emphasis in the Act on preserving parliamentary sovereignty, it is not a perspective which guarantees effective remedies for breaches of Convention rights.

THE INTERNATIONAL PERSPECTIVE ON THE CONFLICT BETWEEN PARLIAMENTARY SOVEREIGNTY AND HUMAN RIGHTS PROTECTION

The fact that Parliament has enacted legislation which contravenes Convention rights is of course no defence in proceedings in Strasbourg. For example, the European Court decided that the closed shop legislation breached freedom of association in *Young James & Webster* v. *United Kingdom*.[71]

The inability of a court to strike down legislation which infringes human rights has also attracted considerable criticism by the Human Rights Committee, the body which supervises state compliance with

---

[68] Above n 44.

[69] 2001 SI 2001/3712 which came into force on 26 November 2001 amending sections 72(1) and 73(1) by moving the word "not" in each provision. The effect is that the wording now requires the Mental Health Review Tribunal to satisfy itself of the existence of criteria justifying detention, rather than to presume their existence at the outset.

[70] See generally, A. Lester, "Parliamentary Scrutiny of Legislation under the HRA 1008" (2002) EHRLR 432.

[71] (1981) 4 EHRR 38.

the International Covenant of Civil and Political Rights.[72] The New Zealand Bill of Rights Act prevents the courts from overriding legislation[73] (although the courts have considered they may have the power to indicate inconsistencies between a statute and the Bill of Rights).[74] The Human Rights Committee therefore recommend that:[75]

> The Bill of Rights be revised in order to . . . give the courts the power as soon as possible to strike down or decline to give effect to legislation on the ground of inconsistency with Covenant rights and freedoms as affirmed in the Bill of Rights.

The Human Rights Committee took the same view in *Ballantyne* v. *Canada*.[76] A communication was made to the Committee concerning the prohibition on English outdoor signs by the Quebec National Assembly. The laws could not be challenged under the Canadian Charter of Rights and Freedoms because they had been enacted under the "notwithstanding" clause of the Charter.[77] The

---

[72] See generally, A. Butler, "Judicial Review, Human Rights and Democracy" in G. Huscroft and P. Rishworth (eds), *Litigating Rights* (Oxford: Hart Publishing, 2002).

[73] S 4 of the Act states:

No court shall, in relation to any enactment (whether passed or made before or after the commencement of this Bill of Rights), –
(a) hold any provision of the enactment to be impliedly repealed or revoked or to be in any way invalid or ineffective;
(b) decline to apply any provision of the enactment –
by reason only that the provision is inconsistent with any provisions of this Bill of Rights.

[74] See the remarks of the Court of Appeal in *Moonman* v. *Film and Literature Board of Review* [2000] 2 NZLR 695; however, the Court of Appeal has subsequently declined to express a view on whether it can make such an order: see *R* v. *Pora* [2001] 2 NZLR 37; and see generally, A. Butler, "Declarations of incompatibility or interpretation consistent with Human Rights in New Zealand" (2001) *PL* 28.

[75] In its Suggestions and Recommendations on the Final Report on the Third Periodic Report of New Zealand in 1995: see A/50/40, para 185.

[76] Comm Nos 359/1989 and 385/1989.

[77] S 33(1) states:

Parliament or the legislature of a province may expressly declare in an Act of Parliament or of the legislature as the case may be, that the Act or provision thereof shall operate notwithstanding a provision included in section 2 or sections 7 to 15 of this Charter.

Canadian Government sought to have the communication declared inadmissible because the complainants had failed to exhaust their domestic remedies by seeking a declaration that the laws infringed their freedom of expression. However, the Committee decided that the domestic courts did not provide the complainants with an effective remedy: even if a declaration of incompatibility had been made under the Charter, the legislation would have remained "operative and intact".[78]

Thus, the absence of an effective remedy for breaches of Convention rights which result from the Government's decision to preserve parliamentary sovereignty will provide it with cold comfort in defending cases before the European Court of Human Rights; and is out of line with international human rights standards.

THE OMISSION OF THE CONVENTION RIGHT TO AN EFFECTIVE REMEDY

The decision to omit the right to an effective remedy under Article 13 was one of the most controversial issues debated when the Human Rights Act was enacted. In fact, the Government also chose not to enact the Article 1[79] obligation to secure to everyone within its jurisdiction the rights and freedoms set out in Articles 2 to 18 of the Convention as well as the two Convention Protocols the UK has not ratified: the Fourth Protocol[80] and the Seventh Protocol.[81]

---

[78] Comm No 359/1989 and 385/1989.

[79] Art 1 has not played a significant role in Convention case law. However, the Court has relied on Art 1 in *Young James and Webster* v. *United Kingdom*, above n 71, in holding that the State was responsible for breaches of the right of association under Art 11 where employees were dismissed as a result of the closed legislation; and again in *A* v. *United Kingdom* (1998) 27 EHRR 611 in deciding that the failure of the State to ensure that individuals were not subjected to inhuman treatment contrary to Art 3 made it liable because the defence of reasonable chastisement to a charge of assaulting a child gave inadequate protection to children

[80] The Fourth Protocol contains a prohibition against deprivation of liberty on the ground of an inability to fulfil a contractual obligation, a right to freedom of movement, a right of non-expulsion from a home state, a right of entry to the State of which a person is a national and a prohibition from the collective expulsions of aliens. In *Rights Brought Home: The Human Rights Bill*, above n 11, the Government explained that the Fourth Protocol has not been ratified because of concerns about

The Lord Chancellor, Lord Irvine justified the decision against incorporating Article 13 during the passage of the Act because:[82]

> We have set out in the Bill a scheme to provide remedies for the violation of Convention rights. We also believe it is undesirable to provide for Articles 1 and 13 in the Bill. . . . The courts would be bound to ask what was intended beyond the existing scheme of remedies set out in the Act. It might lead them to fashion remedies other than [section] 8 remedies, which we regard as sufficient and clear. We believe that [section] 8 provides effective remedies before our courts.

As Lord Hope observed in *Brown* v. *Stott*,[83] the decision to omit Article 13 from the Act shows sections 7–9 are intended to lay down an appropriate remedial structure for giving effect to Convention rights. Nevertheless, the Government's reasoning is not entirely convincing; and the failure to enact Article 13 has provoked discussion in some Human Rights Act cases. However, it is first necessary to examine the Convention right to an effective remedy.

THE RIGHT TO AN EFFECTIVE REMEDY UNDER ARTICLE 13

Article 13 of the Convention was modelled on Article 8 of the Universal Declaration of Human Rights[84] and was inspired by

the exact nature of the obligation regarding rights of entry and indicated that there were no immediate plans to ratify it.

[81] The Seventh Protocol contains a prohibition on expulsion of aliens without a decision in accordance with the law or opportunities for a review, a right to a review of conviction or sentence after criminal conviction, a right to compensation following a miscarriage of justice, a prohibition on double jeopardy in criminal cases and a right of equality between spouses. In *Rights Brought Home: The Human Rights Bill*, above n 11, the Government stated that it proposed to remove certain inconsistencies between the Protocol and domestic law (such as in relation to the property rights of spouses) and would then ratify the Protocol.

[82] *Hansard HL*, 18 November 1997, col 475.

[83] [2001] 1 WLR 817, 847.

[84] Art 8 states:

Everyone has the right to an effective remedy by the competent national tribunal for acts violating the fundamental rights granted to him by the constitution or the law.

English lawyers who attached importance to the idea of effective remedies.[85] The right to a remedy is expressly guaranteed by most global and regional human rights instruments, including the United Nations' International Covenant on Civil and Political Rights, the European Convention, the American Convention on Human Rights and the African Charter on Human and Peoples Rights. This international guarantee of a remedy implies that a wrongdoing state has the primary duty to afford redress to the victim of a violation and the role of international tribunals are subsidiary and only become necessary when the State has failed to afford the required relief.[86]

Article 13 of the Convention states:

> Everyone whose rights and freedoms as set forth in this Convention are violated shall have an effective remedy before a national authority notwithstanding that the violation has been committed by a person acting in an official capacity.

In *Askoy* v. *Turkey*[87] the European Court of Human Rights set out some general principles:

> Article 13 guarantees the availability at a national level of a remedy to enforce the substance of the Convention rights and freedoms in whatever form they might happen to be secured in the domestic legal order. The effect of this article is thus to require the provision of a domestic remedy allowing the competent national authority both to deal with the substance of the relevant Convention complaint and to grant appropriate relief, although contracting states are afforded some discretion as to the manner in which they conform to their obligations under this provision. The scope of the obligation under Article 13 varies depending on the nature of the applicant's complaint under the Convention. Nevertheless, the remedy under article 13 must be "effective" in practice as well as in law, in particular, in the sense that its exercise must not be unjustifiably hindered by the acts or omissions of the authorities of the respondent state.

---

[85] B. Simpson, *Human Rights and the End of Empire* (Oxford University Press, 2001).

[86] See generally, D. Sheldon, *Remedies in International Human Rights Law* (Oxford University Press, 1999), ch 1.

[87] (1997) 23 EHRR, 533 para 95.

The nature and effect of Article 13 can be summarised as follows:

It is not a free standing right but is breached where there is an arguable contravention of a substantive Convention right.[88] Its object is to guarantee in general terms that a suitable national remedy is available which is capable of providing a remedy in an appropriate case.[89]

The fundamental requirement is that the substance of the Convention complaint is put in the domestic forum.[90] Article 13 will therefore be breached where a civil claim has no realistic prospect of making a Convention challenge;[91] where primary legislation excludes any possible challenge;[92] or where the Executive refuses to comply with a court order.[93] Article 13 will also be infringed where the applicant has no right of recourse in the domestic courts – as in *Halford* v. *United Kingdom*[94] where the applicant had no domestic remedy for interception of her office telephone calls since this type of activity was not regulated by the Interception of Communications Act 1985. In *Keenan* v. *United Kingdom*[95] the Court held that the inability of a prisoner to challenge within time an award of 28 additional days imprisonment for breach of discipline by judicial review proceedings contravened Article 13; and that the inability of the parents to prove the prisoner had suffered "damage" in the sense

---

[88] *Silver* v. *United Kingdom* (1983) 5 EHRR 347 para 113.

[89] *Soering* v. *United Kingdom* (1989) 11 EHRR 439, para 120; *Murray* v. *United Kingdom* (1994) 19 EHRR 193, para 100.

[90] *Soering* v. *United Kingdom*, ibid para 122; *Vilvarajah* v. *United Kingdom* (1991) 14 EHRR 248 paras 117–127.

[91] See, eg *Costello-Roberts* v. *United Kingdom* (1993) 19 EHRR 112 Com Rep, para 59 where the Commission said there was no prospect of challenging corporal punishment as amounting to inhuman treatment in breach of Art 3 because of the defence of reasonable chastisement; but see *A* v. *United Kingdom* (1998) 27 EHRR 611 which held that where a stepfather, who assaulted a child successfully invoked the defence of reasonable chastisement, the State failed to provide adequate protection for the child contrary to Art 3.

[92] See, eg *Baggs* v. *United Kingdom* (1985) 9 EHRR 235 (where in certain circumstances the Civil Aviation Act 1982 excluded liability in nuisance for aircraft noise) and *Firsoff* v. *United Kingdom* (1993) 15 EHRR CD 111 (where s 29 of the Post Office Act 1969 gave the Post Office a statutory immunity from liability in tort for interfering with the mail).

[93] *Iatridis* v. *Greece*, Judgment, 25 March 1999.

[94] (1996) 24 EHRR 523.

[95] *The Times*, 18 April 2001.

recognised in domestic law and the absence of any remedy which established where responsibility for his death lay also breached the right to an effective remedy

The question of whether a *Wednesbury*[96] review of an administrative decision satisfies Article 13 has been considered on numerous occasions. In general, the European Court has decided that the *Wednesbury* standard is sufficient.[97] However, in *Chahal v. United Kingdom*[98] the balancing exercise carried out by the Court of Appeal[99] failed to satisfy Article 13 because there was no independent scrutiny of a refugee's Article 3 claim since this had to be carried out without taking account of the perceived security threat he posed. In *Smith and Grady v. United Kingdom*[100] the European Court decided that the Divisional Court and Court of Appeal in *R v. Ministry of Defence ex p Smith*[101] breached the right to an effective remedy because they had placed the irrationality threshold so high when deciding the lawfulness of the ban on homosexual servicemen so that they failed to address whether the interference with Article 8 answered a pressing social need and was proportionate.

The national authority which provides the remedy must be sufficiently independent of the body which is said to have breached Convention rights. Thus, in *Khan v. United Kingdom*[102] the Court held that the system for investigating police complaints was not sufficiently independent to satisfy Article 13.[103]

ARTICLE 13 AND THE HUMAN RIGHTS ACT CASES

The failure to incorporate Article 13 figured prominently in *In Re S (Care Order: Implementation of Care Plan)*.[104] Lord Nicholls

---

[96] *Associated Provincial Picture House* v. *Wednesbury* [1948] 1 KB 223.

[97] See, eg *Soering* v. *United Kingdom*, above n 90; *Vilvarajah* v. *United Kingdom*, above n 90; *D* v. *United Kingdom* (1997) 24 EHRR 413; *Bensaid* v. *United Kingdom*, Judgment 6 February 2001.

[98] (1996) 23 EHHR 413 paras 145–55.

[99] *R* v. *Secretary of State for the Home Department ex p Chahal* [1995] 1 WLR 526.

[100] (1999) 29 EHRR 493.

[101] [1996] QB 517.

[102] (2000) 31 EHRR 1016.

[103] Ibid.

[104] Above n 20.

observed that a failure of a local authority to carry out its responsibilities properly under the Children Act could not properly be characterised as a failure of the legislation to be compatible with the right to family life under Article 8. The complaint really amounted to the absence of an adequate remedy under Article 8 if the authority failed to discharge its parental responsibilities properly and the rights of the child or parents were violated.[105] He stated that:

failure by the state to provide an effective remedy for a violation of article 8 is not itself a violation of article 8. This is self-evident. So, even if the Children Act does fail to provide an adequate remedy, the Act is not for that reason incompatible with article 8. This is the short and conclusive answer to this point.

However, I should elaborate a little further. In Convention terms, failure to provide an effective remedy for infringement of a right set out in the Convention is an infringement of article 13. But article 13 is not a Convention right as defined in section 1(1) of the Human Rights Act 1998. So legislation which fails to provide an effective remedy for infringement of article 8 is not, for that reason, incompatible with a Convention right within the meaning of the Human Rights Act.

Where, then, does that leave the matter so far as English law is concerned? The domestic counterpart to article 13 is sections 7 and 8 of the Human Rights Act, read in conjunction with section 6. This domestic counterpart to article 13 takes a different form from article 13 itself. Unlike article 13, which declares a right ("Everyone whose rights . . . are violated shall have an effective remedy"), sections 7 and 8 provide a remedy. Article 13 guarantees the availability at the national level of an effective remedy to enforce the substance of Convention rights. Sections 7 and 8 seek to provide that remedy in this country. The object of these sections is to provide in English law the very remedy article 13 declares is the entitlement of everyone whose rights are violated.

Thus, if a local authority fails to discharge its parental responsibilities properly, and in consequence the rights of the parents under article 8 are violated, the parents may, as a longstop, bring proceedings against the authority under section 7.

The upshot of Lord Nicholls' analysis was that the widely recognised failures of local authorities in discharging their responsibilities under

---

[105] Above n 20, at 735, 736, paras 56–58.

the Children Act (and the subsequent routine breaches of Article 8) attracted no remedy under the Human Rights Act – except to the extent they constitute infringements of the right of access to the court.

However, the implications of Lord Nicholls' reasoning should not be overstated. The case heard before the House of Lords may not have been the appropriate vehicle to argue a claim of systemic breach of Article 8 resulting from the local authorities' failure to carry out their obligations under the Children Act. In this context it is useful to distinguish between a general attack on the statute and an individual claim focused on the particular circumstances of his case. The position in *Re S (Care Order: Implementation of Care Plan)* was not dissimilar to the proceedings brought against the prison policy which separated mother from child after 18 months, where the Court of Appeal was careful to differentiate between a challenge directed at general policy and one concerned with its application to an individual's particular circumstances.[106]

In any event, the failure to include Article 13 has a further consequence. Relief under the Human Rights Act is discretionary, as I shall discuss in a moment. The inclusion of a right to an effective remedy would assist in structuring the exercise of a discretion – which is otherwise expressed in very open textured language. It would mean that the courts would lean towards granting relief in line with the expectations created by international human rights instruments (as I highlighted earlier).

Nevertheless, it is striking to note that there are *no* remedial provisions in modern domestic bills of rights which are comparable to Article 13 whereas such a stipulation is commonplace in an international human rights instrument. However, I shall defer further discussion about the omission of Article 13 from the Human Rights Act until I examine the problems caused by its discretionary remedy's provision.

---

[106] *R (P)* v. *Secretary of State for the Home Department* [2001] 1 WLR 2002.

THE DISCRETIONARY NATURE OF RELIEF
UNDER THE ACT

Section 8(1) of the Human Rights Act states:

> In relation to any act (or proposed act) of a public authority which the court finds (or would be) unlawful, it may grant such relief or remedy, or make such order, within its powers as it considers just and appropriate.

Its breadth was illustrated by *A-G Reference (No 2 of 2001)*[107] where the Court of Appeal rejected the argument that a breach of the obligation to determine a charge within a reasonable time under Article 6(1) compelled the court as a public authority to stay the proceedings even though the defendant had suffered no prejudice as a result. By contrast, in Scotland a stay must be granted.[108]

The starting point in section 8(1) fundamentally conflicts with the principle that violating a right entitles a claimant to a remedy as of right. However, the private law model of rights championed by Dicey is not a very reliable touchstone.

First, the modern common law development of fundamental or constitutional rights has taken place almost entirely in the public law field.[109] Fordham[110] has catalogued the following claims to fundamental rights which have been canvassed in public law proceedings: the rights to access to the court, liberty, freedom of expression, privacy, due process, property, freedom from destitution, religious freedom, the right to silence, legal professional privilege, the right to trial by jury, freedom of association, access to information and citizen rights. This trend has led to the emergence of a rights based theory of public law which Loughlin[111] has described as "liberal normativism";

---

[107] [2001] 1 WLR 1861.

[108] See *R* v. *HM Advocate, The Times*, 6 December 2002; and note the strong dissenting judgment of Lords Steyn and Hope.

[109] Allison argues that the public law/private law divide in English law is a modern development which lacks systematic principles and has generated procedural confusion: see J. Allison, *A Continental Distinction in the Common Law* (Revised edn) (Oxford: Clarendon, 1999).

[110] M. Fordham, *Judicial Review Handbook* (3rd edn) (Oxford: Hart Publishing, 2001), 10.5

[111] M. Loughlin, *Public Law and Political Theory* (Oxford: Clarendon, 1992) at p 206 referring, in particular, to the views of TRS Allan, Lord Lester and Jeffrey Jowitt.

and encouraged Sir John Laws to argue that the High Court might become the guardian of fundamental common law rights by developing different standards for the substantive principles of judicial review.[112]

Secondly, public law remedies have traditionally been discretionary; and its discretionary character has very strong support.[113] Consequently, there is no principle of domestic law which demonstrates that discretionary nature of relief under the Human Rights Act is seriously flawed.

Thirdly, international human rights standards do not call into question this principle. The various methods used by the Member States of the Council of Europe to give effect to the European Convention into their domestic law are outside the scope of this chapter.[114] However, the remedies provision in the Canadian Charter of Rights and Freedoms,[115] the Hong Kong Bill of Rights Ordinance[116] and South

---

[112] He argued that if a decision overrode a fundamental right without sufficient objective justification, it should be struck down on proportionality grounds; that cases involving fundamental rights required a decision maker to give reasons; and that interference with fundamental rights could only be justified if the policy of the legislature permitted such an inference: see "Is the High Court the Guardian of Fundamental Constitutional Rights" [1993] PL 59.

[113] See, eg Sir Thomas Bingham, "Should Public Law Remedies be Discretionary?" [1991] *PL* 64; Lord Cooke, "The Discretionary Heart of Public Law" in C. Forsythe and I. Hare, *The Golden Metwand and the Crooked Cord* (Oxford: Clarendon, 1998). The Law Commission sought views on the discretionary nature of relief in its Consultation Paper No 126. See *Administrative Law: Judicial Review and Statutory Appeals*. It reported that the majority of consultees accepted the proposition that the mere fact of discretion was no cause of concern if it was strictly limited and clearly understood; and made no recommendations on this issue: see *Administrative Law:Judicial Review and Statutory Appeals* Law Com 116 paras 8.17–8.21.

[114] See generally, R. Blackburn and Jorg Polakiewicz, *Fundamental Rights in Europe* (Oxford University Press, 2001).

[115] S 24(1) of the Charter states:

Anyone whose rights or freedoms, as guaranteed by this Charter, have been infringed or denied may apply to a court of competent jurisdiction to obtain such remedy as the court thinks appropriate and just in the circumstances.

[116] S 6(1) of the Ordinance states:

A court or tribunal . . . may grant such remedy or relief or make such order, in respect of such violation or threatened violation as it has the power to grant or make in those proceedings as it considers just and appropriate in the circumstances.

Africa Constitution Act[117] are couched in very similar terms to section 8(1) of the Human Rights Act. The New Zealand Bill of Rights Act contains no remedies provision at all: so that in *Simpson* v. *A-G*[118] the New Zealand Court of Appeal had to imply the principle that effective remedies would be available for its breach; and went on to hold that the plaintiff had a public law right to damages.

However alien the conclusion might appear in Dicey's eyes, the fact that relief is discretionary is consonant both with domestic principle and international human rights law.

DISCRETIONARY REMEDIES AND THE OMISSION OF ARTICLE 13

The complaint about the omission of Article 13 is that the absence of an express obligation to an effective remedy may prevent litigants from securing one. This issue, however, ultimately depends on the attitude of the judiciary deciding individual cases. At present proceedings brought under the Act do not show that effective remedies are being denied to claimants. Furthermore, because the Human Rights Act is a constitutional statute[119] which should be interpreted in a broad and generous way, there are powerful reasons why breaches of Convention rights should be remedies unless there are cogent reasons to the contrary. In the final analysis, the absence of Article 13 and the existence of a discretionary remedies provision may not be objectionable in principle – provided that it is properly recognised that litigants will walk away empty handed if relief is refused where breaches of Convention rights are proved.

---

[117] S 38 of the Constitution Act states:

> Anyone listed in this section shall have the right to approach a competent court, alleging a right in the Bill of Rights has been infringed or threatened and the courts may grant appropriate relief, including a declaration of rights. . . .

[118] [1994] NZLR 667.

[119] The Act has been described by Lord Bingham as "an important constitutional instrument": see *Brown* v. *Stott* [2003] 1 AC 681 at 703; Lord Steyn described the Convention as "our Bill of Rights": see at 708. Similarly, Lord Woolf CJ in *R* v. *Offen* ([2001] 1 WLR 254 at 275) stressed that it is important to recognise that the 1998 Act is a constitutional instrument introducing Convention rights into domestic law; and see, generally, Laws LJ in *R (International Transport Roth)* v. *Secretary of the Home Department* above n 45, paras 69–75.

THE DEFICIENCIES OF THE DAMAGES PROVISION

Any analysis of damages under the Human Rights Act is necessarily tentative even though the Act has been in force for a substantial time. For reasons which are difficult to explain, decisions on damages under the Act have been very rare; and many issues remain unresolved.

One exception to this trend was in *Marcic* v. *Thames Water Utilities (No 2)*[120] where HHJ Havery QC awarded damages under the Human Rights Act having earlier decided[121] that the failure of the defendant to carry out works to bring to an end repeated flooding on the claimant's home was a breach of Article 8. He refused to grant a mandatory injunction compelling the defendant to carry out the works and awarded damages in lieu of an injunction, rejecting the submission that an award of damages for future wrongs is contrary to the Strasbourg jurisprudence. But the Court of Appeal[122] decided that the defendant was liable for nuisance; and the right to damages at common law displaced any right to damages the claimant otherwise might have under the Human Rights Act.

The court has a power under section 8 of the Act to award damages and there are two particular elements which may cause difficulty cumulatively:

(3) No award of damages is to be made, unless, taking account of all the circumstances of the case, including –

(a) any other relief or remedy granted, or order made, in relation to the act in question (by that or any other court), and

(b) the consequences of any decision (of that or any other court) in respect of that act,

the court is satisfied that the award is necessary to afford just satisfaction to the person in whose favour it is made.

(4) In determining –

(a) whether to award damages, or

(b) the amount of an award,

---

[120] [2002] 2 WLR 1000.
[121] *Marcic* v. *Thames Water Utilities* [2002] 2 WLR 932.
[122] [2002] 2 All ER 55.

the court must take account of the principles applied by the European Court of Human Rights in relation to the award of compensation under Article 41 of the Convention.

The broad discretion in section 8(1) is circumscribed by section 8(2). Section 8(2) is an important aid in structuring the discretion to be exercised when awarding damages under the Act. The real problem in securing an effective remedy is the requirement under the Act to take account of Strasbourg cases when applying the discretion under section 8(2).

The obligation to take account of the Strasbourg case law under section 8(4) is curiously drafted. Article 41 of the Convention is in terms directed to a situation in which domestic law fails to make adequate provision and states:

> If the Court finds that there has been a violation of the Convention or the protocols thereto, and if the internal law of the High Contracting Parties allows only partial reparation to be made, the Court shall, if necessary, afford just satisfaction to the injured party.[123]

The Court of Human Rights explained in the *Vagrancy* case[124] that the Convention's just satisfaction provision originated from arbitration clauses in international treaties. It appears that the purpose of this provision is to place the English Court in the same position as the Court of Human Rights when making damages awards.[125]

Unfortunately, the jurisprudence of the European Court of Human Rights on damages is notoriously weak. Shelton has quoted one former judge of the Court as saying privately "We have no principles" and another judge responded "We have principles, we just do not apply them".[126] Lester and Pannick rightly point out that the

---

[123] Art 41 came into force on 1 November 1998 when the Eleventh Protocol came into effect and replaced Art 50 which provided that "If the Court finds a decision or measure taken by a legal authority or any other authority of a High Contracting Party is completely or partially in conflict with the obligations arising under the present Convention, and if the internal law of the said Party allows only partial reparation to be made for the consequences of this decision or measure, the decision of the Court shall, if necessary, afford just satisfaction to the injured party."

[124] *De Wilde Ooms and Versyp* v. *Belgium No 2* (1971) 1 EHRR 373 at para 16.

[125] Cf S. Grosz, J. Beatson and P. Duffy, *Human Rights: The 1998 Act and the European Convention* (Sweet & Maxwell, 2000), paras 6–19.

[126] See D. Shelton, *Remedies in International Human Rights Law*, above n 86, at p 1.

case law lacks coherence and that advocates and judges are in danger of spending time attempting to identify principles that do not exist.[127]

The European Court does not routinely award compensation to successful applicants. Between 1972 and 1981 the Court made awards in seven cases[128] and rejected three such claims.[129] Between 1982 and 1991 applicants sought non-pecuniary damages in 51 cases where the Court held that the judgment alone gave just satisfaction. It has been argued that these cases share certain general characteristics:

1. the Court was very divided on the merits;
2. a large majority of cases concerned individuals who were accused of (or were guilty of) criminal offences; and
3. they often involved procedural errors in civil or administrative hearings.

The same pattern continued from 1992 until the new Court was established in November 1998. The Court found its judgment sufficient to meet the moral injury caused in 79 of the cases.[130]

An analysis of the case law on just satisfaction is likely to be of limited help in Human Rights Act cases. Serious concerns[131] have been expressed about the lack of consistency in the case law (for example,

---

[127] A. Lester and D. Pannick, *Human Rights Law and Practice* (Butterworths, 1999), para 2.8.4.

[128] *Ringeisen* v. *Austria* (1971) 1 EHRR 455 (wrongful and excessive detention); *Engel* v. *Netherlands* (1976) 1 EHRR 706 (unlawful arrest, excessive detention and military proceedings in camera); *Deweer* v. *Belgium* (1980) 2 EHRR 439 (coercion of applicant to waive his right to a fair hearing); *Konig* v. *Germany* (1978) 2 EHRR 170 (unreasonable proceedings to revoke doctor's licence to practice); *Artico* v. *Italy* (1980) 3 EHRR 1 (distress for denial of legal assistance in fraud trial); *Guzzardi* v. *Italy* (1980) 3 EHRR 557 (Mafia suspect detained on island pending trial); *Airey* v. *Ireland* (1979) 3 EHRR 592 (denial of legal aid to enable wife in judicial separation proceedings).

[129] *Neumeister* v. *Austria* (1968) 1 EHRR 91; *Golder* v. *United Kingdom* (1975) 1 EHRR 524; *Marckx* v. *Belgium* (1979) EHRR 330.

[130] See D. Shelton, *Remedies in International Human Rights Law* above at 204–11.

[131] See generally, A. Mowbray, "The European Court of Human Right's Approach to Just Satisfaction" [1997] *PL* 647 (based on a study of case law from 1991 to 1995).

over the treatment of criminal fines as financial loss[132] and the appropriate methodology for valuing property),[133] about the obscure nature of the basis on which the European Court makes awards of specified amounts of compensation[134] and about the moral judgments the Court makes when evaluating different types of applicants (such as the claims of convicted criminals and terrorists to just satisfaction).

In particular, the subjective and unreasoned way in which the European Court refuses to award damages in the exercise of its discretion does not provide a satisfactory set of principles for the English courts. The guidance it provides for compensating victims of human rights infringements will do little to assist the courts in providing an effective remedy. These difficulties were highlighted in the important case of *R (Bernard)* v. *Enfield LBC*.[135] In that case Sullivan J awarded damages under the Human Rights Act of £10,000, holding that the award made should not be minimal because that would diminish respect for the public policy underlying the Act. The council had failed to comply with its duty to re-house a severely disabled woman and her husband and breached its duty to secure the claimants' private and family life. Sullivan J did not derive any assistance from the principles or damages awards made by the European Court. The

---

[132] Whereas the Court refused to award compensation paid by an administrative body which exercised a criminal jurisdiction in breach of Art 6 in *Schmautzer* v. *Austria* (1995) 21 EHRR 511, it failed to distinguish earlier cases where it awarded compensation for criminal fines paid on convictions: see *Jersild* v. *Denmark* (1994) 19 EHRR 1; *Oberschlick* v. *Austria* (1991) 19 EHRR 389.

[133] Contrast *Papamichalopoulos* v. *Greece* (1995) 21 EHRR 439 where the Court relied on expert valuation evidence with *Hentrich* v. *France* (1995) 21 EHRR 199 where it did not.

[134] See, eg *Lopes Ostra* v. *Spain* (1994) EHRR 277; *Schuler-Zgraggen* v. *Switzerland* (1995) EHRR 404.

[135] [2003] HLR 4. See also, *R (KB)* v. *Mental Health Review Tribunal* [2003] 2 WLR 185 where a failure to deal speedily with applications made by mental patients to the Mental Health Review Tribunal resulted in modest damages for distress in the range of £750 to £4,000; and *R (Mambakasa)* v. *Secretary of State for the Home Department* [2003] EWHC 319 Richards J said *obiter* that damages of £1,000 to £2,000 would be appropriate for distress for breach of respect for family life resulting from delays in the entry clearance system. The Court of Appeal will set out the principles to be applied in *Anufrijeva* v. *Southwark LBC*, judgment awaited.

most helpful analogies were the awards made for maladministration by the Local Government Ombudsman.

CONCLUSION

I have taken rather a long time to reach the rather unremarkable conclusion that the Human Rights Act does not guarantee effective remedies. There are worrying signs that the rule of construction under section 3 will become diluted, leaving claimants who prove breaches of Convention rights with the sterile remedy of a declaration of incompatibility. The remedial action to be taken confers an open ended discretion on the Government. By contrast, the failure to incorporate Article 13 (coupled with a discretionary remedial provision) may not turn out as badly as some critics fear – provided the courts continue to regard infringements of rights as calling for a remedy. And the drafting of section 8 leaves a lot to be desired as a framework for securing compensation for human rights violations.

At this stage we can say with confidence that the Act has structural weaknesses which ensure it does not guarantee effective remedies. How badly it may fail is too early to tell.

Remedies Under the Human Rights Act: A Community Law Perspective

P. M. Roth QC*

INTRODUCTION

Like the Contracting States to the European Convention on Human Rights ("ECHR"), the Member States of the European Union are bound, at an international level, to give effect to a body of superior legal norms in their domestic legal order. The Human Rights Act 1998 ("HRA") is designed to bring a full, and many would say belated, implementation of the ECHR norms into the legal regimes of the United Kingdom. In the consideration of remedies under the Human Rights Act 1998, there are several reasons why examination of the position under the European Community ("EC") legal order is relevant and appropriate.

First, the principles of the ECHR have long been applicable through EC law. Although there was no reference to human rights in the EC Treaties until the Maastricht amendment of the Treaty on European Union,[1] in the 1970s the Court of Justice ("ECJ") enunciated as a general principle of Community law the protection of fundamental rights as recognised in the constitutional traditions of the Member States and in international treaties for the protection of human rights on which the Member States have collaborated or to which they are signatories.[2] The ECHR is clearly recognised as having special significance in that regard and the ECJ in its judgments has referred to specific provisions of the ECHR[3] and to decisions of the European Court of Human Rights.[4] In

---

* Monckton Chambers, Visiting Professor, King's College, London.
[1] See now Art 6(2) [ex F(2)] of the Treaty on European Union.
[2] See Case 11/70 *Internationale Handelsgesellschaft* [1970] ECR 1125; Case 4/73 *Nold* [1974] ECR 491. For a general statement of the principle, see Case C–260/89 *ERT* [1991] ECR I–2925, para 41.
[3] For the first occasion, see Case 44/79 *Hauer* [1979] ECR 3727.
[4] For the first occasion, see Cases C–74 and 129/95 *X* [1996] ECR I–6609.

consequence, although the HRA came into force only in October 2000, the provisions of the ECHR had, in effect, been directly applicable in the United Kingdom beforehand through EC law in those areas which EC law covers. This limited, "back-door" incorporation, therefore applied both to acts of the UK authorities when implementing EC legislation: see *Johnston v Chief Constable of the RUC*,[5] where the ECJ relied on Articles 6 and 13 ECHR as a ground for holding contrary to Community law a provision of the Northern Ireland Sex Discrimination Order which rendered conclusive a certificate of the Secretary of State that an act was done for the purpose of national security; and to acts of the Community institutions: see *R* v. *Secretary of State for Health ex p Imperial Tobacco*,[6] where one ground of challenge to the EC Tobacco Advertising Directive was that it contravened Article 10 ECHR, a ground which was largely accepted by Advocate General Fennelly, adopting the analytical approach of the European Court of Human Rights.[7] Hence, the ECJ recently had to determine, on two references from the Court of Session, whether orders by the Secretary of State for Scotland for the destruction of infected fish stocks infringed the fundamental right to property derived from Article 1 of the First Protocol ECHR since no compensation was payable. The destruction took place before the HRA came into force in Scotland, but the issue arises because the governing UK regulations implement an EC directive and accordingly their application had to respect fundamental human rights as a matter of EC law.[8]

Secondly, the drafting of the HRA clearly reflects some influence from EC law, notably in section 3 regarding interpretation of legislation. This effectively enacts the principle of consistent interpretation that has long applied under EC law, raising some of the issues now discussed in the context of the HRA.[9] Hence it was application of

---

[5] Case C–222/84 [1986] ECR 1651.

[6] Case C–74/99 [2000] ECR I–8599.

[7] Since it annulled the Directive on other grounds, the ECJ did not address this point.

[8] Cases C–20 and 64/00 *Booker Aquaculture* v. *The Scottish Ministers*, judgment of 10 July 2003. The ECJ held that the orders did not contravene the right to property: they were made in the general interest, were not disproportionate and did not impare the very substance of the protected right.

[9] The doctrine originated with Case 14/83 *Von Colson and Kamann* [1984] ECR 1891. For the extent of, and limit to, its application, see Case C–106/89 *Marleasing* [1990] ECR I–4135; Case C–91/92 *Faccini Dori* v. *Recreb* [1994] ECR I–3325.

that principle of EC law which led the House of Lords to "read in" words to secondary legislation in the field of employment.[10]

Thirdly, EC law has engaged and addressed the question of how extensive as a matter of policy should be the remedies that apply against a State, beyond the annulment of measures and actions which contravene Community rights or obligations. As will be seen, the crafting of a damages remedy, in particular, has been a careful exercise in case law jurisprudence by the ECJ. Now that these same issues are being confronted under the HRA, it seems instructive to look at the EC approach.

Indeed, EC law has already had an effect on remedies in English public law outside the Community law field. The requirement as a matter of EC law that an interim injunction can issue against the Crown, determined by the ECJ in *Factortame I*,[11] was clearly influential in the subsequent decision of the House of Lords holding that the courts had jurisdiction to issue injunctive relief, including an interim injunction, against the Crown in any judicial review case: *M* v. *Home Office*.[12]

Fourthly, above and beyond examination of EC case law for analogy and comparison, there is naturally an incentive for the courts to fashion a single, coherent, set of remedies instead of maintaining a multiplicity of different principles and criteria, each applicable according to which area of norms is engaged: EC law, the ECHR under the HRA, or liability of public bodies under common law principles of negligence or misfeasance in public office. As Lord Woolf has observed:[13]

> . . . the implementation of the [Human Rights] Act should be used as a catalyst for improving and bringing up to date our existing public law remedies. Where possible the distinctions between public and private law remedies should be eliminated. Our approach to the granting of

---

[10] *Litster* v. *Forth Dry Dock and Engineering Co. Ltd.* [1990] 1 AC 546.

[11] See below, n 51.

[12] [1994] 1 AC 377. Referring to the apparent rule to the contrary, Lord Woolf there noted, at 407: "the unhappy situation now exists that while a citizen is entitled to obtain injunctive relief (including interim relief) against the Crown or an officer of the Crown to protect his interests under Community law he cannot do so in respect of his other interests which may be just as important."

[13] "The Human Rights Act 1998 and Remedies" in Andenas and Fairgrieve (eds), *Judicial Review in International Perspective* (The Hague: Kluwer, 2000), 429, 430.

remedies for the infringement of human rights and other unlawful activities of public bodies should, as far as possible be harmonised.

THE RIGHT TO REPARATION

The HRA of course does not establish a *right* to damages against a public body for violation but gives the court power to award damages; and section 8(3) indicates that this discretion is to be exercised as something of a "fall-back" when other remedies, which are to be considered first, do not afford "just satisfaction". Conceptually, the approach developed by EC law is different in that it is framed in terms of a right to reparation against the State, but this right does not accrue in respect of all infringements. However, the underlying problem which has been addressed by EC law is essentially the same: in what circumstances should public institutions be liable to pay compensation for breaches of the law?

It was in the seminal judgment in *Francovich and Others*[14] that the ECJ in 1991 established the principle of state liability in damages for breach of Community law. In that case, the principle was developed as the corollary to the doctrine of the "direct effect" of directives, which enables the enforcement of a directive against a State (or its emanation) if the directive meets certain conditions, although the State has failed to implement the directive in its domestic law.[15] Where a directive did not meet those conditions because it left various options to the individual Member State regarding its implementation, protection of individuals whom the directive was intended to benefit could be achieved only by giving them a right of reparation against the State. But the right to what are often called "*Francovich* damages" was developed into a principle of more general application and not restricted to cases involving the non-implementation, or mis-implementation, of directives which lacked direct effect. Indeed, the EFTA Court (which performs a similar role under the EEA

---

[14] Cases C–6 and 9/90 [1991] ECR I–5357.

[15] It will be recalled that under the EC Treaty, a directive – as distinct from a regulation – is not directly applicable but is addressed only to the Member States: Art 249 (ex 189). Hence the doctrine of direct effect does not apply "horizontally" as between private parties but the State cannot rely on the breach of its Treaty obligation.

Agreement to the ECJ under the EC Treaty) has recently adopted the same principle to govern state liability to individuals for breach of the EEA Agreement although the doctrine of direct effect does not apply as regards the rules made under that Agreement.[16]

The landmark judgment of the ECJ which established this fundamental principle, while seeking to define its scope, was given in the conjoined cases of *Brasserie du Pêcheur and Factortame ("Factortame III")*[17] which arose on references from, respectively, the German and English courts. In the first case, a French company had been required to discontinue its exports to Germany of beer which it lawfully marketed in France, because its beer was held by the German authorities not to comply with the requirements of the German beer purity law. Imposition of those requirements was subsequently held by the ECJ to contravene the right of free movement of goods under the Treaty,[18] and the company then brought proceedings claiming damages against the German State for its violation of EC law. In the second case, Spanish owners of fishing vessels challenged the compatibility with the right of establishment under the Treaty of the Merchant Shipping Act 1988, which imposed requirements of British nationality, residence and domicile of the owners in order for a vessel to be registered on the UK register of fishing vessels, and therefore benefit from UK fishing quota. In *Factortame II*[19] the ECJ had held that these aspects of the UK regime (but not the requirement that the vessels must be operated out of the United Kingdom) were contrary to the Treaty and the owners then sought to recover damages from the Secretary of State for their prior exclusion.

The ECJ held that the full effectiveness of EC law would be impaired if individuals who were given directly effective rights under EC law could not obtain reparation before their national courts for infringement of those rights. In that regard, it did not matter which organ of the State, including the legislature, may have been responsible for the violation. Noting that the subject-matter of both cases

---

[16] Case E–4/01 *Karlsson* v. *Iceland*, Judgment of 30 May 2002. The EEA Agreement between the European Communities, the EC Member States, Iceland, Liechtenstein and Norway set up the European Economic Area with effect from 1 January 1994.

[17] Cases C–46 and 48/93 [1996] ECR I–1029.

[18] Case 178/84 *Commission v Germany* [1987] ECR 1227.

[19] Case C–221/89 [1991] ECR I–3905.

involved areas where EC law allowed a measure of discretion to the Member States, the Court set out the conditions for state liability as follows:[20]

> In such circumstances, Community law confers a right to reparation where three conditions are met: the rule of law infringed must be intended to confer rights on individuals; the breach must be sufficiently serious;[21] and there must be a direct causal link between the breach of the obligation resting on the State and the damage sustained by the injured parties.

Fulfilment of the first condition can be assessed on the basis of the established jurisprudence. It is the second condition that is here of particular interest. As to that, the ECJ stated:[22]

> As to the second condition, . . . the decisive test for finding that a breach of Community law is sufficiently serious is whether the Member State . . . concerned manifestly and gravely disregarded the limits on its discretion.
>
> The factors which the competent court may take into consideration include the clarity and precision of the rule breached, the measure of discretion left by that rule to the national . . . authorities, whether the infringement and the damage caused was intentional or involuntary, whether any error of law was excusable or inexcusable, the fact that the position taken by a Community institution may have contributed towards the omission, and the adoption or retention of national measures or practices contrary to Community law.

The ECJ proceeded to hold that this right of reparation supersedes any narrower rule of national law, such as the high criteria for liability for misfeasance in public office under English law. And it made clear that while the factors connected with the concept of fault under a national legal system may be relevant for determining whether or not a breach was sufficiently serious:[23]

---

[20] Above n 17, para 51.

[21] In the original French text, this is expressed as "que la violation soit suffisament caracterisée." That appears to point more to the obvious nature of the breach as opposed to any reference to its consequences and the habitual English translation as "sufficiently serious" can be misleading. But see below n 37.

[22] Ibid, paras 55–56.

[23] Ibid, para 79.

The obligation to make reparation for loss or damage caused to individuals cannot, however, depend upon a condition based on any concept of fault going beyond that of a sufficiently serious breach of Community law. Imposition of such a supplementary condition would be tantamount to calling in question the right to reparation founded on the Community legal order.

Although the computation of reparation was a matter for the national courts, the ECJ further emphasised what are known as the principles of "effectiveness" and "equivalence". The reparation for loss or damage must be commensurate with the loss or damage sustained so as to ensure effective protection of the individuals' rights. And the criteria set by the national legal systems for determining compensation,[24]

> must not be less favourable than those applying to similar claims based on domestic law and must not be such as in practice to make it impossible or excessively difficult to obtain reparation.

In subsequent cases, the ECJ emphasised that the question of whether a breach was sufficiently serious to satisfy the second condition of liability was a matter for the national court. But sometimes the ECJ has considered that it had sufficient factual material before it to answer that question itself. Accordingly, it has held that the misapplication of one provision in a directive, where that had been done in good faith and where that provision was reasonably capable of having the meaning attributed to it, was not a sufficiently serious breach to found liability in damages. That is the case whether the error was made by domestic secondary legislation: eg, *R* v. *HM Treasury ex p British Telecommunications*;[25] or by administrative decision: eg, *Brinkmann*.[26] On the other hand, complete non-implementation of a directive by the due date is regarded as *per se* a serious breach: eg, *Dillenkofer*[27] and *Rechberger*.[28] And beyond the area of directives, infringement of a right under the Treaty will

---

[24] Ibid, para 99
[25] Case C–392/93 [1996] ECR I–1631.
[26] Case C–319/96 *Brinkmann Tabakfabriken* v. *Skatteministeriet* [1998] ECR I–5255.
[27] Cases C–178/94, etc *Dillenkofer and Others* v. *Germany* [1996] ECR I–4845.
[28] Case C–140/97 *Rechberger and Others* [1999] ECR I–3499.

constitute a sufficiently serious breach where no legislative choice is involved: eg, *Hedley Lomas,*[29] where the British authorities refused to grant licences for the export of live animals to Spain in violation of the Treaty right of free movement of goods.

It is worth noting in this context that there is no requirement in EC law that the State itself should provide the reparation. The right under EC law is to reparation for the loss and damage and that is satisfied if compensation is payable by the public body whose actions were responsible for the infringement: *Haim II.*[30] How liability is allocated as between the internal organs of the State is of no concern to EC law provided that the right is effectively protected. Therefore the fact that *Francovich* damages are commonly said to be payable by "the State" is not in itself a material distinction with liability under the HRA.

The subsequent developments in the three leading cases in which the principle was established, *Brasserie du Pêcheur, Factortame* and *Francovich* itself, cast some light on the way in which the liability principle is applied.

Brasserie du Pêcheur

Following the ruling of the ECJ, the German Federal Supreme Court held that there was no liability to pay reparation. The German beer purity law involved two relevant infringements of Article 30 [now Article 28] of the Treaty: a prohibition on marketing under the designation "*Bier*" beers lawfully manufactured by different methods in another Member State; and a prohibition on importing beers containing additives. The ECJ held that the designation restriction could not be regarded as excusable in the light of its existing case law but

---

[29] Case C–5/94 *R* v. *MAFF ex p Hedley Lomas* [1996] ECR I–2553. Similarly under the EEA Agreement: *Karlsson* v. *Iceland,* above n 16, where Iceland's maintenance of the state monopoly on the importation of alcoholic beverages was held a sufficiently serious breach. See also the formulation of the principle in Case C–127/95 *Norbrook Laboratories* v. *MAFF* [1998] ECR I–1531 at para 109: ". . . where, at the time when it committed the infringement, the Member State in question was not called upon to make any legislative choices and had only considerably reduced, or even no, discretion, . . .".

[30] Case C–424/97 [2000] ECR I–5213, where an Italian dentist brought his claim against the Nordrhein Association of Dental Practitioners of Social Security Schemes, a public law body, which had refused to enrol him on the register.

that the question whether the additives restriction contravened EC law was less clear until the ECJ's prior ruling.[31] On that basis, the German court found that although on the question of additives the ECJ had in that case rejected the Government's arguments, there was nothing to indicate that the Government's legal position was "so far removed from the requirements of Community law that it was necessary to hold that there was a manifest and grave transgression of the boundaries placed on the discretion of the national legislature".[32] And since the Court also found that the controls placed on the imports of the claimant's beer concerned only the additives restriction and not the designation restriction, the latter infringement, although serious, had not caused any loss.

Factortame

On the return of the *Factortame* case to the House of Lords, the Secretary of State mounted a sustained argument that the violation was not a sufficiently serious breach to establish liability. This contention was unanimously rejected.[33] It was held that although the Government had acted in good faith and obtained legal advice, the deliberate adoption of legislation which was plainly discriminatory on grounds of nationality was a fundamental breach of clear and unambiguous provisions of the EC Treaty.[34] The Secretary of State's position was made difficult by the fact that the Commission had expressed the view to the UK Government that the legislation conflicted with the Treaty, and some of the speeches also refer to the legal advice which the Government had received which indicated that the Government had only an arguable case.[35] Lord Hope significantly

---

[31] ie, the 1987 judgment in *Commission* v. *Germany*, above n 18.

[32] Judgment of 24 October 1996, [1997] 1 CMLR 971, paras [17]–[18].

[33] *R* v. *Sec. of State ex p Factortame Ltd (No 5)* [2000] 1 AC 524.

[34] Lord Slynn expressed some hesitation as regards the residence condition, but in the end found that it was artificial to treat this separately from the nationality and domicile conditions.

[35] The Secretary of State waived privilege and disclosed the advice, a strategy that proved doubtful in the case itself and creates problems for later cases if the content of such advice might be relevant. The better view is that of Lord Hoffmann that the question of whether the error of law is excusable or inexcusable is an objective one and the content of legal advice received is irrelevant: see at 548. In *R* v. *Dept of Social Security, ex p Scullion* [1999] 3 CMLR 798 (decided after the Court of Appeal but

based his conclusion[36] on three factors: (a) that the subject-matter of the breach involved key areas of the Treaty, the freedom of movement of persons and of establishment ("The more fundamental the breach, the easier it will be to regard it as sufficiently serious."); (b) the potential for obvious and immediate damage;[37] and (c) the method of implementation by primary legislation which made it impossible for those adversely affected to obtain interim relief on the law as it then stood.

Francovich

Finally, in *Francovich* the issue arose from Italy's failure to implement Directive 80/987 which required Member States to provide for a guarantee institution that would pay a part of employees' outstanding claims for pay in the event of their employer's insolvency. Following the decision, Italy implemented the directive by a government decree that was retroactive to the required date. That decree incorporated one of the alternative limitations of liability (by reference to the period of earnings covered) that were available under the directive on the amount for which the Italian guarantee institution ("the INPS") was liable. Several Italian courts hearing claims by employees whose employers had become insolvent before the date of the decree referred to the ECJ the

prior to the House of Lords judgments in *Factortame*), Sullivan J held that a breach of Dir 79/7 regarding equal treatment in the field of social security gave rise to a right to damages on the grounds, *inter alia*, that no legal advice was sought by the Government ("or if sought it has not been produced"), nor had formal advice been sought from the Commission. The obligation there concerned invalid care allowance and the fact that this affected particularly vulnerable individuals clearly weighed heavily with the judge.

[36] *Factortame (No 5)*, above n 33, at 550–51. Lords Nicholls and Hoffmann agreed with his speech: ibid, at 547 and 549.

[37] See also *R v. Home Secretary, ex p Gallagher* [1996] 2 CMLR 951, where the Court of Appeal interpreted the ECJ's criterion of "grave" in *Factortame III* as importing a requirement that the breach must have significant consequences. Accordingly, a minor breach that did not obviously disadvantage the affected party was held not to satisfy the condition for an award of damages although the breach could be characterised as "manifest". That judgment preceded the House of Lords decision in *Factortame* but is consistent with its tenor. The claim in that case was also dismissed on the ground that the breach made no difference to the applicant's position, so the requirement of causation was not fulfilled (the argument that causation was to be determined on the basis of the loss of a chance was rejected).

question whether such a legislative solution satisfied the liability to make reparation established by the *Francovich* judgment. In its rulings, the ECJ held that retroactive and proper implementation of a directive should enable the harmful consequences of the breach to be remedied and will therefore constitute adequate reparation for the loss and damage, unless the beneficiaries can establish that they sustained additional loss by reason of the delayed implementation in which case "such loss must also be made good".[38] Moreover, neither the principle of effectiveness nor the principle of equivalence were infringed by the imposition of a limitation period of one year for claims under the decree, although the limitation period for non-contractual claims against public authorities under Italian law was five years. This one-year period corresponded to the time limit for claims by employees from the INPS for unpaid wages in all other cases.[39]

Accordingly, beneficiaries of Community rights whose claims meet the *Factortame* conditions are not necessarily entitled to a *damages* remedy. Indeed, where a directive provides a legislative choice which the non-implementing Member State necessarily has not made, it is difficult to see on what basis the State should be deprived of that choice so long as individuals are fully protected. It has accordingly been suggested that in reality *Francovich* introduced not a right to damages but a more general right to reparation "in whatever form the Member State finds it most convenient to provide".[40] For a defaulting State (or public body) to provide a remedy by a legislative or administrative scheme of compensation may have considerable practical advantages. This approach could similarly be appropriate in the context of the HRA. For example, where a public authority is found to have infringed Article 1 of the First Protocol because disturbance of a right to property was not covered by reasonable compensation, a satisfactory remedy might be for the public authority to introduce a scheme providing such compensation

---

[38] Cases C–94 and 95/95 *Bonifaci and Others* v. *INPS* [1997] ECR I–3969, para 53; Case C–373/95 *Maso and Others* v. *INPS and Italy* [1997] ECR I–4051, para 41. Mrs Bonifaci had been one of the claimants in the earlier reference that led to the *Francovich* judgment.

[39] Case C–261/95 *Palmisani* v. *INPS* [1997] ECR I–4025.

[40] See Dougan, "The *Francovich* Right to Reparation: Reshaping the Contours of Community Remedial Competence" (2000) *EPL* 103, 109. In *Bonifaci*, above n 38, AG Cosmas notably described the beneficiaries' rights as: "a right to reparation": Opinion at para 63.

retrospectively rather than for the court to determine individual claims for damages.

In addressing the question whether a breach justifies an award of damages under section 8(3) HRA where the claimants have suffered non-pecuniary loss, the early decisions of the English courts making such an award have emphasised the seriousness of the violation on the particular facts of the case as the major reason why "just satisfaction" required a damages remedy.[41] The circumstances taken into account involve both the nature and the consequences of the breach. The analysis therefore has much in common with that deployed in applying the *Factortame III* principles under EC law.

THE EFFECTIVENESS PRINCIPLE

The HRA has not incorporated Article 13 ECHR on the basis that the Act itself, within the general legal regimes applicable in the United Kingdom, will provide an effective remedy. As mentioned above, under EC law a general principle of effectiveness applies and will control the remedies available under national legal systems. The effective exercise of rights derived under EC law may require a national court not to apply a particular procedural or substantive rule of national law. If one asks whether incorporation of Article 13 was indeed unnecessary, it is worth considering briefly some instances where the EC law principle of effectiveness has been applied.

Limitation

The extent to which the ECJ in its rulings has questioned national limitation has undergone considerable recent fluctuation and the case law is not altogether consistent. This is not the occasion for a full review of

---

[41] See *R (Bernard)* v. *Enfield LBC* [2002] EWHC 2282 (Admin), [2003] HRLR 4 (p111); *R (KB)* v. *S London Mental Health Tribunal* [2003] EWHC 193 (Admin), [2003] 1 WLR 187; *R (N)* v. *Sec of State for the Home Dept* [2003] EWHC 207 (Admin), [2003] HRLR 20 (p 583) (appeal to the Court of Appeal pending). Although HRA s 8(4) requires the court to "take into account the principles" applied by the European Court of Human Rights in relation to an award of compensation, it is widely recognised that it is impossible to discern consistent principles in that regard in the Strasbourg case-law: eg, *R (KB)*, at [24] and [41].

the various decisions,[42] and it should be remembered that the ECJ is very conscious of its position as an international court which therefore seeks to leave as much autonomy as possible to national legal systems. The high point of control of national limitation periods came in *Emmott*.[43] Directive 79/7 on the abolition of sex discrimination in social security should have been implemented by the end of 1984, but in Ireland full implementation occurred only in 1988 after a ruling by the ECJ on a reference from the High Court. When Ms. Emmott then brought judicial review proceedings against the Minister for Social Welfare seeking to recover the benefits which should have been paid to her in the period 1984–88, she was met with the defence that she was well outside the three-month time limit for judicial review.[44] The High Court referred to the ECJ the question whether it was contrary to EC law for the public authorities to rely on national procedural time limits in such circumstances. The ECJ stated:[45]

> So long as a directive has not been properly transported into national law, individuals are unable to ascertain the full extent of their rights. That state of uncertainty for individuals subsists even after the Court has delivered a judgment finding that the Member State in question has not fulfilled its obligations under the directive and even if the Court has held that a particular provision or provisions of the directive are sufficiently precise and unconditional to be relied upon before a national court.

On that basis the Court held that only proper transposition of the directive creates the necessary legal certainty so that until that time, a limitation period laid down by national law cannot begin to run.

The ruling on its full breadth had significant implications for the coherence of national procedural rules as to limitation (eg if a claim based on a constitutional right under national law was subject to a shorter limitation period).[46] This may have been one of the

---

[42] See Flynn, "Whatever Happened to *Emmott?* The Perfecting of Community Rules on National Time-Limits" in Kilpatrick et al (eds), *The Future of Remedies in Europe* (Oxford: Hart Publishing, 2000), 51.

[43] Case C–208/90 [1991] ECR I–4269.

[44] The Irish rule was equivalent to the English rule and incorporated a discretion in the court to extend the time period, but the Irish High Court nonetheless referred the issue of principle to the ECJ.

[45] At para 21.

[46] Flynn, above n 42, at 54. And note the primary limitation period of one year under HRA, s 7(5).

considerations which led the ECJ substantially to qualify the position in its subsequent decisions. But the principle that national time limits must not operate so as to frustrate protection of EC rights has been preserved.

Damages

The effectiveness principle has been applied to overrule national rules concerning damages that might preclude or hinder the grant of full compensation. Following the ruling in *Marshall (No 1)* that Ms Marshall could claim directly under the Equal Treatment Directive against an Area Health Authority, as an emanation of the State, for applying to her an earlier retirement age than applied to male employees, Ms Marshall pursued her claim in the industrial tribunal for compensation. Although the tribunal calculated her actual loss at about £18,000, including some £7,700 interest, the statutory ceiling for compensation under the Sex Discrimination Act 1975, which was intended to implement the directive, was at that time only £6,250 and the tribunal did not have power to award interest. In *Marshall (No 2)*,[47] the ECJ held that an award of compensation must be adequate and cannot be limited to an *a priori* upper limit or by excluding interest.

In the *Comateb* judgment,[48] ruling on a series of French cases where traders claimed repayment of port dues that had been unlawfully collected, the ECJ held that the French customs authority could resist repayment only to the extent that they established that the traders had passed on the charge to their customers and that repayment would therefore involve unjust enrichment. No such assumption could be made simply on the basis of either commercial practice or legal requirements. Any national rule on the burden of proof which requires the claimants to establish that the charges had not been passed on is contrary to EC law.[49] Moreover, on the question of

---

[47] Case C–271/91 *Marshall v. Southampton and South-West Area Health Authority (No 2)* [1993] ECR I–4367.

[48] Cases C–192/95 to C–218/95 *Comateb and Others v. Directeur Général des Douanes et Droits Indirects* [1997] ECR I–165.

[49] Cases C–441 and 442/98 *Kapniki Mikhailidis* [2000] ECR I–7145, paras 36–42. See also the Opinion of AG Jacobs of 20 March 2003 in Case C–147/01 *Weber's Wine World* (pending).

unjust enrichment, other damage which traders may have suffered, such as a decrease in sales by reason of the increase in price, was to be taken into account.[50]

Jurisdiction

In the first round of the *Factortame* litigation before the English courts, the application to suspend the Merchant Shipping Act 1988, pending a reference to the ECJ on its conformity with EC law, came into conflict with both the English common law rule prohibiting injunctive relief against the Crown and the presumption that legislation conformed with the law until it had been held to be incompatible. On a reference by the House of Lords, the ECJ responded in *Factortame I* with a resounding declaration of the primacy of EC law over such national rules:[51]

> . . . any provision of a national legal system and any legislative administrative or judicial practice which might impair the effectiveness of Community law by withholding from the national court having jurisdiction to apply such law the power to do everything necessary at the moment of its application to set aside national legislative provisions which might prevent, even temporarily, Community rules from having full force and effect are incompatible with those requirements, which are the very essence of Community law.

The supremacy of EC law over national legislation had of course been established long before and is an obvious distinction with the deference under the HRA afforded to primary legislation which is inconsistent with the ECHR. But the judgment in *Factortame I* is a striking illustration of the extent to which remedies must prove fully effective and national obstacles must be swept aside irrespective of their ostensible significance within the domestic legal order. The principle of effectiveness developed in EC law may be seen as an expression of the right set out in Article 13 ECHR and the case law of the ECJ demonstrates how valuable and varied the application of this fundamental principle can be. The principle may require the

---

[50] The ECJ noted that the traders might be able to bring a separate claim for damages in respect of that loss, subject to conditions governing such liability: *Comateb*, above n 48, paras 34–35; *Kapniki Mikhailidis*, above, paras 36–42.

[51] Case C–213/89 *Factortame and Others* [1990] ECR I–2433, [1991] AC 603, para 20.

grant of a remedy where none may be available under national law and thus presents a contrast with the traditional English view that public law remedies are discretionary, an approach formally preserved in section 8(1) HRA.[52]

OTHER DAMAGES ISSUES

There seems to be little in EC law to provide assistance on quantification issues that may arise under the HRA, but two areas which have arisen in the Community context are worth brief mention: exemplary damages and damages for delay.

Exemplary Damages

Although the principle of awarding exemplary, or punitive, damages remains controversial, the House of Lords in *Kuddus* v. *Chief Constable*[53] has recently made clear that the jurisdiction to award such damages is not confined to particular causes of action but applies in all cases that fall within either of Lord Devlin's two categories in *Rookes* v. *Barnard*. The second category, cases in which the defendant has calculated that his action should make him a profit that may exceed the compensation otherwise payable, could clearly apply as regards infringement of the right to privacy, a right that appears to be emerging as against private defendants through direct or indirect application of the HRA. It is the first category, "oppressive, arbitrary or unconstitutional action by the servants of government," that is more problematic. In *Kuddus*, Lord Mackay reserved his view as to whether the principles governing damages under the HRA may affect the propriety of and the need for a power to award exemplary damages and Lord Hutton wondered whether such damages could be awarded where a claimant is entitled to compensation under the HRA.[54] By contrast, Lord Nicholls provided a clear endorsement for the power to award exemplary damages, in exceptional cases, on grounds that resonate in the context of the HRA:[55]

---

[52] See generally Jacobs, "Public Law – The Impact of Europe" (1999) PL 232.
[53] [2001] UKHL 29, [2002] 2 AC 122.
[54] Ibid, at 36 and 92.
[55] Ibid, at 63.

The availability of exemplary damages has played a significant role in buttressing civil liberties, in claims for false imprisonment and wrongful arrest. From time to time cases do arise where awards of compensatory damages are perceived as inadequate to achieve a just result between the parties. The nature of the defendant's conduct calls for a further response from the courts. On occasion conscious wrongdoing by a defendant is so outrageous, his disregard of the claimant's rights so contumelious, that something more is needed to show that the law will not tolerate such behaviour. Without an award of exemplary damages, justice will not have been done. Exemplary damages, as a remedy of last resort, fill what otherwise would be a regrettable lacuna.

In the *Factortame* litigation, the claims included a plea of exemplary damages. In *Factortame III*, one of the questions referred by the House of Lords to the ECJ asked whether EC law required any special consideration to be applied to such claims. The ECJ ruled that the application of such a head of damages was a matter of domestic law and that there were no particular considerations under EC law except as regards the principle of equivalence. On the basis that such damages may be awarded in English law where public authorities acted oppressively, arbitrarily or unconstitutionally, the ECJ held that insofar as such conduct may constitute or aggravate a breach of EC law, "an award of exemplary damages pursuant to a claim or an action founded on Community law cannot be ruled out if such damages could be awarded pursuant to a similar claim or action founded on domestic law".[56] However, on the return of the case to the English court, the Divisional Court held that the applicants were not entitled to claim exemplary damages since the nature of their claims, had they been under English law, would not satisfy the "cause of action" test which was then regarded as conclusive for the power to award exemplary damages.[57] This part of the judgment was not appealed. But this reasoning has, in effect, been overruled by *Kuddus* which determined that the "cause of action" test is inappropriate.

The position therefore seems to be as follows. For so long as there is power to award exemplary damages for conduct falling within Lord Devlin's second category under English law,[58] this must apply similarly

---

[56] Above n 17, para 89.
[57] *R* v. *Secretary of State for Transport ex p Factortame* [1997] EuLR 475 at 524–32.
[58] Such damages are not awarded in Scottish law.

if the claim is brought in the English courts under EC law. There should accordingly be a power to award exemplary damages for breach of a fundamental right derived from the ECHR that applies through the medium of EC law.[59] But if it becomes clear that there is no power to award exemplary damages under the HRA (see section 8(4)(b)),[60] then it seems arguable that a claim in the field of EC law for the breach of a fundamental right falling within the ECHR should not be able to attract exemplary damages since the "equivalent" domestic claim for the purposes of comparison is an HRA claim.

Damages for Delay

The quantification of non-pecuniary damages is likely to prove one of the most difficult areas under the HRA. Little consistent guidance can be derived from the judgments of the European Court of Human Rights, which in any event necessarily reflect a consensus of opinion of judges from very different legal cultures in their treatment of compensation for non-pecuniary loss.[61] Accordingly, it is becoming clear that the English courts will seek to develop their own approach, drawing on their own precedents in related fields.[62]

Nonetheless, it may be worth noting the decision of the ECJ regarding non-pecuniary loss in *Baustahlgewebe*.[63] The applicant was one of 14 companies fined by the Commission under the EC competition rules for participation in a cartel concerning welded steel mesh. Its appeal to the Court of First Instance ("CFI") led to a reduction in the fine imposed from ECU 4.5 million to ECU 3 million. On further appeal to the ECJ, the applicant argued as an additional ground that the proceedings before the CFI infringed Article 6 ECHR because of the time taken by that court to resolve the case.

---

[59] See above.

[60] Lord Woolf LCJ, writing extra-judicially, has expressed the view that neither exemplary nor aggravated damages should be awarded: above n 13, at 434. It has been held that s 9(3) HRA precludes an award of exemplary damages for a judicial act done in good faith: *R (KB)* v. *S London Mental Health Tribunal*, above n 41, at [60]; but it is difficult to see how such an act could attract an award of exemplary damages in any event.

[61] See Carnwath, "ECHR Remedies from a Common Law Perspective" (2000) 49 *ICLQ* 517.

[62] See especially *R (Bernard)* v. *Enfield LBC*, above n 41, at [45]–[47]; *R (KB)* v. *S London Mental Health Tribunal*, ibid, at [53].

[63] Case C–185/95P *Baustahlgewebe* v. *Commission* [1998] ECR I–8417.

The ECJ accepted this argument, holding that, even allowing for the great complexity of the case, the time of 32 months that elapsed between the end of the written procedure and the opening of the oral procedure, and a further 22 months between the close of the oral procedure and the delivery of judgment, meant that the time taken to complete the case exceeded the bounds of reasonableness.[64] However, the ECJ unsurprisingly rejected the submission that the decision should therefore be annulled in its entirety since there was no indication that the excessive length of the proceedings had affected their outcome. Instead, it made a very modest deduction of ECU 50,000 from the fine as "reasonable satisfaction".[65]

Baustahlgewebe is notable in the present context not only for the measure of compensation but because under the HRA no damages at all would presumably be recoverable in analogous circumstances where the delay was by a UK court: section 9(3). The CFI is of course a Community institution. It seems strongly arguable that the obligation to resolve the proceedings within a reasonable time is similarly imposed *as a matter of EC law* on a national court determining a case under EC law. *Francovich* reparation may accordingly be recoverable for judicial delay in such a case. This raises the prospect, admittedly only in exceptional circumstances, of circumventing the section 9(3) immunity. Furthermore, it should be observed that the "right to good administration" set out in Article 41 of the Nice Charter of Fundamental Rights may in due course give rise to decisions considering the quantum of compensation for administrative delays by Community institutions.[66]

TEMPORAL LIMITATION

The ECJ has on occasion restricted the effect of its judgment to the applicant in the case before it and those who had commenced

---

[64] Ibid, paras 26–47.

[65] Ibid, paras 48–49, 141.

[66] Although the Charter is not formally binding, it is becoming clear that the Community courts are according to it considerable significance: Case T–177/01 *Jégo-Quéré* v. *Commission* [2002] ECR II–2365; see also per AG Léger in Case C–353/99P *Council* v. *Hautala* [2001] ECR I–9565, opinion at paras 80–86. The Charter applies only to the institutions of the European Union and to the Member States when they are implementing EU law: Art 51.

proceedings before the date of its decision. Others were not entitled to start new claims arising out of past actions or loss but could rely on the judgment only prospectively. In *R* v. *Governor of Brockhill Prison, Ex p Evans (No 2)*,[67] there was discussion in argument before the House of Lords whether such a doctrine of temporal limitation could apply under English law and the Solicitor General submitted that this possibility would assume considerable importance in some cases under the HRA. *Brockhill* itself arose from a prison governor's decision as to a prisoner's conditional release date, which he had calculated in accordance with the law as it was generally understood at the time but which was then held to be incorrect on a proper interpretation of the relevant statutory provision. On the correct interpretation, the applicant should have been released 59 days earlier. Her claim for damages for false imprisonment succeeded and Lords Hope and Browne-Wilkinson held that there was similarly a contravention of Article 5 ECHR which would give a right to compensation under Article 5(5).[68] All their Lordships considered that there could be no basis for applying any temporal limitation to their judgment on the facts of the case. But whereas Lord Hobhouse was hostile to the concept in principle (although his criticism appears to be directed more at the different United States formulation which excludes relief for the parties in the case itself),[69] several of their Lordships expressly reserved their view as to whether introduction of such a concept might be valuable in an appropriate case.[70] Lord Hope noted that a statutory power to limit the retrospective effect of decisions as to whether legislation is within the legislative competence of the regional parliaments is contained in the devolution statutes.[71] Accordingly, it is pertinent to consider the development and application of the concept of temporal limitation by the ECJ.

---

[67] [2001] 2 AC 19.

[68] Ibid, at 37–39 and 27. The case is accordingly also of interest in the human rights context for the quantification of damages.

[69] [2001] 2 AC 19, at 48. But Lord Hobhouse accepted its application as regards matters of practice and procedure and, interestingly, remedies. See further below.

[70] Lord Slynn at 27; Lord Browne-Wilkinson, *idem*; Lord Steyn at 29; Lord Hope at 35–37.

[71] ie, Scotland Act 1998, s 102; Government of Wales Act 1998, sect. 110; Northern Ireland Act 1998, s 81.

The concept was originally introduced by the ECJ in the second *Defrenne* case.[72] The then Article 119 (now 141) of the EC Treaty provided that each Member State should ensure application of the principle that men and women should receive equal pay for equal work. However, many Member States delayed the implementation of this principle by national legislative measures. On a reference from the Belgian court hearing the claim by an air hostess against Sabena for paying her less than male cabin crew, the ECJ held that Article 119 had direct effect and so could be relied on in national courts of States which had failed to adopt implementing legislation. But in what was clearly a response to the dire warning given by the Irish and UK governments of the serious financial consequences of a potential multitude of claims against private employers going back the full periods of limitation, based on a principle of law that employers could not have reasonably foreseen, the ECJ ruled:[73]

> . . . it is appropriate to determine that, as the general level at which pay would have been fixed cannot be known, important considerations of legal certainty affecting all the interests involved, both public and private, make it impossible in principle to reopen the question as regards the past.
>
> Therefore the direct effect of Article 119 cannot be relied on in order to support claims concerning pay periods prior to the date of this judgment, except as regards those workers who have already brought legal proceedings or made an equivalent claim.

The ECJ has subsequently introduced such a temporal limitation in its ruling that university education in veterinary medicine constituted "vocational training", so that charging students from another Member State supplementary fees not payable by students from the home State fell within the Treaty prohibition of discrimination on the grounds of nationality;[74] in determining that Article 119 (now 141) applies to private occupational pension schemes, so that

---

[72] Case 43/75 *Defrenne* v. *Sabena* [1976] ECR 455.

[73] Ibid, paras 74–75.

[74] Case 24/86 *Blaizot* v. *University of Liège and Others* [1988] ECR 379. The ECJ's reasoning meant that many university courses constituted vocational training. In applying a temporal limitation, the judgment states that reopening past legal relationships more widely "would throw the financing of university education into confusion and might have unforeseeable consequences for the proper functioning of universities" (para 34).

different retirement ages for men and women were not permitted,[75] and as regards the payment of footballer transfer fees which it found contravened the right of free movement of persons.[76] The *Defrenne* ruling was undoubtedly a policy-based decision and it has been criticised as conflicting with sound legal principle.[77] But although the ECJ has continued to incorporate a temporal limitation, the concept is used very cautiously. In those cases where a limitation is imposed, the ECJ generally notes that the Member State may have been misled by the attitude of the Commission to the subject matter, or that the mistake as to the legal position was widespread across the Community. Indeed, attempts by Member States to persuade the ECJ to incorporate a temporal limitation are usually unsuccessful. Hence the ECJ has recently rejected requests for such a limit by the United Kingdom, in ruling that the British authorities had misinterpreted certain agricultural regulations and so excluded land which should have qualified for the purpose of arable area payments;[78] by Belgium, in ruling that entitlement to non-contributory social benefits, available to Belgian students, cannot be withheld from students from other Member States who were studying in Belgium;[79] and by France, in ruling that the grant of family service credits only to women for the purpose of retirement pensions of civil servants was discriminatory because it excluded men who assumed the task of bringing up children.[80]

In each case, the ECJ has emphasised that financial consequences alone cannot justify a temporal limitation. As it explained in *Griesmar*:[81]

> The Court has taken that step only in quite specific circumstances, where there was a risk of serious economic repercussions owing in particular to the large number of legal relationships entered into in good faith on the

---

[75] Case C–262/88 *Barber* v. *Guardian Royal Exchange Assurance Group* [1990] ECR I–1889.

[76] Case C–415/93 *Union Royale Belge des Sociétés de Football Association* v. *Bosman* [1996] ECR I–4921.

[77] Eg, Hartley, *The Foundations of European Community Law* (4th ed., Oxford: OUP, 1998), 81.

[78] Case C–372/98 *R* v. *MAFF ex p J.H. Cooke & Sons* [2000] ECR I–8683.

[79] Case C–184/99 *Grzelczyk* [2001] ECR I–6193.

[80] Case C–366/99 *Griesmar* [2001] ECR I–9383.

[81] Ibid, para 76.

basis of rules considered to be validly in force and where it appeared that both individuals and national authorities had been led into adopting practices which did not comply with Community law by reason of objective, significant uncertainty regarding the implications of Community provisions, an uncertainty to which the conduct of other Member States or the Community institutions may even have contributed.

The reference to individuals seems significant. Problems for public bodies alone make it much more difficult to justify such a limitation. But in exceptional circumstances that is not impossible. In *EKW and Wien & Co.*,[82] the ECJ held that Austrian municipal taxes on the sale of alcoholic drinks contravened the EC excise duty directive. The Austrian government pointed out the catastrophic financial consequences of a judgment that required repayment of the duty levied in the past. It would cover millions of transactions; most consumers do not keep appropriate records; and the potential cost was beyond the capacity of many municipalities to pay. Noting that the relevant provision of the directive had not previously received judicial interpretation and that the Austrian government could reasonably have been misled by the Commission to believe that the tax complied with EC law, the ECJ imposed a temporal limitation, holding that:[83]

> overriding grounds of legal certainty preclude calling into question legal relations which have exhausted their effects in the past; to do so would retroactively cast into confusion the system whereby Austrian municipalities were financed.

Where a temporal limitation is introduced, the form in which it is framed is significant. In all those cases where the ECJ has acceded to the request for such a limitation, the declaratory nature of the judgment is formally preserved. Accordingly, the ruling applies retroactively: it is the right to *rely upon* the judgment that is restricted to the

---

[82] [2000] ECR I–1157.

[83] Ibid, paras 58–59. Although the ECJ stated that it was not considering the global amount involved, it is hard to suppose that the Court was not influenced by the Austrian government's statement that the amount that would otherwise be recoverable for the years 1995–98 was equivalent to 0.9% of GNP: see *Weber's Wine World*, above n 49, for the consequential proceedings. Cp the stricter approach of the ECJ six months later in rejecting France's request for a temporal limitation of a ruling concerning monies recoverable under a VAT directive: Cases C–177 and 181/99 *Ampafrance and Sanofi* [2000] ECR I–7013.

parties to the proceedings and those who had raised equivalent claims prior to the date of the judgment. The limitation therefore goes to the remedy. Moreover, the introduction of a temporal limitation is acceptable in the framework of the ECHR. In *Marckx* v. *Belgium*,[84] the European Court of Human Rights held that the rules of Belgian law that circumscribed the right to dispose of property to illegitimate children violated the Convention. Noting the statement by the Belgian Government that giving the judgment retroactive effect would render many distributions of estates over the previous 24 years open to challenge in the courts, the Strasbourg Court, referring expressly to the ECJ judgment in *Defrenne*, held that the principle of legal certainty "dispenses the Belgian State from re-opening legal acts or situations that ante-date the delivery of the present judgment".[85]

Not only is it wholly exceptional for the ECJ to introduce a temporal limitation in its ruling, but the different nature of proceedings in Luxembourg is a further reason why a court in the United Kingdom should be cautious when contemplating such a course. Imposition of such a limitation precludes the granting of relief to potential claimants not before the court. They are accordingly denied the opportunity to present the arguments against a limitation, whereas the parties to the case itself may have no incentive to resist a limitation. For the claimant, introduction of a limitation overcomes a "floodgates" objection advanced against his claim, whereas for the defendant a limitation provides an effective means of preventing the flood. In addressing this question, the ECJ has the benefit of an Advocate General, acting as a sort of judicial *amicus curiae*, and of interventions by Member States who are able to present the broader public policy implications. If a court in the United Kingdom were to consider adopting the concept of a temporal limitation, it would be important to ensure that an independent party – whether an *amicus* assuming a broader role than merely to assist as to the law, or the relevant government department – could similarly present to the court the overall policy considerations with the supporting facts.

In the United States, submission of a range of *amicus* briefs by interested bodies and third parties is accepted practice in the highest

---

[84] [1980] 2 EHRR 330.
[85] Ibid, para 58.

appellate courts. A similar concept to temporal limitation was accepted in the United States in the 1930s in the form of "prospective overruling".[86] Under that approach, the old rule is applied to the case before the court and in other pending cases, but it is set aside as regards future cases. The concept gained particular currency in the 1960s but subsequently the United States Supreme Court has reaffirmed the principle of the retroactivity of its decisions, first in criminal cases[87] and, more recently, but with vehement judicial division, in civil cases as well.[88] Prospective overruling, as distinct from an EC-style temporal limitation, carries the disadvantage that it may remove the incentive for a party to bring a case in the first place which challenges the existing rule, since success in that challenge may not benefit the party who made it but only others thereafter. It has been justified as a more consistent application of the policy of protecting parties' legitimate expectations where those are based on a widely recognised interpretation of legal rules (perhaps based on an existing precedent that is being reversed). But even that is questionable insofar as cases commenced in the future but arising out of transactions carried out before the judgment will be based on the new rule.[89]

In *R v. National Insurance Commissioner, ex p Hudson*,[90] four members of a seven-member House of Lords considered that the construction placed on industrial injury benefit legislation by a decision of the House of Lords given five years previously was wrong but a differently constituted majority declined to overrule that earlier decision. In the "Afterthoughts" with which he concluded his speech,[91] Lord Simon expressed the view the most satisfactory outcome to the case would have been by way of prospective overruling of the earlier judgment, and that such an extension of the powers of the House should be seriously considered. Lord Diplock concurred

---

[86] See the judgment of Cardozo J in *Gt Northern Ry* v. *Sunburst Oil and Refining Co*, 287 US 358 (1932).

[87] *Griffith* v. *Kentucky*, 479 US 314 (1987).

[88] *James B. Beam Distilling Co* v. *Georgia*, 501 US 529 (1991); *Harper* v. *Virginia Dept. of Taxation*, 509 US 86 (1993). See also *Reynoldsville Casket Co* v. *Hyde*, 514 US 749 (1995).

[89] There are of course different ways in which the application of prospectivity can be formulated to try to deal with this situation, but there are almost always factual possibilities which will lead to unequal application.

[90] [1972] AC 944.

[91] Ibid, at 1026–27.

with these remarks,[92] which echoed his previous, extra-judicial observations:[93]

> . . . the rule that a new precedent applies to acts done before it was laid down is not an essential feature of the judicial process. It is a consequence of the legal fiction that the Courts merely expound the law as it has always been. The time has come, I suggest, to reflect whether we should discard this fiction.

In *Ex p Hudson*, Lord Simon suggested that any limitation to the general principle of retroactivity required legislative authority. However, the temporal reach of their decisions seems pre-eminently a matter for the courts and there is no reason why it should require statutory sanction any more than the House of Lords' announcement in the 1966 Practice Statement that it would no longer be invariably bound by its previous judgments. But if authority from Parliament is required, arguably it has now been provided in the broad discretion of section 8(1) of the HRA. Admittedly, section 8(1) applies only to the "relief or remedy" once the court has found that an act is unlawful. But it is as regards the relief or remedy that the problem of retroactivity arises in its acute form and, as seen above, it is to the remedy that the EC approach is directed. The HRA now enables the courts to declare an act unlawful, but to limit the remedy in the instant case while making clear that in the future parties behaving similarly to the defendant may expect to pay damages.[94]

The divisions of opinion regarding any limitation to the general retroactivity of judicial decisions can be seen to reflect differences of

---

[92] Ibid, at 1015F–G.

[93] Address to the Holdsworth Club, University of Birmingham (1965), p. 17. At the time Lord Diplock was a judge of the Court of Appeal. For subsequent discussion by the House of Lords of the declaratory theory in a different context, see *Kleinwort Benson Ltd* v. *Lincoln CC* [1999] 2 AC 349.

[94] Equally, any substantive as opposed to compensatory relief may be tailored to the justice of the case. In the landmark case of *Brown* v. *Board of Education*, 347 US 483 (1954), 349 US 294 (1955), holding that segregated schooling violated the Constitution, the US Supreme Court did not require that it must be halted as of the date of the judgment (which would have caused chaos, or worse) but that desegregation must be introduced "with all deliberate speed." In the *Brockhill* case, Lord Hobhouse significantly envisaged, *obiter*, that in appropriate circumstances a remedy might be prospective: above n 69.

approach to the judicial process.[95] But whether US-style prospective overruling or EC-style temporal limitation, such techniques should best be recognised as an explicit departure, on grounds of public policy, from the normal rule in exceptional circumstances. Faced with the prospect of upholding an interpretation which the court is convinced is wrong, because of the serious hardship which would be caused to many innocent third parties who had reasonably relied on that interpretation if it were now discarded, these techniques enable a court to strike a balance in a way that minimises injustice.[96]

CONCLUSION

Any analogy drawn from EC law for the potential operation of the HRA must bear in mind the different substantive scope and distinct legislative architecture of the regime of the Community as compared to the regime of the Convention. Several aspects may be noted:

1. The EC is a single market and EC law operates as a single body of law, which comprises not just the Treaty but detailed legislation in areas such as the CAP and VAT. That law has to be applied uniformly and to avoid economic distortion. By contrast, the ECHR is largely confined to the enunciation of more general principles and although those are considerably elaborated in the jurisprudence of the European Court of Human Rights, individual contracting States are left with a considerable margin of appreciation.

2. While the reach of EC law extends much more widely than many had expected, it nonetheless operates within boundaries. By contrast, the ECHR may apply across the whole field of public activity and public rules, broadly interpreted. The early cases in the English courts under the HRA have already made this clear: it has applied to pawn-broking agreements;[97] the flooding of a res-

---

[95] See Tribe, *American Constitutional Law* (3rd edn, New York: Foundation Press, 2000), Vol. 1, 232–35.

[96] See generally, Traynor, "Quo Vadis. Prospective Overruling: A Question of Judicial Responsibility" (1977) 28 *Hastings LJ* 533. This article, by the highly respected former Chief Justice of California, has been very influential in the United States

[97] *Wilson* v. *First County Trust (No. 2)* [2001] EWCA Civ 633, [2002] QB 74 (appeal to the House of Lords pending).

idential garden;[98] and the right to amend pleadings in a personal injuries action.[99] That very breadth of application may make general rules difficult to articulate at this early stage. And whereas EC law in a sense *displaces* national law within its field, the ECHR, through the HRA, *underpins* national law with its own fundamental norms.

3. The Community has a central court, with which national courts at every level may engage directly by the procedure of referring questions of EC law for preliminary ruling in the case before them, and to which the highest court *must* make a reference of a question to which the answer is not altogether clear. Not only does the absence of such a reference procedure make the Strasbourg court appear more remote from the national system, but the level of operation of the ECHR means that its judgments may be less intrusive into national rules.

4. The EC legal order includes a supra-national Commission, which has the role of monitoring the Member States' compliance with EC law and bringing defaulting states before the ECJ under the Article 226 (ex 169) procedure. Violation of the ECHR can be addressed only by individual enforcement, at least in the United Kingdom.

However, the EC regime effectively incorporates not only the fundamental rights of the ECHR but its own fundamental rights, notably the four fundamental freedoms under the Treaty (free movement of persons, goods, services and capital). The Amsterdam Treaty introduced several provisions which may lead to the creation of new Community rights, such as protection against many forms of discrimination.[100] The very fact that, within its field, EC law seeks to be a more comprehensive system means that some of the problems encountered under EC law resemble some of the problems now arising under the new combination of the ECHR with English or Scots law.

---

[98] *Marcic* v. *Thames Water Utilities Ltd.* [2002] EWCA Civ 64, [2002] QB 929; *(No. 2)* [2001] EWHC Technology 394, [2002] QB 1003 (appeal to the House of Lords pending).

[99] *Goode* v. *Martin* [2002] EWCA Civ 1899, [2002] 1 WLR 1828.

[100] Art 13 EC provides for the Council to take action to combat discrimination based on sex, racial or ethnic origin, religion or belief, disability, age or sexual orientation.

Moreover, both the EC regime, through the principles of effectiveness and equivalence, and the domestic incorporation of the ECHR through the HRA, are intended to provide effective remedies to those injured by violations. Yet the questions how far to impose costs on public bodies through liability to pay damages, and whether the court should have power, exceptionally, to prevent its rulings disturbing a multitude of settled arrangements, arise in both contexts. It cannot be argued that since the ECHR concerns fundamental human rights, any limitation on remedies found in EC law is inappropriate. Already the experience since October 2000 has shown that the HRA may apply in a range of situations, some of them much graver than others, whereas some provisions of EC legislation concern fundamental rights.

In recent years the courts have been alert to the policy implications raised by the imposition of obligations on public bodies and this has clearly influenced judges' approach to such questions.[101] Although the HRA is intended to foster a culture of human rights, there is nonetheless an evident concern that it should not introduce a culture of public law damages.[102] The reference in section 8(1) HRA to the court granting such relief or remedy as "it considers just and appropriate", and the circumscription of the damages power under section 8(3), appear to acknowledge to the policy questions at issue. As the above discussion has shown, the ECJ has developed through its decisions a body of law addressing some of these policy issues, seeking to create a balance between public liability, legal certainty and the effective protection for individual rights. In some respects, this has led Community law to override restrictions under English law; in others, the ECJ has introduced limitations which the courts in the UK do not, as yet, generally recognise. Altogether, the EC jurisprudence provides a fertile and appropriate guide when developing the remedies to deliver rights under the HRA.

---

[101] See, eg, *per* Sir Thomas Bingham M R in *R* v. *Cambridge HA, ex p B* [1995] 1 WLR 898 at 906; *per* Lord Hoffmann in *Stovin* v. *Wise* [1996] AC 923 at 958; *per* Lord Hoffmann (with whom Lords Bingham, Hope and Walker agreed) in *Runa Begum* v. *Tower Hamlets LBC* [2003] UKHL 5, [2003] 2 WLR 388 at [42]–[45].

[102] Lord Woolf, above n 13, at 433.